Linux E-mail

Set up, maintain, and secure a small office e-mail server

Ian Haycox

Alistair McDonald

Magnus Bäck

Ralf Hildebrandt

Patrick Ben Koetter

David Rusenko

Carl Taylor

BIRMINGHAM - MUMBAI

Linux E-mail
Set up, maintain, and secure a small office e-mail server

First published: June 2005

Second edition: November 2009

Production Reference: 1051109

Published by Packt Publishing Ltd.
32 Lincoln Road
Olton
Birmingham, B27 6PA, UK.

ISBN 978-1-847198-64-8

www.packtpub.com

Cover Image by Vinayak Chittar (vinayak.chittar@gmail.com)

Credits

Authors
Ian Haycox
Alistair McDonald
Magnus Bäck
Ralf Hildebrandt
Patrick Ben Koetter
David Rusenko
Carl Taylor

Reviewers
Patrick Chan
Aric Pedersen

Acquisition Editor
David Barnes

Development Editor
Ved Prakash Jha

Technical Editors
Gaurav Datar
Neha Patwari

Editorial Team Leader
Gagandeep Singh

Project Team Leader
Lata Basantani

Project Coordinator
Poorvi Nair

Proofreader
Lesley Harrison

Indexer
Rekha Nair

Graphics
Nilesh Mohite

Production Coordinator
Aparna Bhagat

Cover Work
Aparna Bhagat

About the Authors

Ian Haycox is a freelance IT consultant based in France and actively contributes to open source projects. He has twenty-five years of software development experience in the enterprise integration, telecommunications, banking, and television sectors.

Ian has a degree in Computer Science from the University of Hertfordshire, UK, and now runs his own web design company (http://www.ianhaycox.com/) and Linux programming consultancy.

> My thanks to Debbie for supplying me with copious amount of coffee and cheese sandwiches.

Alistair McDonald is a software developer and IT consultant. He has worked as a freelancer in the UK for 15 years, developing cross-platform software systems in C, C++, Perl, Java, and SQL. He has been using open source software for over 20 years and implementing systems using it for the past 10 years.

Last year, he gave up his freelance career and joined JDA Software, working in a technical role in their Service Industries division.

Alistair is also the author of the book *SpamAssassin: A practical guide to integration and configuration*, published by Packt .

> I would like to thank my wife Louise for the support she has given me throughout the writing of all my books.

Magnus Bäck has been playing and working with computers since his childhood days. He is interested in everything in the computer field, from digital typography and compilers, to relational databases and UNIX. His interests also include e-mail services, and he is an active contributor to the Postfix mailing list. Besides computers, he enjoys photography, cars, and bicycling.

Magnus holds a Master's degree in Computer Science and Engineering from Lund Institute of Technology, Sweden, and currently works with software configuration management for mobile phone software at Sony Ericsson Mobile Communications.

Ralf Hildebrandt is an active and well-known figure in the Postfix community, working as a Systems Engineer for T-Systems, a German telecommunications company.

He speaks about Postfix at industry conferences and hacker conventions, and contributes regularly to a number of open source mailing lists. Ralf Hildebrandt is the co-author of *The Book of Postfix*.

Patrick Ben Koetter is an active and well-known figure in the Postfix community, working as an Information Architect. Patrick Koetter runs his own company, consulting and developing corporate communication for customers in Europe and Africa.

He speaks about Postfix at industry conferences and hacker conventions, and contributes regularly to a number of open source mailing lists. Patrick Koetter is the co-author of *The Book of Postfix*.

David Rusenko was born in Paris, France, and spent most of his childhood overseas. He began working as a freelance Web Designer in 1996 and had his first experience with open source, a box copy of Red Hat 5.2, shortly after in 1999. After six years and as many versions of Red Hat, he now creates appealing web pages and devises solutions implementing high availability through clustering and alternate security models.

He founded Aderes (`http://www.aderes.net`) in 2001, a company that provides e-mail and web-based security solutions. His search for an appropriate Webmail Platform for the company led him to SquirrelMail. Initially managing all aspects of the business—from the technical concerns to customer support—gave him the experience that he now contributes to the Webmail chapter of this book.

David has studied both, Information Sciences and Technology (IST) and Management Information Systems (MIS) at the Pennsylvania State University. He speaks English and French fluently, and is conversational in Arabic. During his free time and vacations, he enjoys scuba diving, backpacking, playing racquetball, and playing electronic music records.

Carl Taylor has worked over 20 years in the IT industry and has spent the majority of that time working on UNIX type systems, mainly communications or office automation projects. He was an early user of the UseNet network and taught himself to program in C through working on a variety of open source software. His experience covers roles including pre and post sales support, product development, end user training and management.

Carl now runs his own web solutions development company "Adepteo", where they specialize in intranet and workflow products building on the best open source applications available. Whilst not working or looking after his children, Carl is something of a dance addict and is currently learning Latin Ballroom and Salsa.

About the Reviewers

Patrick Chan is a programmer at Computer Bank, a not-for-profit organization that recycles and distributes donated computers to disadvantaged individuals and community groups.

He has used Linux for quite a number of years, and has fond memories of starting off learning Linux as a newbie using the Gentoo distribution. His favorite tools include vim, GNU Screen, Z shell (zsh), Secure Shell (SSH), and Mutt.

Aric Pedersen is the author of *cPanel User Guide and Tutorial* (ISBN 978-1-904811-92-3) and *Web Host Manager Administration Guide* (ISBN 978-1-904811-50-3), both written for Packt Publishing. He also served as a reviewer for *CUPS Administrative Guide* (ISBN 978-1-84719-258-5), published by Packt Publishing.

Aric has over 8 years of experience working as a System Administrator. He currently works for Hostdime.com, the world-class web host; and also for Netenberg.com, makers of Fantastico, the world's most popular web script installer for cPanel servers.

I would like to thank Mike Kahn for all of his assistance over the past few years and also my good friend, Capt John "Jack" Grimes, Esq. USAF JAG Corps, who is the best friend a fellow could hope for, and his new wife, Kristin, who has shown incredible fortitude by marrying Jack (*smile*). I don't want to forget Francene Brown who is a good friend and a straight shooter (so rare to find these days).

Finally, I'd like to thank my mother and Allen, because without them, nothing I've done would have been possible.

Table of Contents

Preface

Many businesses want to run their e-mail servers on Linux for greater control and flexibility of corporate communications, but getting started can be complicated. The attractiveness of a free-to-use and robust e-mail service running on Linux can be undermined by the apparent technical challenges involved. Some of the complexity arises from the fact that an e-mail server consists of several components that must be installed and configured separately, then integrated together.

This book gives you just what you need to know to set up and maintain an e-mail server. Unlike other approaches that deal with one component at a time, this book delivers a step-by-step approach across all the server components, leaving you with a complete working e-mail server for your small business network.

What this book covers

Chapter 1: Linux and E-mail Basics takes you through the essential elements of a Linux e-mail server and the network and mail protocols that make e-mail possible. Like it or not, running a Linux e-mail server does require some understanding of the underlying networking, and this chapter is where you will start to get that understanding. This chapter explains the benefits and disadvantages of running your own e-mail server and provides some guidance on hardware sizing for a typical organization.

Chapter 2: Setting Up Postfix speaks about basic Postfix setup. Postfix is our chosen Mail Transfer Agent (MTA), which forms the heart of any e-mail server. The MTA is responsible, among other things, for moving messages between the various mail servers on the Internet.

Chapter 3: Incoming mail with POP and IMAP covers what to do with incoming e-mails. It will show you how to set up IMAP and POP access to mailboxes. This means users will be able to send and receive messages using their familiar e-mail clients.

Chapter 4: Providing Webmail Access shows how to set up webmail access using SquirrelMail. This will give users an easy, out-of-office access to their e-mail.

Chapter 5: Securing Your Installation looks at how your installation can be secured to prevent misuse of your users' data and the e-mail facility itself.

Chapter 6: Getting Started with Procmail discusses the basics of Procmail and gets you familiar with the various files that Procmail uses to load recipes, the core principles of filtering, and the options available.

Chapter 7: Advanced Procmail explores Procmail and explains a large number of services and a large amount of functionality that it can provide in getting mail under control. It also discusses the advanced features of Procmail and their benefits.

Chapter 8: Busting Spam with SpamAssassin shows the use of SpamAssassin in conjunction with Procmail to filter out the wide range of spam that afflicts the modern e-mail user.

Chapter 9: Antivirus Protection shows another way to protect users from rogue e-mail—this time the spread of e-mail viruses. Using ClamAV you can scan mail for viruses and schedule tasks to maintain an up-to-date antivirus database.

Chapter 10: Backing up your System will show you how to protect all your hardwork by backing up not only the e-mail itself, but also all of the configuration options that make up your e-mail server. Examples are provided to create an automated backup schedule to minimize data loss. Of course, you'll also learn how to restore data from these backups.

Who this book is for

This book is aimed at beginner or intermediate level System Administrators in small businesses, who want to set up a Linux-based e-mail server without spending a lot of time in becoming expert in individual applications.

Basic knowledge of Linux is also expected.

Conventions

In this book, you will find a number of styles of text that distinguish between different kinds of information. Here are some examples of these styles, along with an explanation of their meaning.

Code words in text are shown as follows: " The configuration file entry that you need to modify is `DatabaseMirror`.

A block of code is set as follows:

```
##
## Example config file for freshclam
## Please read the freshclam.conf(5) manual before editing this file.
## This file may be optionally merged with clamd.conf.
##
```

When we wish to draw your attention to a particular part of a code block, the relevant lines or items are set in bold:

```
$ grep score.*BAYES /usr/share/spamassassin/* /etc/mail/spamassassin/*
~/.spamassassin/local.cf
```

Any command-line input or output is written as follows:

```
# ls -al /etc/init.d/clamsmtpd
```

New terms and **important words** are shown in bold. Words that you see on the screen, in menus or dialog boxes for example, appear in the text like this: "Save the file using the browser (normally, the **File** menu has a **Save as** option)."

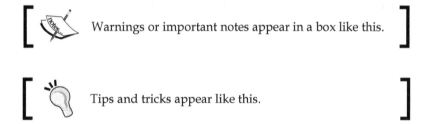

Warnings or important notes appear in a box like this.

Tips and tricks appear like this.

Reader feedback

Feedback from our readers is always welcome. Let us know what you think about this book—what you liked or may have disliked. Reader feedback is important for us to develop titles that you really get the most out of.

To send us general feedback, simply send an e-mail to feedback@packtpub.com, and mention the book title via the subject of your message.

If there is a book that you need and would like to see us publish, please send us a note in the **SUGGEST A TITLE** form on www.packtpub.com or e-mail suggest@packtpub.com.

If there is a topic that you have expertise in and you are interested in either writing or contributing to a book on, see our author guide on www.packtpub.com/authors.

Customer support

Now that you are the proud owner of a Packt book, we have a number of things to help you to get the most from your purchase.

Errata

Although we have taken every care to ensure the accuracy of our content, mistakes do happen. If you find a mistake in one of our books—maybe a mistake in the text or the code—we would be grateful if you would report this to us. By doing so, you can save other readers from frustration, and help us to improve subsequent versions of this book. If you find any errata, please report them by visiting http://www.packtpub.com/support, selecting your book, clicking on the **let us know** link, and entering the details of your errata. Once your errata are verified, your submission will be accepted and the errata added to any list of existing errata. Any existing errata can be viewed by selecting your title from http://www.packtpub.com/support.

Piracy

Piracy of copyright material on the Internet is an ongoing problem across all media. At Packt, we take the protection of our copyright and licenses very seriously. If you come across any illegal copies of our works, in any form, on the Internet, please provide us with the location address or web site name immediately so that we can pursue a remedy.

Please contact us at copyright@packtpub.com with a link to the suspected pirated material.

We appreciate your help in protecting our authors, and our ability to bring you valuable content.

Questions

You can contact us at questions@packtpub.com if you are having a problem with any aspect of the book, and we will do our best to address it.

1
Linux and E-mail Basics

If you are one of those thousands of system administrators who manage the networks and computers of small to medium-sized companies and you are thinking of hosting your own e-mail service, this book is for you.

We will start with the most basic components of an e-mail system. Together those components will allow your users to send or receive mail to or from anyone on the Internet. This might be all you need, but many companies also want to provide their users with an accessible webmail service that people can use from home or when they are on the road. Another feature that many people unfortunately cannot be without today is proper protection against viruses spread via e-mail as well as the filtering of spam messages.

We will also cover the most important aspects of security to prevent unauthorized or malicious use of the server. We will then discuss how to retain an archive of all e-mails received or sent by the server. Finally, we shall describe a process to backup and restore the server to protect all messages against data loss.

This book will cover the major features of the software in question, which will give you a solid foundation to work from.

By the end of this book, you will have a functioning e-mail server suitable for most small companies.

As the technical platform for our endeavor, we have chosen the GNU/Linux operating system and a proven selection of free software tools that will help us achieve the goal of a secure and reliable e-mail server for smaller companies. The tools we have chosen are widely known and used, written by software professionals, and are supported by a large community of users.

In this very first chapter of the book, we start with what you need to know before you even start working on your server.

- We discuss the advantages and disadvantages of running your own e-mail server.

- Guidance is given for choosing the appropriate hardware and network connection needed for the server.

- We give a brief introduction to the protocol used for exchanging mail over the Internet and the main protocols available to allow users to access their e-mails.

- In order to correctly route e-mail, we discuss the configuration options required on the server connected to the Internet.

- Finally, we provide a brief introduction to backup e-mail servers.

By the end of this chapter, you will have a basic understanding of the main components required to run an e-mail server.

Why manage your own e-mail server

Most **Internet Service Providers** (**ISPs**) already give customers the ability to send and receive e-mail on their servers, so why would we want to own and manage it by ourselves? As you are after all reading this book, you may already have your reasons, but let us examine this question and some possible answers to it.

The most important reason for hosting and managing your own e-mail server is control. For many organizations, e-mail is an important part of the Information Technology infrastructure. Keeping control over your e-mail has many advantages.

- If a company has offices in multiple places, you have full freedom when choosing how to connect them. A virtual private network between the offices, Transport Layer Security (TLS) connections between the offices, a single server for all offices, one server per office, and so on.

- By keeping your own messaging in-house, you can send messages to each other without having them travel across unsecured lines to and from the ISP. This also gives you a more reliable service if your Internet connection fails, and it avoids unnecessary latencies.

- You are not dependent on the competence of the provider's staff. If you manage your own server and need to solve a difficult problem or implement a custom solution for something, you can. Or if necessary, you can hire a consultant to help you.

- If the provider goes bankrupt, all of your data resides safely in your server room and on your backup media.

- You are not subject to the limitations that our provider may set regarding, say, use of disk space or the maximum size of messages.

- You can implement any policies for message archiving, antispam, or antivirus that you choose.

More control requires more responsibility and more knowledge, and that is where this book comes in.

These hopefully compelling arguments aside, there are also downsides to hosting your own e-mail server. This is a task that requires a certain level of knowledge and commitment, and so should not be undertaken by everyone. With your own server, you are not only responsible for the service you provide to your users, but you also have a responsibility towards the whole Internet community. An ill-configured e-mail server can help worms and spam to spread, which is not only is a disservice to the community but can also get your server blacklisted. Even though a properly set up server can run for years without requiring much maintenance, you must keep yourself reasonably updated and be prepared to act upon new threats that may arise. This is not meant to scare you off, but just to make you think carefully before embarking on this project.

What you need to host an e-mail server

Your server needs to be available through a permanent Internet connection with a fixed IP address. In theory, it is possible to run an e-mail server with a non-fixed (dynamic) IP address but it will not be reliable when the IP address is changed, and you will risk losing messages. With a dynamic IP address, you will also face a bigger risk of being put on one of the blacklists for dynamic IP address ranges.

If you are serious about running an e-mail server, get a decent business-class Internet connection. These are relatively inexpensive these days, and investing in one will save a lot of trouble later on. E-mail traffic does not depend on high bandwidth, so the capacity of a simple DSL line should be more than adequate.

Even though you will need a fixed IP address, you do not necessarily need a public IP address dedicated to the mail server. If your company only has a few external IP addresses and uses private RFC 1918 addresses (192.168.x.y) on the inside with a **Network Address Translation (NAT)** router, this is not a problem. The NAT router connects the private network to the rest of the world, and it is possible to set up the router to forward the ports required by the e-mail services to the internal e-mail server.

The next table shows which TCP ports are most likely to be used for this.

Port	Service
25	Simple Mail Transfer Protocol (SMTP)
110	Post Office Protocol (POP)
143	Internet Message Access Protocol (IMAP)
993	IMAP over TLS

If employees want to access their messages from home or from the road, all that is required is to make sure that no firewall is blocking access to the required ports, and that the NAT router (if any) forwards these ports correctly. If users want to send messages via the e-mail server, some extra configuration will be necessary to allow the host to perform authentication to prevent unregistered users sending e-mail.

Sizing the hardware of your e-mail server

When choosing a computer to use as an e-mail server, a lot of people have misconceptions regarding the hardware required to perform this task well. The constantly increasing performance of computers seems to lead people into thinking that they really need the latest and most buzzword-compliant stuff, even if they only want to handle a few thousand messages per day.

Although a certain expertise is required to assess the hardware needs for an organization, common sense goes a long way. For a company with 100 users, a reasonably high upper limit for the number of messages per day would be 5,000. That would allow each user to send or receive 50 messages every day. Even if we say that each and every message is sent within the eight hours of the working day, on an average, the system will not have to cope with more than 10 messages per minute. It is reasonable that a modern computer can receive and act upon a single e-mail message, often only a few kilobytes in size, in less than six seconds.

This little back-of-the-envelope exercise is obviously very rough and does not, for example, take into account the fact that messages typically do not arrive uniformly distributed in time, but it is still a pretty good way of estimating.

Let us now take a deeper look into what to think about when choosing the server. For an e-mail server that does not perform any content scanning (viruses, spam, and so on), the performance is typically not bound by the CPU but by the I/O performance, specifically the seek time of the hard disk(s) and the quality and configuration of the I/O controller. Throwing more CPU horsepower at the problem will not help. Modern computers are relatively better equipped CPU wise than I/O wise, so investing in a multiple gigahertz multi-core CPU configuration is probably useless. For any reasonably modern 1 GHz-class PC, a handful of messages per second is no problem. That load equates to almost 20,000 messages every hour.

Adding content scanning will probably increase the CPU load quite a lot, and the I/O system will also require more power to keep up. Still, one or two messages per second should not place a noticeable load on the system.

What we have been discussing so far is just the e-mail server. All it does is receive messages and deliver them to other hosts or local mailboxes. When choosing a server, you should not forget that people are going to want to read their e-mail too. This service is provided by additional server software. Just like the message handling software, the key requirement is I/O and not CPU. The number of users of the system is by itself an irrelevant figure; what is important are the usage patterns. How often will the users poll their mailboxes? If 100 users poll their mailboxes once every five minutes, on average there will be one every three seconds. Checking if a mailbox has any new messages, takes a fraction of a second, so the burden will not be significant.

The final, and arguably the hardest thing to consider, is disk storage. Using the expected traffic numbers, we can make some rough estimates. Let us assume 80% of our messages are under 1 KB, 15% have document attachments of 200 KB with the remainder being videos and other large files of 1 MB. Therefore, using a 200 day working year, that equates to a storage requirement of approximately 80 GB per year. A typical 1 TB disk drive would have the capacity for more than 12 years messages assuming no messages are deleted.

These guidelines may appear vague and non specific, but it is impossible to give exact figures. The performance one would expect from a given piece of hardware depends on so many factors that trying to give anything but general guidelines would be misleading. Use common sense and simple back-of-the-envelope calculations; do not buy the fanciest server you can find unless you are sure you really need it, but also do not use any old abandoned desktop machine you can find. Even if the performance of the old desktop machine may suffice, the components may be old and the service agreement or warranty may be out of date.

Main e-mail protocols: SMTP, POP, and IMAP

Why are we discussing basic network communication protocols in this book? Are we not running advanced software? Indeed we are, but knowing one's way around the protocols cannot only assist debugging a possibly non-working system but also increases the understanding of a mail system's behavior. We will start with a rather non-technical overview of the protocols, after which we will focus on the protocol details.

Overview

In the UNIX environment, traditional mail applications did not use any network protocol at all. They have instead accessed the locally stored mailbox files directly through the file system. Typically, the inbox of each user is stored in a single file in either the /var/mail or the /var/spool/mail directory with the same name as that of the user (for example, /var/spool/mail/joe). The focus of this book is to discuss Linux based e-mail solutions for a small office where users do not wish to log on to a central server with a terminal application in order to access their mail, so local mail storage will be covered only briefly.

The most important protocol in Internet mailing is the **Simple Mail Transfer Protocol** (**SMTP**). Its purpose is to transport e-mail messages between two systems. Both these computers may either be servers, or one of them may be a client machine on which the user runs the mail application—Outlook, Thunderbird, Eudora, or whatever. To collect new messages, the end user does not utilize SMTP. This is where the **Post Office Protocol** (**POP**) and the **Internet Message Access Protocol** (**IMAP**) come in.

Some proprietary systems such as Microsoft Exchange and Lotus Notes use their own protocols to access messages, and we will not discuss them here.

POP protocol

POP is the older and more widely used protocol of the two. It focuses on giving the users access to their inboxes, from which the users can download the new messages to their local computers and then delete them from the server. POP servers are not meant to be used for permanent storage of messages. The POP services of some Internet providers even prohibit users from leaving messages on the server after they have been downloaded once. The chief disadvantage of POP is that it only provides an intermediary storage medium and the users must store their messages permanently someplace else (for example, on their local hard drives). This is not only impractical for users who want to access their e-mail messages from multiple locations, but it is also a hassle for the System Administrator who may have to implement a backup solution for the users' messages on their local hard drives. POP also does not have any notion of providing multiple folders for every user; with POP a user can access his/her inbox only.

IMAP protocol

IMAP is meant as an access method to a first class mail store, that is, it is designed to allow the user to store the messages permanently on the server. This solves the System Administrator's backup problem and allows the user to access all messages from any place in the world (firewall restrictions aside). IMAP also has a more widespread implementation of TLS-secured connections, making IMAP safe to use in hostile environments. To improve performance and allow users to work with their mailboxes while not being connected to the mail server, most mail applications with IMAP support caching the downloaded mailboxes and messages in the local hard drive.

Unlike POP, IMAP supports multiple folders and stores message state information (whether or not the message has been read, replied to, or deleted) on the server. This means that a user accessing their message store from different locations, with possibly different e-mail clients, will be presented with a consistent, up-to-date view of their messages. IMAP also supports server-side searching, so the client application does not need to download all the messages to search for an e-mail.

The SMTP protocol

SMTP is a line-oriented text protocol that runs over TCP, which makes it trivial to decode SMTP transcripts and to initiate SMTP sessions using the regular telnet client found on just about any computer. An SMTP client starts a session by connecting to port 25 on the SMTP server. After the server has greeted the client, the client must respond by saying hello, or actually HELO or EHLO, followed by the client's hostname. If the server accepts the cordial greeting, the client may begin the first mail transaction.

An SMTP mail transaction consists of three parts—a sender, one or more recipients, and the actual message contents. The sender is specified with the MAIL FROM command, each recipient with an RCPT TO command, and the start of the message contents with a DATA command. If the server accepts the message, the client may continue with additional transactions or issue the QUIT command to terminate the SMTP session.

Let's be less abstract and look at an actual SMTP session to illustrate the protocol. The bold face print represents what the client sends to the server.

```
220 mail.example.com ESMTP Postfix (2.12.6.2)
EHLO gw.example.net
250-mail.example.com
250-PIPELINING
250-SIZE
250-VRFY
250-ETRN
250 8BITMIME
250-STARTTLS
250-ENHANCEDSTATUSCODES
MAIL FROM:<jack@example.net> SIZE=112
250 Ok
RCPT TO:<jill@example.com>
250 Ok
RCPT TO:<jack@example.com>
250 Ok
RCPT TO:<joe@example.com>
550 <joe@example.com>: Recipient address rejected: User unknown in
local recipient table
DATA
354 End data with <CR><LF>.<CR><LF>
Subject: Test mail
To: <root@example.com>
Date: Sun, 15 May 2009 20:23:22 +0200 (CEST)
This is a test message.
.
250 Ok: queued as B059D3C2B
QUIT
221 Bye
```

This example shows a host that claims to be named gw.example.net connecting to an SMTP server that calls itself mail.example.com. Because the server's first response contains ESMTP, the client decides to try **Enhanced SMTP (ESMTP)** and greets the server with EHLO instead of HELO. The server accepts this greeting and responds with a list of the supported ESMTP extensions.

Together with the sender address, the client sends the SIZE attribute to indicate the size of the message to the server. This is allowed because the server has stated that it supports the SIZE extension. If the size specified by the client exceeds the message size limit set by the server, the message can be rejected at once rather than after the whole message has been received and the server can assess the size.

An SMTP message can obviously have more than one recipient. This has a few consequences that must be remembered while implementing a mail system and inventing policies. In the previous example, the mail server accepts the first two recipients but rejects the third one. As two recipients have been accepted by the server, the client will try to send the message contents. Here the message is accepted by the server and queued for delivery (250 Ok: queued as B059D3C2B), which means that the SMTP server has taken over the responsibility for the delivery of the message to the accepted recipients. If the message cannot be delivered, the server will send a non-delivery message (bounce) back to the sender. The server could also have chosen to reject the whole message. If so, it would have rejected it for all recipients and not delivered it at all. In other words, in response to the message contents the server must either reject the message for all recipients or accept it for all recipients.

It is vital to understand the difference between the envelope and the header. The envelope of a message consists of the information given in the MAIL FROM and RCPT TO commands, that is, the sender and recipient information that are used to deliver the message. An SMTP server pays no attention what so ever to the From, To, and Cc message headers. In our example the To header contains just a single address with no other relation to the actual recipient addresses than the domain, but that is just a coincidence. Bounces are always sent to the envelope sender address, in this case jack@example.net. The sender address of bounce messages is the empty sender address, often called the null sender. However tempting it may be for some people, the null sender address must not be blocked.

So far, we have not commented on the numerical codes given by the server at the beginning of each line. Each number has a specific meaning and it is important to learn the correct interpretation of the first digit.

Digit	Meaning
2	Server has accepted the previous command and is awaiting your next command.
3	Used only in response to the DATA command, and means that the server is ready to accept the message contents.
4	Temporary error: The request cannot be performed at the moment, but it may be successfully serviced later.
5	Permanent error: The request will never be accepted.

In SMTP, error conditions can be either temporary or permanent. Both 4 and 5 are used to signal errors. A client that receives a temporary error designated by 4 should disconnect, keep the message in the queue, and retry at a later time. Typical temporary error conditions include a full mail queue disk, a server configuration error that must be resolved before messages can be accepted, or a temporary DNS lookup error. Permanent errors are indicated by the first digit being 5 and mean that the request will never be accepted, so a client will have to remove the message from the queue and send a bounce to the sender telling him or her that the message could not be delivered.

There is a lot more to SMTP than this quick introduction has covered. For further reading there are a number of documents that cover Internet networking related topics known as **Request for Comments** (**RFC**). RFCs are memorandums published by the **Internet Engineering Task Force** (**IETF**), which are generally adopted as standards. For SMTP the most important ones are **RFC 821** (Simple Mail Transfer Protocol) and **RFC 822** (Standard for the format of ARPA Internet text messages).

E-mail and DNS

The **Domain Name System** (**DNS**) plays an important role in e-mailing. The DNS is used by both, e-mail clients and e-mail servers. Even if you do not intend to maintain your own DNS server, a thorough understanding of DNS's role in e-mailing is a necessity for the mail server operator. This section assumes that the reader has basic knowledge of how DNS works in general.

DNS record types used by e-mail applications

In many networking scenarios, only two DNS record types are used — the **A record** and **PTR record**. These map hostnames to IP addresses and IP addresses to hostnames respectively. These record types are also used for e-mail, but there is also a third DNS record type that is uniquely available for e-mail.

How does an SMTP server discover to which host a message for a certain domain should be delivered? The recipient domain is, not surprisingly, used as the key in one or more DNS lookups. The first lookup that is made is for the mail-specific **MX record** — the **mail exchanger** record type. The MX entry allows the DNS operator to specify the hostname or hostnames of servers that can receive mail for a certain domain. For example, MX records can be used to specify that messages to someone at example.com should be sent to mail.example.com. If the recipient domain does not have an MX record, an attempt is made to find an A record for the recipient domain. If the A record lookup succeeds, the mail will be delivered to the host. If both the MX and A lookups do not return any results, the message is deemed undeliverable and is returned to the sender.

There are two good reasons to having MX records:

- Firstly, it might not be desirable to be forced to map the A record of a domain to the mail server. For example, Company Inc. with the WWW address `http://www.example.com/` wants to allow visitors to use the shorter `http://example.com/` URL, but does not want to run the web server application on the mail server (or vice versa).

- The more important reason is that the result of an MX lookup not only contains a list of hostnames, but rather a list of (hostname, priority) tuples. The priority field is an integer describing the priority of the hostname within the list. The absolute magnitude of the priority number does not matter, but it is used in relation to the priority of any other hostnames to create an ordered list of hostnames to try when delivering a message. The list is in ascending order, so the hostname with the lowest priority number will be contacted first. If two hostnames have equal priority, they will be tried in random order.

Equal-priority MX records can be used as a very crude form of load balancing between two or more servers. This is also possible with A records that map to multiple IP addresses. A hierarchy of backup mail servers with different priorities can be set up for a domain using MX records that cannot be made to happen with A records. Let us look at a constructed example of an organization that uses a lot of mail servers.

Priority	Hostname
10	mx1.example.com
10	mx2.example.com
20	mx3.example.com
30	mx4.example.com

If this DNS configuration is set for the domain example.com, SMTP servers are expected to try to deliver messages for example.com to mx1.example.com or mx2.example.com first. If both connections fail, mx3.example.com should be tried, and if even that server does not respond in a timely way, mx4.example.com is the last resort. Should that fail too, the message is kept and delivery is retried at a later time.

Backup mail servers

Having a backup mail server that can receive messages if the primary server is unavailable sounds like a really good idea, but today's reliable Internet connections together with spam, worms, and other rubbish have for the most part made backup mail servers unnecessary and often even harmful. The rationale for having a backup server is that it can receive messages while your primary server is down, and then deliver them to the primary server when it is up again. However, the advantage of this is very small, as all SMTP servers are required to queue undeliverable messages for at least five days before they are returned to the sender. Granted, by having a backup server it is possible to store unavailable messages for longer time than five days. However, if the main SMTP server is unavailable for longer than five days at a stretch then there are probably bigger problems than a few lost messages.

Because a backup mail server typically does not have the same spam-thwarting configuration as the primary server, spammers often specifically target backup servers in order to bypass the stricter rules of the primary server.

Another strong reason to avoid backup mail servers is that they typically do not perform recipient validation. This means that they do not know which recipient addresses are valid for the domains they act as backup servers for. This requires a backup server to accept all messages for the backed-up domains and attempt to deliver them to the primary server. The primary server will reject invalid recipients, causing the backup server to bounce such message back to the sender. This is known as backscatter and is bad for two reasons:

- Sender addresses are often spoofed, so the bounces may be sent to an innocent bystander.
- It may fill the mail queue with bounced messages that cannot be delivered because the receiving server is unavailable.

A busy server that does not perform recipient validation and is hit heavily with spam may have thousands or tens of thousands of undeliverable messages residing in the queue.

Summary

In this chapter, we started by discussing why you should even consider hosting your own e-mail server. Then, we looked at some questions that need to be answered before starting work with the server—the kind of network connection, computer power and disk space requirements that are expected.

To manage an e-mail server successfully, an understanding of the network communication protocols used is important. We gave an overview of POP and IMAP, and delved more deeply into the most important of them all, SMTP.

Finally, we looked at the vital role that the DNS plays in routing messages to the correct server or a backup server if one is available.

2
Setting up Postfix

The **Mail Transfer Agent** (**MTA**) is perhaps the most important part of a mail system. It is responsible for receiving messages from the Internet or from your own users and doing what it can to make sure that the messages arrive at their destinations—other mail servers or mailboxes of your users.

Postfix has been chosen as the mail transfer agent to be covered in this book. Postfix has a large feature set, it has an excellent security track record, it is fast, easy to configure, and under active development.

This book assumes that you are running Postfix 2.0 or later. Any feature or behavior of Postfix that is specific to releases later than 2.0 will be noted.

Introduction to Postfix

This first section gives a brief introduction to Postfix, how it works, and describes how its behavior can be controlled.

What is Postfix

Postfix is a modular mail transfer agent developed by IBM researcher Wietse Venema. It is free software and was released publicly for the first time in 1998 under the name **VMailer**. It is written in **C** and currently consists of about 105,000 lines of code (comments excluded), which makes it fairly small. It works on most non-historic variants of UNIX and Linux.

As a pure mail transfer agent, Postfix does not provide any service for allowing users to collect their mail via the **POP or IMAP** protocols. That task must be carried out by some other piece of software. The software discussed in this book for facilitating retrieval of mail from the host is **Courier IMAP**.

All official Postfix documentation, as well as the source code and links to third-party software and archives of the very active mailing list can be found at the Postfix website at `http://www.postfix.org/`.

Postfix architecture: An overview

This section will describe the different parts of the Postfix mail transfer agent and explain what really goes on when you send a message through the system. Although this might not be the most exciting text you have ever read, understanding the basics of how Postfix works is essential if you wish to successfully manage a Postfix server.

Postfix is divided into a number of separate **daemons**, or background processes, that communicate with each other. The daemons have distinct areas of responsibility, may run in different security contexts, and may have different rules for the number of processes of their type that may be created. All daemon processes are created as needed and are supervised by a mother daemon, the `master`. Some daemons are rarely or never restarted, but most of them will commit suicide after having served a configurable number of requests or after they have been idle for a configurable duration of time. The following figure shows how messages flow through a Postfix system, and can be used to accompany the text that follows. The solid lines show the path of the message content while dotted lines show other forms of communication.

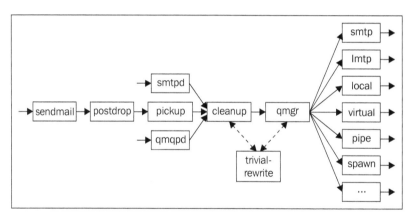

Not all Postfix daemons will be described here, just the important ones. A complete rundown of all daemons can be found in the *Postfix Architecture Overview* document at `http://www.postfix.org/OVERVIEW.html`.

New message arrival

New messages can arrive into the Postfix system in three ways. The most common way is, of course, via the **Simple Mail Transfer Protocol (SMTP)**. The daemon responsible for receiving messages via SMTP is named smtpd. The uncommon **QMQP Submission Protocol**, introduced in Daniel J. Bernstein's MTA **qmail**, is also supported with the qmqpd daemon. However, this book will not discuss QMQP.

The third way in which a message can arrive is via local submission with the sendmail program. This is the standard way to submit mail messages from programs and scripts running on a UNIX host. Postfix provides a sendmail program that in most regards is compatible with the sendmail program of the sendmail mail transfer agent (http://www.sendmail.org/). Many UNIX mail user agents such as Mail, Pine, and Mutt, as well as webmail software such as SquirrelMail and IMP use the sendmail interface to submit new messages, although some software offer the option to submit messages via SMTP instead.

The sendmail program hands messages on to the **postdrop** program, which places message files in the maildrop directory within the Postfix queue directory. The pickup daemon waits for messages to arrive into the maildrop directory, and passes them on to the cleanup daemon. From there on, sendmail-submitted messages take the same road as messages submitted via SMTP or QMQP. Messages can be submitted via sendmail even if Postfix is not running on the machine at the moment. When Postfix starts the next time, pickup will discover the queued-up message files and process them.

When smtpd, qmqpd, or pickup receives a new message, it hands it to the cleanup daemon. This daemon enforces restrictions on the message's size, acts on any content restrictions configured by the user, rewrites sender and/or recipient addresses as required by the configuration, adds any required headers that are missing, and does a few other things. The cleanup daemon uses the trivial-rewrite daemon for some address rewriting operations. When done with its business, cleanup puts the queue file in the incoming queue and notifies the queue manager.

Scheduling message deliveries

The **queue manager**, qmgr, is responsible for scheduling the delivery of messages. To decide how a message should be delivered to each recipient (namely the delivery method and the next destination), qmgr gets help from trivial-rewrite. The queue manager requests delivery agent processes from the master daemon and collects the results of the deliveries.

The queue manager is responsible for all messages from the point when the `cleanup` daemon hands them over until they are removed from the queue. The removal can be either because they have been successfully delivered to all recipients or because they have been in the queue for so long that Postfix decides that they are undeliverable. By default, messages will remain in the queue for a maximum of five days. The queue manager calls upon the `bounce` daemon to send a `bounce` message to the sender.

The queue manager uses a number of directories for different purposes. The incoming queue is monitored for new messages, and the next stop is the **active queue**. The active queue contains the messages that are ready for delivery and are waiting to be dispatched to a delivery agent. If a delivery attempt fails, the message is moved to the **deferred queue**. That queue will be scanned periodically and, if it is time to retry the delivery of a message, the queue file for the message will be moved back into the active queue. Whether a delivery of a message should be reattempted when the queue is scanned depends on two factors—how much time has passed since the message arrived and the two configuration parameters that set a minimum and maximum time interval between the reattempts.

In addition to these queues, there is also a special-purpose queue named **hold**. This queue contains messages that have been put on hold by the system administrator using the `postsuper` command. Postfix will not touch these messages at all until they are taken off hold with the same command. The hold queue can be used to temporarily stall the delivery of certain messages, for example because they are large and need to be delivered during off-peak hours, or because they are deemed suspicious and need to be inspected before they are allowed to be delivered.

The different queues used by Postfix are described in detail in the *QSHAPE_README* document (`http://www.postfix.org/QSHAPE_README.html`). This document also describes `qshape`, a script that ships with Postfix and analyzes the contents of the queues, and helps you identify bottlenecks.

Message delivery

Postfix comes with a number of delivery agents that are used to deliver messages using various means and protocols. The delivery agents are the last daemons that touch the messages before they leave your system.

The Postfix SMTP client, `smtp` (not to be confused with the SMTP server, `smtpd`), is used to deliver messages to other hosts via the SMTP protocol. It is very similar to the LMTP client, `lmtp`, which delivers messages via the **Local Mail Transfer Protocol (LMTP)**. As a network protocol, LMTP is very similar to SMTP, but where SMTP is used to transport messages between MTAs, LMTP is used for the final delivery of messages to the mail store from which users can access the messages.

The local delivery agent, `local`, delivers messages to users with normal accounts on the system. It supports aliases for simple mailing lists or role addresses as well as `.forward` files so that users themselves can set up forwarding of their messages.

If you have virtual mailbox users—users that do not have real accounts (for example, shell accounts) on the system—their messages are delivered with `virtual` Postfix daemon.

If Postfix's standard delivery agents do not suffice, you can write your own delivery agent and have Postfix invoke it for some (or all) messages. In that case, you can either use the `pipe` daemon to have the message bodies given to your delivery agent via the standard input stream, or you can use the `spawn` daemon if you want to write a delivery agent that accepts messages via some network protocol.

Supporting programs

Postfix contains a number of supporting programs that you can use to control, test, and debug your Postfix system. This list is not exhaustive and gives only a brief description of each program, but some of the programs will be used later in the chapter. It is a good idea to get acquainted with them so that you at least know what sort of problems they can help you solve.

Program	Description
`mailq`	Views the current contents of the Postfix queue. The output includes the size, time of arrival, sender address, and recipient address/addresses of each message. Internally `mailq` just invokes the `postqueue` command and exists only for backwards compatibility with the `sendmail` mail transfer agent.
`newaliases`	Uses the `postalias` command to rebuild all local alias files. Local aliases will be covered in the *Virtual alias domains and local aliases* section.
`postalias`	Rebuilds a single alias file or queries an alias lookup table.
`postcat`	Shows the contents of a binary queue file residing in the Postfix queue.
`postconf`	Shows the current or default values of Postfix's configuration parameters. Can also modify the main configuration file, which can be useful in scripts.
`postfix`	Starts, stops, or restarts Postfix, or reloads its configuration. Can also be used to check the integrity of the queue directories and a few other seldom-used administrative tasks.
`postmap`	Rebuilds an indexed database file used for table lookups or queries any lookup table. The *Troubleshooting lookup tables with postmap* section discusses how this can be used to debug a Postfix setup.

Program	Description
postqueue	Apart from carrying out the work for the mailq program, postqueue can also be used to flush the queue. Flushing a queue means moving all messages in the deferred queue to the active queue. This can be useful to schedule immediate message delivery, but be careful. If your server is heavily loaded and performing badly, flushing the queue will only make matters worse. The sendmail program can also be used to flush the queue, again for compatibility reasons.
postsuper	Allows you to take actions on already queued messages, for example deleting or re-queuing them. It can also perform a structural check on the queue directories and fix problems such as queue files having the wrong names. Such a check is, for example, necessary if the whole queue directory has been moved or restored from a backup.

Installation and basic configuration

In this section, we will take a look at how to obtain and install Postfix as well as how to make basic configuration changes. By the end of this section, you will be able to use Postfix to send and receive e-mail messages.

Choosing the Postfix version

There are two separate branches of Postfix development— the official release and the experimental release. The official release is sometimes referred to as the stable release, but that is somewhat misleading as it implies that the experimental release is unstable. That is not the case. The experimental release is used to introduce all new Postfix features. When the implementations of the features and their interfaces (for example, their configuration parameters) have stabilized sufficiently, they are brought into the official release. Normally, the only changes made to the official release are bug fixes and fixes for portability problems.

The experimental release is usable in production environments, but the code is of course less tested, and configuration parameters and their semantics may change between releases. If you run the experimental builds, you are more likely to run into bugs and other oddities that the stable release should not have. On the other hand, you get access to new features before those using stable builds. If you choose to use the experimental release, you should build and install Postfix from source code instead of using some package management system (say RPMs). This will allow you to easily apply any patches for newly discovered problems.

The experimental release has a version number that indicates the number of the upcoming official release together with the release date of the experimental release in question. For example, at the time of writing the current official release was 2.6.3 and the current experimental release was 2.7-20090807.

Installing from a package

Most Linux distributions include Postfix as a package that can easily be installed. You are better off with the distribution's package unless you are comfortable building software from source and, if required, debugging any build problems that might occur. Most packages come prebuilt with some extra features that would otherwise require a more complicated build process.

Because there are many different packaging systems, the actual process of installing the Postfix package(s) will not be covered in this book. Please consult the documentation of your package management system for details.

A word of caution for users of distributions that allow multiple mail transfer agents to be installed at the same time: If you are installing Postfix to replace another mail transfer agent, you should make sure the previous software is properly removed from your system. As probably all mail transfer agents provide a sendmail program, this file is installed with a name such as sendmail.postfix, and a symbolic link points from sendmail to sendmail.postfix or whatever mail transfer agent's sendmail program is chosen to be the main one. If that symbolic link does not point to Postfix's sendmail program, you might get surprised when you attempt to send a message.

Installing from source code

Installing Postfix from the original source code is not very difficult and enables you to run any version you want and not just the version chosen by the package maintainer of your Linux distribution. The Postfix source code can be downloaded from a number of mirrors accessible from the main Postfix website http://www.postfix.org/download.html.

Once you have downloaded and unpacked the archive in a suitable directory (for example)/usr/local/src, you will notice that the Postfix build system does not use GNU autotools and therefore does not have the configure script that one normally finds in the root directory of the unpacked source code archive. The Postfix build system will automatically take care of this step. Do not worry if you want to install Postfix in some non-standard location, you will have an opportunity to set various installation directories later.

If you need to enable non-standard features such as support for MySQL or LDAP lookups, you must inform the build system about this and where to find the libraries and header files for each feature. For exact instructions and details about each non-standard feature, please review the README file for each and every one of them. For example, the MySQL instructions found in README_FILES/MYSQL_README tell you to run the following command to enable MySQL support when building Postfix:

```
$ make -f Makefile.init makefiles \
  'CCARGS=-DHAS_MYSQL -I/usr/local/mysql/include' \
  'AUXLIBS=-L/usr/local/mysql/lib -lmysqlclient -lz -lm'
```

Adjust the paths to where the MySQL header files and shared libraries are located on your system. You must have the development header files and libraries for MySQL installed. Depending on your Linux distribution these may have to be installed separately.

If you need more than one extra feature, you will have to combine the commands given in each of the README files. Pay close attention when doing this. All quotes, equal signs, and spaces need to go at precisely the right places. The CCARGS and AUXLIBS variables must be set only once, so the general form of combining several configuration commands is this:

```
$ make -f Makefile.init makefiles \
  'CCARGS=<feature 1 CCARGS setting> <feature 2 CCARGS setting>' \
  'AUXLIBS=<feature 1 AUXLIBS setting> <feature 2 AUXLIBS setting>'
```

After this, you are all set to build Postfix using the following command:

```
$ make
```

When the build is complete (hopefully without errors), it is time to create a user and some groups that Postfix can use for many of its daemons. Start by adding two groups—postfix and postdrop. For example, you can use the groupadd tool that probably is available in your Linux distribution.

```
$ groupadd postfix
$ groupadd postdrop
```

Verify this by checking the contents of /etc/group. It should by now contain lines similar to this:

```
postfix:x:123:
postdrop:x:321:
```

The next step is to create a user named `postfix`. This user requires neither shell access nor a valid home directory. The primary group of this new user should be the newly created `postfix` group. Here is how to do it using the `useradd` tool:

```
$ useradd -c postfix -d /tmp -g postfix -s /bin/false postfix
```

Again, verify by checking the contents of `/etc/passwd`:

```
postfix:x:12345:123:postfix:/tmp:/bin/false
```

The next and final step is to install your newly built Postfix. If you are installing Postfix for the first time in this particular Linux installation, run the following command:

```
$ make install
```

This command will guide you through an interactive installation procedure where you get to choose various installation directories and file locations.

If you are upgrading Postfix from a previous release, run the following command instead:

```
$ make upgrade
```

All right! Postfix is now installed on your system and you will soon be ready to use it.

To make sure that Postfix starts when your system boots, some extra measures are needed. Most Linux systems have a `SysV-style init`, so you need to construct an `init` script and make proper links in the runlevel directories.

The Postfix configuration

Like most UNIX software, Postfix reads its configuration from text files stored in the `/etc` directory or a subdirectory thereof. Postfix configuration files are usually stored in `/etc/postfix`, but you can configure Postfix to use any other directory. Postfix uses two main configuration files, `master.cf` and `main.cf`, and any auxiliary files that you set up yourself.

After a change to any of these files, Postfix must be reloaded. This can be done with the same program that started Postfix, either via the `init` scripts or via some other service management tool that your distribution provides.

```
postfix reload
/etc/init.d/postfix reload
/etc/rc.d/init.d/postfix reload
```

> **Postfix restart required after changing `inet_interfaces`:**
> If the `inet_interfaces` parameter is changed, a reload is not enough. Postfix must be stopped and restarted for the changes to take effect. This is also true for the `inet_protocols` parameter introduced in Postfix 2.2.

main.cf

The file you will be editing most frequently is `main.cf`. This file defines the parameters that control the behavior of Postfix's daemon processes. Each line has the following form:

```
parameter = value
```

This simply means that the configuration parameter named `parameter` is assigned the contents `value`. A parameter may only be specified once in `main.cf`. If you mistakenly give the same parameter different contents at different places in `main.cf`, the last occurrence will be the one used by Postfix. Apart from this, the order in which parameters are listed in `main.cf` is insignificant. However, within the parameter contents the order of the keywords may matter. For example, the following two parameter settings are not necessarily equivalent:

```
parameter = A, B
parameter = B, A
```

If the value of a parameter is not specified in `main.cf`, Postfix will use a default. The default for most parameters is hardwired in the source code, but some default values are determined at build time and a few of them at run time.

Lines in `main.cf` can be marked as comments by starting them with #.

```
# These two lines are comments. They can be used to temporarily
# disable parameters, or to explain the configuration.
mydomain = example.com
mydestination = $mydomain, localhost
```

This short example also shows how the current value of another parameter can be inserted when setting a parameter value; simply type a dollar sign directly followed by the name of the parameter whose value you wish to obtain. The last line in the previous code snippet is equivalent to the following:

```
mydestination = example.com, localhost
```

Sometimes it is not convenient to have everything on one line. By starting a line with whitespace, you tell Postfix that the line is a continuation of the previous line. For example, the following two are equivalent:

```
smtpd_recipient_restrictions = permit_mynetworks, reject
smtpd_recipient_restrictions =
        permit_mynetworks,
        reject
```

Starting with Postfix 2.1, the format of the `main.cf` configuration file is documented in the `postconf(5)` manual page that also describes all available configuration parameters. The manual page is available online from `http://www.postfix.org/postconf.5.html`.

The `postconf` program is very useful for examining the current and default value of `main.cf` parameters. Start the program with one or more parameter names as options and it will report the values that Postfix would use. If you use the `-d` option, `postconf` will report the default value of the parameter(s) you list.

For example, here is how to compare the current value of `mydestination` with its default value:

```
$ postconf mydestination
mydestination = $mydomain, localhost.$mydomain

$ postconf -d mydestination
mydestination = $myhostname, localhost.$mydomain, localhost
```

Using this method is often quicker than looking in `main.cf` or wading through a huge manual page to find the default value. It also reveals the actual value that Postfix thinks a parameter has, making it easier to spot typing errors.

In addition to displaying `main.cf` configuration parameters, the `postconf` program can edit `main.cf` for you. This is especially useful if you want to automate configuration changes in scripts. This is done with the `-e` option that expects one or more parameter assignments to follow.

```
$ postconf relay_domains
relay_domains =

$ postconf -e relay_domains=example.com
$ postconf relay_domains
relay_domains = example.com
```

master.cf

The `master.cf` file configures the Postfix master daemon that was discussed earlier. For most simple Postfix setups, `master.cf` does not need to be touched at all.

Each line in `master.cf` defines a service that a certain program carries out. For example, the daemon that receives and processes SMTP connections, `smtpd`, is one service. The program that delivers messages to the local users, `local`, is another service. In addition to the 15–20 services that Postfix defines from the start, you can add your own services.

The fifth column in `master.cf` controls whether each service should be run in a `chroot` environment. `chroot` is a UNIX feature that changes the root of the file system, making it impossible to access a file outside the new root directory even if a running process is compromised by an evildoer with root privileges. The source distribution of Postfix disables `chroot` completely by default, but some Linux distributions have it enabled. Although `chroot` is a security feature that can be quite useful as an extra safety net, it makes Postfix more difficult to maintain and is more or less useless unless the rest of your system is tightly secured.

In Postfix 2.2 and later, the format of the `master.cf` configuration file is documented in the `master(5)` manual page. In earlier releases, most of that information can be found in comments in the `master.cf` file itself.

Lookup tables

Some information cannot be conveniently represented in `main.cf` or `master.cf`. Postfix's concept of lookup tables allows information to be stored in external files, relational databases, or LDAP directories.

To Postfix, a lookup table is an abstract entity that maps one string, the **lookup key**, to another string, the **lookup result**. Those who are mathematically inclined may look upon it as a function or as a collection of (key, value) tuples, and programmers may recognize it as a hash table. Basically, it functions like a phonebook; you look up a name and get a phone number or an address back.

Postfix supports many different kinds of lookup tables. Some of them are referred to as *indexed*, meaning that the `postmap` command is used to compile the input file written by the user to a binary format the Postfix reads. This is done for performance reasons and allows the tables to contain tens of thousands or even hundreds of thousands of entries without affecting performance. This means you need to remember to use `postmap` after editing the file.

The following table describes the most important lookup table types:

Type	Description
cdb	An indexed map type that uses the CDB library. Very fast for large number of entries. Supported by Postfix 2.2 and later versions.
cidr	Allows lookups of IP addresses using the CIDR notation. Supported by Postfix 2.1 and later versions.
dbm	DBM is a classic UNIX indexed database format that is available on Linux too, but its use is discouraged because it uses two files to represent the database. This increases the risk of inconsistencies as the two files cannot be updated atomically. Use hash or cdb instead.
hash	This indexed lookup table type is probably the most commonly used, and utilizes the Berkeley DB library.
ldap	LDAP directories are often used in corporate and university environments to store user databases. Microsoft's Active Directory is also accessible through LDAP, simplifying the use of Postfix in a heterogeneous environment.
mysql	The well-known MySQL relational database engine is supported, allowing you to make almost any type of SQL query.
pcre	Allows matching the looked-up strings against a list of regular expressions where the first matching expression wins. Uses the widespread **Perl Compatible Regular Expressions (PCRE)** library.
pgsql	The PostgreSQL relational database engine is also supported.
proxy	The proxy type is a special lookup table type that is used to wrap other lookup tables. This is useful for reducing the number of concurrent connections when lookup tables are being used from services with a high process count. For example, accessing LDAP directories from the SMTP server can cause the maximum number of connections in the LDAP server to hit the roof, but accessing the LDAP directory through the proxy lookup table will reduce the concurrency.
regexp	Works such as pcre but without the dependency to the PCRE library. The regular expression grammar supported is limited and the performance may be worse than with pcre. If possible, choose pcre rather than regexp.
static	This type is a special-purpose one that always returns a given string regardless of what is being looked up. This can be used in cases where Postfix expects a lookup table reference instead of a fixed string, but you really want to specify a fixed string.

You can use any type of lookup table for any purpose; Postfix does not impose any limitations except that security considerations require that some features of regular expression tables are disabled under some circumstances. That said, not all lookup table types make sense to use for each and every purpose.

Many of the lookup table types are always supported by Postfix, but some of them are optional and require support to be compiled into Postfix. Many Linux vendors provide additional packages that you can install to obtain, for example, LDAP support. To find out which lookup table types your Postfix installation supports, use the `postconf` command.

```
$ postconf -m
static
cidr
nis
regexp
environ
proxy
btree
unix
hash
pcre
ldap
sdbm
```

In most cases, the simple indexed lookup table types will be the most convenient ones. An indexed lookup table is nothing more than a text file that you can edit using your favorite text editor. The first part of each line, up to the first space or tab, will be taken as a lookup key and the rest of the line will be taken as the corresponding value.

```
key                          value
```

One possible drawback with indexed lookup table types is that you do have to remember to run `postmap` when you have updated the table. You do not have to reload or restart Postfix after updating an indexed file with `postmap`. Postfix will discover the updated file itself and restart its daemon processes as required.

The topic of lookup tables could fill a whole chapter by itself, so this section will just touch upon them. We will use lookup tables in a few places later in this chapter, for example, when we set up policies for spam control.

For a more elaborated discussion of lookup tables and a list of all available lookup table types, see DATABASE_README (http://www.postfix.org/DATABASE_README.html) and the manual pages that document the use of some of the more complex lookup table types.

Getting Postfix up and running

Now that you have installed Postfix, let's make some basic configuration changes, fire it up, and take it for a test drive. If you installed Postfix from a package you may already have answered some configuration questions and have had Postfix started for you.

Domains and hostnames

Before starting Postfix, let's review some fundamental settings in `main.cf`. The first ones concern the names of your domain and your mailhost. The `mydomain` parameter should be set to your main Internet domain. If you run Example Inc. having the domain `http://www.example.com/`, the following setting would be reasonable:

```
mydomain = example.com
```

The value of `mydomain` will affect how Postfix transforms hostnames that are not fully qualified. This means that all bare hostnames encountered in places such as sender and recipient addresses will be qualified with this domain—a hostname such as `jeeves` will, in this case, be turned into `jeeves.example.com`. We will also refer to `mydomain` in other parameters using the `$parameter` notation described earlier. Note that the feature of appending `mydomain` can be disabled by setting the `append_dot_mydomain` parameter to `NO`, and some Linux distributions make this modification by default. In general, the value should be left as `YES`.

A related parameter is `myhostname` that incidentally tells Postfix the hostname of the machine. The hostname is among other things used as default when the Postfix SMTP server greets a client and when the SMTP client says HELLO to a server. Postfix is normally able to determine this by itself, but sometimes you want to override this. Use the `postconf` command to see if the current value looks good.

```
$ postconf myhostname
myhostname = jeeves
```

Yes, this looks fine. Note that this hostname is not fully qualified, so the actual hostname used in various places will include `mydomain`.

A parameter that is related to `mydomain` is `myorigin`. This parameter specifies the domain that should be used to qualify e-mail addresses that have no domain part at all. This may seem highly irregular, but it is actually pretty common. Messages submitted with the `sendmail` program will by default get the current username as the sender address and, because usernames do not have domains, the username will be qualified with `myorigin` before the message is delivered anywhere. By default, `myorigin` is set to the same value as `myhostname`.

```
$ postconf -d myorigin
myorigin = $myhostname
```

This should be fine, but you might want to set it to `mydomain` instead.

```
myorigin = $mydomain
```

The next parameter that we will give attention to is `mydestination`. This parameter is quite important because it tells Postfix which domains are considered local, that is, which domains should be delivered to UNIX accounts on this machine. Unlike `mydomain` and `myorigin`, `mydestination` may contain multiple domains separated by space or commas. By listing `example.com` here, Postfix will accept messages addressed to `joe@example.com` and deliver them to the UNIX user "joe".

One important property of local domains is that they are all considered equal. If `example.com` and `example.net` are both listed in `mydestination`, `joe@example.com` will be equivalent to `joe@example.net`. If you need additional domains where the users are not equal, that is `joe@example.com` and `joe@example.net` should lead to different mailboxes, you need to implement virtual alias domains, described in the *Virtual alias domains* section.

Returning to Example Inc. you will want to have `example.com` listed in `mydestination` as it is your primary domain. The old domain, `example.net`, should also work for the time being so that one should be included too. Additionally, it is wise to list the value of `myhostname` in `mydestination` as well as make sure that mail addressed to `localhost` gets delivered properly. This yields the following complete list of local domains for Example Inc.:

```
mydestination = $mydomain, example.net, $myhostname,
localhost.$mydomain
```

So why `localhost.$mydomain` instead of just `localhost` if we want messages to `root@localhost` to be delivered locally? Remember that `mydomain` is used to qualify all hostnames that are not already fully qualified (one may argue that `localhost` in fact already is a fully qualified hostname, but Postfix does not make a special case for that hostname). The address `root@localhost` will be rewritten to `root@localhost.example.com`, so `localhost.example.com` is what we want to list in `mydestination`.

Two very important Postfix parameters, `mynetworks` and `mynetworks_style`, control which hosts are allowed to use your server as a relay. Setting these incorrectly may allow your server to be abused by spammers and the likes, so it is important that you get them right. By default, all hosts on the subnets that your server is directly connected to will be allowed access. This should be secure in most cases. These parameters and other methods of allowing relay access will be discussed in depth in Chapter 5.

Indirect mail delivery through your ISP

Some **Internet Service Providers (ISP)** do not allow their customers to directly access remote mail servers via the standard SMTP port (25). Instead they provide a relay server that all outbound messages must go through. This policy is common for residential cable or DSL connections, but some providers have the same policy for commercial-grade connections. If such is the case, you need to configure Postfix to deliver all outbound messages indirectly via your ISP's relay server.

This is done with the `relayhost` parameter that contains the hostname or IP address of the relay server to use. The following forms are allowed:

```
relayhost = example.com
relayhost = [mail.example.com]
relayhost = [1.2.3.4]
```

The first form will cause Postfix to perform an MX lookup on the hostname, just as it would do for a normal message delivery. Enclosing the hostname in square brackets as in the second example suppresses the MX lookup. The square brackets are also required in the third case when an IP address is specified.

Optionally, the hostname or address can be followed by `:port` to specify an alternative TCP port. Note that you cannot specify multiple hostnames or addresses to achieve fallback or load balancing behavior. If you need fallback hosts when the normal relay server is unreachable, take a look at the `fallback_relay` parameter. Refer the *Other useful configuration parameters* section for additional information on other parameters.

Choosing network interfaces

The `inet_interfaces` parameter decides the network interfaces that Postfix will use for both listening to new connections and sending out messages. If you have multiple network interfaces and you do not want Postfix to use all of them, you can adjust this parameter to list the addresses or hostnames of the interfaces you do want Postfix to use.

Some Linux distributions set `inet_interfaces` to `localhost` by default, which means that Postfix will listen only on the loopback interface. This makes at least some sense for workstations, but it is obviously completely unusable for servers that need to receive messages from foreign hosts. If the Postfix packaging of your Linux distribution has this feature, just delete or comment the `inet_interfaces` line from `main.cf` to disable it. Postfix will then use the default value of `all`, which of course means that all interfaces should be used.

Changing `inet_interfaces` requires Postfix to be restarted. A reload is not enough.

Choosing mailbox format for local deliveries

By default, Postfix delivers local messages (messages to domains listed in `mydestination`) into files in `mbox` format. The `mbox` format for mailboxes stores all messages of a mailbox in a single text file. These files are named after the user and go into the directory specified by `mail_spool_directory` (normally `/var/mail` or `/var/spool/mail`). If the user desires additional mailboxes to store messages, those files are stored somewhere in the user's home directory (often in `$HOME/mail` or `$HOME/Mail`).

The `mbox` format has a few flaws that make it rather undesirable. The single-file format makes message deletion expensive as the whole file must be rewritten completely unless the message deleted is the last one, in which case the file can just be truncated. `mbox` also puts up hurdles when multiple processes need to access the same mailbox concurrently, which happens when a user uses a POP server to retrieve and delete messages while new mail is being delivered. This requires that some method of exclusive locking is used to avoid the concurrent access that might corrupt the files. Such locking is not a big problem if all software run on the same machine, access the same local file system, and agree on which locking method to use, but it is a royal pain if mailboxes need to be accessed over the network via network file systems such as NFS where reliable file locking can be a problem. Finally, `mbox` causes problems if used together with disk quotas. While the mailbox is being rewritten, it will use up to twice the original storage.

To avoid these problems, D. J. Bernstein, the author of software such as `qmail` and `djbdns`, designed the `maildir` format for mailboxes. As the name implies, `maildir` uses directories and one file per message. Deletion of messages is always very fast, but on the other hand it may take longer to scan a mailbox and produce a list of all messages as all message files have to be opened and read. `maildir` is safe to use with NFS. In the `maildir` delivery format, the inbox of a user is typically found in `$HOME/Maildir`.

To configure Postfix to deliver new messages to local users to `$HOME/Maildir`, set the `home_mailbox` parameter like this:

```
home_mailbox = Maildir/
```

Note the slash at the end of the line; it is important! Postfix follows the convention used by many other programs that a mailbox location ending with a slash denotes `maildir`. If you omit the slash, Postfix will try to deliver messages to the mbox file `$HOME/Maildir`.

The `home_mailbox` parameter is only effective for local domains when Postfix performs the delivery itself. If delivery is made by some other delivery agent such as Procmail or Maildrop, you have to configure that software for `maildir` delivery.

The rest of this book assumes that you have chosen `maildir` delivery. The IMAP/POP server you will be introduced to later, Courier IMAP, does not support the `mbox` format at all. Converting mailboxes between `mbox` and `maildir` is not difficult, so if you want to switch formats later that would not be a problem.

Error reporting

The final step is to make sure that Postfix and real people around the world can notify you as a postmaster about error conditions. Internet standards require all domains to have a postmaster address, but you do not need to create an account with that name. Instead you can use the aliasing feature of Postfix to redirect messages addressed to the postmaster address to yourself and any other people that manage the mail system. Also, you should redirect messages to the root account.

Aliases will be discussed in more detail in the *Local Aliases* section, but this step should be done right now so we will take a quick look anyway. To make Postfix redirect root's messages and accept messages addressed to postmaster even though no such user account exists, the local alias table must be modified. The configuration parameter `alias_maps` controls the location of the lookup tables that define such mappings:

```
$ postconf alias_maps
alias_maps = hash:/etc/aliases
```

On this particular system, the local aliases are stored in the file `/etc/aliases`. Edit that file so that it contains two lines similar to these:

```
postmaster: root
root: jack, jill
```

This means that messages addressed to the postmaster will be sent to the root user, and messages to the root user will be redirected to the users, "jack" and "jill". Save the file and run the `newaliases` command so that Postfix will pick up the changes to the file.

Note that alias lookups are recursive—Postfix does not stop when the `postmaster` lookup has succeeded, it continues to look up `root`, and finally `jack` and `jill`. `jack` and `jill` may not have alias entries, in which case Postfix stops the lookup recursion.

The type of problems that Postfix will report to the postmaster is configurable with the `notify_classes` parameter. By default, only resource issues such as out-of-disk-space problems and software problems will be reported, but you may configure Postfix to report more types of problems. For example, you might also want to know about SMTP protocol violations:

```
notify_classes = resource, software, protocol
```

When Postfix reports a problem, a transcript of the SMTP session is included. This can be a valuable debugging aid.

Opt for more extensive error reporting rather than terse reporting. If you receive too many error reports, see if you can use the filtering features of your delivery agent or your mail client to remove the error reports that you are not interested in. Protocol violations by incoming spam mail generated by badly written spam software can typically be ignored, but if one of your own computers behaves badly you will want to know about it.

Other useful configuration parameters

In addition to the configuration parameters covered so far, a few others that can be useful to know about will be mentioned. You will most likely do fine using their default values. If you want more information about them, please consult the documentation that came with your version or Postfix or read the documentation online at `http://www.postfix.org/documentation.html`.

Parameter	Description
always_bcc	Sends a copy of each message to a specified recipient. This can be used for e-mail archiving. If you need more fine-grained control over which messages are copied, take a look at `sender_bcc_maps` and `recipient_bcc_maps`. The latter two parameters require Postfix 2.1 or later.
defer_transports	Contains names of transports (delivery agents, more or less) whose deliveries should be temporarily deferred. This allows you to suspend local message deliveries if the file system for the home directories is broken or unavailable but the rest of the system works fine.

Parameter	Description
delay_warning_time	By default, Postfix does not send a warning if a message cannot be delivered for some time. Setting this parameter to a particular duration, say 5h for five hours, will cause Postfix to send a single warning message for each message that has been undeliverable for that period of time.
	A word of caution, though: Your users may not be able to interpret this warning message correctly. Even though Postfix clearly states that it is only a warning and that the message does not need to be resent, many users do not understand this and resend their delayed message anyway.
mailbox_size_limit	This parameter controls the maximum size of a local mailbox or maximum size of a message when using maildir mailboxes. Nowadays the default of 50 MB may be too low, especially if you are using the default mbox format for mailboxes.
maximal_queue_ lifetime	Specifies how long Postfix will retry failed deliveries of messages before they are returned to the sender. The default of five days is reasonable and should not be changed without good reasons. From Postfix 2.1 onwards, there is also bounce_queue_lifetime that is the same thing, but for bounce messages with an empty sender address.
message_size_limit	This parameter controls the maximum size of a message. The default value of 10 MB is reasonable (mail is not the best transport method for large files), but may need to be adjusted. Remember that messages are sent using only 7 bits, so if you want to allow 20 MB binary files, you must add about 35% to compensate for the overhead of the 7 bit encoding of the file.
proxy_interfaces	If your server is connected to the Internet via a proxy or NAT device so that Postfix cannot determine all network addresses that can be used to reach the server, add those addresses to this parameter.

Starting Postfix and sending the first message

With these settings in place, it is time to start Postfix. Use the following Postfix command to do this:

```
$ postfix start
postfix/postfix-script: starting the Postfix mail system
```

To verify that Postfix is running, take a look in the log file. Postfix logs via the standard `syslog` interface, and the exact location of the log files depends on the `syslog` daemon configuration. The mail logs will typically be named `/var/log/maillog`, `/var/log/mail.info`, or something similar. The configuration of your `syslog` daemon, typically found in `/etc/syslog.conf`, contains the details. This is what you will find at the end of the mail log after you have started Postfix:

```
Jan  3 21:03:28 jeeves postfix/postfix-script: starting the Postfix
mail system
Jan  3 21:03:29 jeeves postfix/master[22429]: daemon started --
version 2.1.5
```

Postfix is now ready to receive and deliver messages. To try it out, use your favorite mail client and send a test mail to yourself. If your mail client uses SMTP, remember to reconfigure it to use your server.

If you get an error message from your mail client when you try to send the test message, read your log again. Does it show any traces of a connection from the host on which you run your mail client? If so, is any error message logged? To get hints on how to debug Postfix problems, see the *Troubleshooting Postfix problems* section.

Once you have sent the message successfully, you will also want to check that it is delivered properly. As you have not yet configured a POP or IMAP server, that road is not an option. But if you have installed a mail client on your server that reads mail directly from the file system (mail, Pine, Mutt, and many more) things should work fine as long as your mail client is configured to look for new messages in the same place as Postfix delivers them. If you have chosen `maildir` delivery, the default settings of your mail client probably won't do.

In any case, reading the mailbox directly from the file system is always an option. With normal `mbox` delivery, the mailbox file has the same name as the user and resides in the directory pointed to by the `mail_spool_directory` configuration parameter. With `maildir` delivery, the message will typically be found in a file of its own in the `$HOME/Maildir/new` directory.

If all has gone well, the message was delivered to the expected place. Whatever delivery method you choose, make sure you know where delivered messages end up. That knowledge will be valuable when you have to debug delivery problems.

Stopping spam and other unwanted messages

This section will discuss the various methods Postfix provides to help stop unwanted messages. Spam, or unsolicited commercial e-mail, is perhaps the biggest problem that e-mail server administrators face, but there may also be other kinds of messages that one does not want to receive.

Postfix by itself will not stop all spam, but it can catch many spam messages. For some people this may be adequate, but if you need to fight large volumes of spam you may need a tool such as SpamAssassin, described in Chapter 8. Even if you use SpamAssassin, Postfix's own lightweight methods can help reduce the load on the server by rejecting the messages before they even reach SpamAssassin.

Postfix's anti-spam methods: An overview

There is no silver bullet to stop all spam, but Postfix provides a number of methods that you can use to help the situation:

- **SMTP restrictions**: SMTP restrictions let you define rules that control whether or not a message is accepted by Postfix. The rules cannot take into account the content of the message, just the envelope information. The SMTP restrictions are not merely a tool for stopping spam, but a general way of defining policies for the usage of the mail system.

- **DNS blocklists**: DNS blocklists are globally published blocklists containing IP addresses of known spammers and other likely sources of junk mail. Postfix lets you use this information to reject messages.

- **Matching header expressions**: The header fields and message bodies can be matched against regular expressions, allowing you to reject certain types of e-mail.

- **After-queue content filtering**: After Postfix has accepted a message, it will not be delivered to the destination right away. Instead, it will be fed to a content filter that can do anything with the message—delete it, scan it for viruses, strip unwanted attachments, and so on. It is the responsibility of the content filter to resubmit messages back into Postfix which will then treat them as any other message.

- **Before-queue content filtering**: The drawback with after-queue content filtering is that Postfix always accepts the message before the message is sent to the content filter. This means Postfix cannot reject a message based on the verdict of the content filter. Before-queue content filters receive the messages during the SMTP session and can choose to reject them. Because one before-queue content filter connection is required for each open SMTP session, this type of content filter is harder to scale for high-traffic sites and requires extra capacity to deal with traffic bursts. This feature requires Postfix 2.1 or later.

- **Milters**: Starting with Postfix 2.3, the Milter plug-in protocol for e-mail content-inspection is supported. Milters were introduced in the `sendmail` mail transfer agent, and there are many available milters for spam protection, antivirus checks, message authenticity and signing in accordance with, for example, the DKIM standard. Third-party Milters can be downloaded from `http://www.milter.org/milters`.

- **Access policy delegation**: If the SMTP restrictions are not sufficiently expressive, you can construct your own access policy server that Postfix can contact during each SMTP session. Using this tool, you can enforce just about any specialized policy you want, as long as the policy can be enforced by looking at the message envelope. Access policy servers will not be supplied with any of the message contents. Postfix comes with a very simple policy daemon for use to implement greylisting, but several other policy daemons have been made by other people. Links to these daemons and other Postfix add-on software can be found at `http://www.postfix.org/addon.html`.

Understanding SMTP restrictions

Postfix has a simple but still expressive notation for defining rules that will be applied to messages that arrive via SMTP. For example, you can express a policy to reject messages sent from certain networks, clients who say `HELO` with certain hostnames, or clients that have no reverse records in DNS unless they are one of your own clients.

Postfix defines a number of configuration parameters, each of which can contain a list of restrictions. Each restriction list may contain zero or more restrictions, and each restriction may or may not return something when evaluated. As in a few other places in Postfix, the "first match wins" principle reigns here too. This means that the restrictions are evaluated in the order they are specified, and the first restriction that returns something terminates the evaluation of the current restriction list.

The restriction lists get evaluated during the SMTP session. The following table contains the restriction lists that Postfix uses and shows at what stage in an SMTP session they are evaluated:

Parameter	Point of evaluation
smtpd_client_restrictions	Directly upon connection.
smtpd_data_restrictions	When the client has sent the DATA command.
smtpd_end_of_data_restrictions	When the client has sent the complete message. This restriction list is available in Postfix 2.2 and later versions.
smtpd_etrn_restrictions	When the client has sent the ETRN command. This command is not used in a normal SMTP session.
smtpd_helo_restrictions	When the client has sent its greeting with HELO or EHLO.
smtpd_recipient_restrictions	When the client has sent a recipient address with RCPT TO.
smtpd_sender_restrictions	When the client has sent the sender address with MAIL FROM.

The default value of the smtpd_delay_reject parameter is yes, which means that all rejections will be postponed until after RCPT TO. The reason for this is that some client software do not like being rejected before RCPT TO, so they will disconnect and try again. Another good reason is that a postponed rejection gives Postfix a chance to log more information. This makes it easier for the administrator to determine whether a message was rejected even though it should not have been.

A common misunderstanding is that only restrictions on the recipient address can be placed in smtpd_recipient_restrictions, only restrictions on the sender address can be placed in smtpd_sender_restrictions,and so on, but because of the default value of smtpd_delay_reject, that is not true. The name of the restriction list only indicates at what stage in the SMTP session the listed restrictions will be applied.

Let's explore what restrictions Postfix imposes by default. We can use the postconf command to inspect the default values of the most commonly used restriction lists.

```
$ postconf -d smtpd_client_restrictions smtpd_helo_restrictions \
    smtpd_sender_restrictions smtpd_recipient_restrictions
smtpd_client_restrictions =
smtpd_helo_restrictions =
smtpd_sender_restrictions =
smtpd_recipient_restrictions = permit_mynetworks, reject_unauth_
destination
```

This tells us that Postfix by default does not have any client, HELO, or sender restrictions. However, it does have two recipient restrictions. The first one, permit_mynetworks, permits the current recipient if the connecting client is within the networks specified by mynetworks. It is this restriction that gives your own clients relay access. If the connecting client is not within mynetworks, the next item in the restriction list will be evaluated. reject_unauth_destination will reject recipients whose domain is not one of the domains that Postfix will accept mail for. In other words, reject_unauth_destination rejects relay attempts. If no rejection takes place here, the end of the restriction list has been reached. If that happens, Postfix accepts the message.

A permit result in one restriction list will not cause the message as a whole to be accepted. Only the remaining restrictions in the same list will be bypassed. This is not true for restrictions that return reject — that result is always terminal and stops the evaluation of all restriction lists.

There are more than 50 standard SMTP restrictions to choose from, and there is no room to cover them all here. This table will present a little smorgasbord with useful restrictions. Additional restrictions will be covered later in this chapter.

Restriction	Description
permit_inet_interfaces	Permit if the connecting client resides in one of the networks listed in inet_interfaces, which typically covers all network that the server running Postfix is connected to.
permit_mynetworks	Permit if the connecting client is listed in mynetworks.
permit_sasl_authenticated	Permit if connecting client has authenticated itself. (SMTP authentication is covered in Chapter 5.)
reject	Reject the request, unconditionally.
reject_invalid_hostname	Reject if the syntax of the HELO/EHLO hostname given by the client is incorrect.
reject_non_fqdn_hostname	Reject if the HELO/EHLO hostname given by the client is not a fully qualified domain name.
reject_non_fqdn_recipient	Reject if the domain part of the recipient address is not a fully qualified domain name.
reject_non_fqdn_sender	Reject if the domain part of the sender address is not a fully qualified domain name.
reject_unauth_destination	Reject the request unless the recipient domain is one of the domains that the Postfix server hosts, or for some reason, will accept mail for.

Restriction	Description
`reject_unknown_client_hostname`	Reject if the connecting client's hostname cannot be determined. This happens if either of the following conditions is true: a) The client's IP address cannot be resolved to a hostname, that is the PTR lookup fails. b) The A record lookup of the resulting hostname(s) fails. c) None of the IP addresses obtained from the A record lookup matches the input IP address. Prior to Postfix 2.3, this restriction was named `reject_unknown_client`.
`reject_unknown_recipient_domain`	Reject if the domain part of the recipient address has no A or MX record in DNS.
`reject_unknown_reverse_client_hostname`	Reject if the connecting client's IP address cannot be resolved to a hostname, that is the PTR lookup fails to return a result. This feature is available in Postfix 2.3 and later.
`reject_unknown_sender_domain`	Reject if the domain part of the sender address has no A or MX record in DNS.
`reject_unlisted_recipient`	Reject if the domain part of the recipient address is a domain hosted by Postfix and the complete address is not a valid recipient address. By default, this restriction is implicitly evaluated at the end of `smtpd_recipient_restrictions`. This behavior is controlled by the `smtpd_reject_unlisted_recipient` parameter. By using `reject_unlisted_recipient`, you can put the restriction into effect earlier on. This restriction is available in Postfix 2.1 and later. Previous versions of Postfix can use the `check_recipient_maps` parameter.
`reject_unlisted_sender`	Reject if the domain part of the sender address is a domain hosted by Postfix and the complete address would not be acceptable as a recipient address. The idea behind this feature is that there is no reason to accept messages with sender addresses known to be incorrect. This restriction is available in Postfix 2.1 and later. See also the `smtpd_reject_unlisted_sender` parameter.

Access maps

In addition to the restrictions already discussed, Postfix defines a number of restrictions that look up information in access maps. An **access map** is a lookup table with contents that affects whether a message will be accepted. The name of the restriction controls what information is used as the lookup key.

For example, the `check_client_access` restriction looks up the client IP address and hostname in a lookup table, allowing you to, say, ban certain clients that are known to send spam. Together with the restriction name you also state the type and name of the lookup table.

```
smtpd_client_restrictions =
        check_client_access hash:/etc/postfix/client_access
```

Although not an exhaustive list, the following are the most important restrictions that use access maps:

Restriction name	Lookup key
`check_client_access`	Client IP address and hostname.
`check_sender_access`	The sender address.
`check_sender_mx_access`	The hostname(s) of the mail exchangers for the sender domain, that is the result of an MX lookup. This feature was added in Postfix 2.1.
`check_sender_ns_access`	The hostname(s) of the name servers for the sender domain, that is the result of an NS lookup. This feature was added in Postfix 2.1.
`check_recipient_access`	The recipient address.
`check_helo_access`	The HELO/EHLO hostname.

For all lookup table types except `regexp` and `pcre`, Postfix makes multiple lookups for each of these restrictions, slightly dependent on what type of data is being looked up (e-mail address or hostname, for example). This makes it possible to make inexact wildcard matches, for example matching all e-mail addresses in a domain.

For `check_client_access`, Postfix makes separate lookups for the client IP address, the client hostname, and parts of the IP address, the latter making it possible to match whole A-, B-, or C-class networks (for better granularity and full CIDR notation use the `cidr` lookup table type). For a client with the address 1.2.3.4 and the hostname `mail.example.com`, the following lookup keys are attempted, in the following order:

- mail.example.com
- example.com
- com
- 1.2.3.4
- 1.2.3
- 1.2
- 1

Items 2 and 3 assume that the default value of the `parent_domain_matches_subdomains` parameter is used. The Postfix author has indicated that this behavior may change in the future.

For restrictions where the lookup key is an e-mail address, such as `check_sender_access`, Postfix looks up the whole e-mail address, the domain part only, followed by the localpart and @. The full list of lookups for the e-mail address `user@example.com` then becomes:

1. `user@example.com`
2. `example.com`
3. `com`
4. `user@`

Again, items 2 and 3 assume that default value of `parent_domain_matches_subdomains`.

Lookups for IPv6 addresses and e-mail addresses containing recipient delimiters have been omitted from these lists for brevity reasons.

The following results are recognized for a given lookup key (this is again not an exhaustive list).

Result	Description
OK	Permit the request.
REJECT [optional text]	Reject the request with a permanent error code and either the specified error message or a generic message.
DUNNO	Pretend that the lookup key was not found, and do not continue with additional lookup keys. For example, if a lookup of `user@example.com` returns DUNNO, Postfix will not look up `example.com` or `user@` like it normally would.
DISCARD [optional text]	If the message eventually gets accepted, it will be discarded and not delivered.

Result	Description
HOLD [optional text]	Place the message in the hold queue. Messages that are held will not be delivered and can be inspected with the postcat program and subsequently released for delivery or deleted. This can be used as a simple way of quarantining messages that might be unwanted.
REDIRECT email address	Scrap all the current message recipient(s) and send the message to the specified address only. This feature was added in Postfix 2.1.
PREPEND header: text	Add an additional header to the message. This feature was added in Postfix 2.1.
WARN [optional text]	Place a warning message in the log file. This feature was added in Postfix 2.1.
restriction, restriction, …	Apply one or more restrictions and use their result. Only simple restrictions that do not refer to any lookup tables are allowed here unless you use restriction classes. Those are not covered in this book, but you can read about them in the *RESTRICTION_CLASS_README* document available at http://www.postfix.org/RESTRICTION_CLASS_README.html.

Full documentation of the access map lookup keys and possible result values can be found in the access(5) manual page or at http://www.postfix.org/access.5.html.

Access map examples

Here are a series of examples with access maps to discuss how they can be used, both alone and along with other restrictions in order to form pretty expressive policies:

```
smtpd_client_restrictions =
        check_client_access hash:/etc/postfix/client_access
```

In this first example, the lookups will be made against the hash-type lookup table /etc/postfix/client_access. This file is not created by Postfix and you may give it any name. From the *Lookup tables* section we recall that hash-type lookup tables are just text files from which binary files (in this case with the file extension .db) should be built with the postmap command whenever the source file changes.

```
postmap hash:/etc/postfix/client_access
```

Here is an example client_access file:

```
# Block RFC 1918 networks
10                      REJECT RFC 1918 address not allowed here
192.168                 REJECT RFC 1918 address not allowed here
```

```
# Known spammers
12.34.56.78              REJECT
evil-spammer.example.com REJECT
```

What does all this mean? The first two non-comment lines are used to reject clients that appear to connect from the networks `10.0.0.0/8` and `192.168.0.0/16`. These are not valid Internet addresses, so no legitimate client will connect from any of these addresses. The rejection will be made with the error message `RFC 1918` **address not allowed here**. If your own clients have such RFC 1918 addresses you need to place a `permit_mynetworks` restriction before the `check_client_access`. Otherwise you will reject your own clients.

```
smtpd_client_restrictions =
        permit_mynetworks,
        check_client_access hash:/etc/postfix/client_access
```

Indexed access maps support network block matching on octet boundaries, but CIDR notation (as in `10.0.0.0/8`) is not supported. If you need to specify network blocks with CIDR notation, consider the `CIDR` lookup table type available in Postfix 2.1 and later. Earlier releases can use a script such as `cidr2access` by Rahul Dhesi (`http://www.rahul.net/dhesi/software/cidr2access`) that expands CIDR blocks to a notation that is acceptable for indexed access maps.

Note how comments are used to explain why and when entries were added. This can be valuable if more than one person is maintaining the files.

The last lines are used to match a couple of notorious spammers (fictional, of course) and demonstrate that both complete IP addresses and hostnames are acceptable here. These rejections will be made with a generic error message.

Here is another example:

```
smtpd_sender_restrictions =
        check_sender_access hash:/etc/postfix/sender_access
```

Contents of `/etc/postfix/sender_access`:

```
hotmail.com              reject_unknown_client
example.com              permit_mynetworks, reject
```

If someone attempts to send a message with a `hotmail.com` sender address, the client attempting to deliver the message will be subject to the `reject_unknown_client` restriction which, as you might recall, rejects client that do not have a valid mapping between IP address and hostname.

The second line exemplifies a useful policy that allows clients only from your networks to use your domain in the sender address.

Finally, if you only use Postfix internally within your network and have no need to allow anyone else to connect, the following two restrictions enforce this policy:

```
smtpd_recipient_restrictions = permit_mynetworks, reject
```

Implementing new policies

Be careful when you implement new policies. Some of Postfix's restrictions are far too strict for general use and may reject significant amounts of legitimate e-mail. For each new restriction you plan to implement, examine the conditions under which messages are rejected and try to come up with cases where legitimate messages fulfill these conditions. To help you determine whether a restriction is safe to use, the warn_if_reject restriction can be used. This restriction affects the restriction that immediately follows it in the restriction list and, if the following restriction should have resulted in a rejection, it will be converted to a rejection warning. A rejection warning places a line in the mail log, but does not reject the message.

For example, you may want to evaluate the reject_unknown_client restriction because you have noticed that many spam messages are received from clients that do not have a reverse pointer in DNS, that is, there is no mapping from their IP address to a name that maps back to the IP address in question.

Here is one way of doing it:

```
smtpd_client_restrictions = warn_if_reject reject_unknown_client
```

This will result in log messages like this one:

```
Dec 31 16:39:31 jeeves postfix/smtpd[28478]: NOQUEUE: reject_warning:
RCPT from unknown[222.101.15.127]: 450 Client host rejected: cannot
find your hostname, [222.101.15.127]; from=<jdoe@example.com> to=<me@
example.com> proto=SMTP helo=<222.101.15.127>
```

This log messages contain all known information about the envelope of the message, and this should hopefully be enough for you to decide whether a message was legitimate or not. After a few days, inspect your mail logs and try to determine whether the ratio between would-be rejected unwanted messages and would-be rejected legitimate messages is acceptable.

There are many spam countermeasures with good accuracy, some of which are covered in this book. Others will emerge in the future depending on how the spammers behave. Be very careful when inventing your own ways to identify spam—picking characteristics from a small number of spam messages and drawing the conclusion that those characteristics are good spam indicators is dangerous and is likely to lead to loss of legitimate e-mails. Choose wisely and avoid methods with low accuracy. Do not forget to examine legitimate e-mails to make sure they do not have the characteristics that you associate with spam.

Using DNS blacklists

Since 1997, the **Domain Name System (DNS)** has been used to thwart spam. The method, **DNS-based Blackhole List (DNSBL)** or **Real-time Blackhole List (RBL)**, also known as **blacklist** or **blocklist**, uses the DNS to publish information about certain clients or sender domains. When a mail server such as your own is contacted by a client, your server can combine the client's IP address or the given sender address with the domain of one or more DNSBLs and perform a DNS lookup. If the address is listed by the DNSBL, the lookup succeeds, and your server may choose to, for example, reject the client.

For example, let's say that you have configured Postfix to use the widely used `zen.spamhaus.org` blacklist. If a client with the address 1.2.3.4 connects, Postfix will look in DNS for an A record for the address `4.3.2.1.zen.spamhaus.org`. If such a record exists, Postfix will not accept a message from the client.

Postfix supports three types of DNSBL lookups—client host address, client hostname, and sender domain. Each lookup type has a restriction of its own, and they all require that you specify the name of the DNSBL domain after the restriction name.

DNSBL type	Syntax	Description
Client host address	`reject_rbl_client rbl_domain`	The IP address of the connecting client is looked up. This is the original and by far most common DNSBL type.
Client hostname	`reject_rhsbl_client rbl_domain`	The hostname of the connecting client is looked up.
Sender address domain	`reject_rhsbl_sender rbl_domain`	The domain of the given sender address is looked up.

Feel free to list multiple DNSBL restrictions. Make sure you use the restriction that corresponds to the DNSBL type—using `reject_rbl_client` with a sender address domain DNSBL does not make sense.

The following code shows one way of configuring Postfix to use the `zen.spamhaus.org` standard-type DNSBL and the `dsn.rfc-ignorant.org` sender domain-DNSBL:

```
smtpd_recipient_restrictions =
        permit_mynetworks,
        reject_unauth_destination,
        reject_rbl_client relays.ordb.org,
        reject_rhsbl_sender dsn.rfc-ignorant.org
```

Notice how these restrictions are listed after both `permit_mynetworks` and `reject_unauth_destination`. This is because DNSBL lookups are comparatively expensive, and there is no use in wasting time on such lookups for your own clients or for clients that might get rejected anyway. To avoid unnecessary delays, be sure to list the DNSBLs that block the most messages, first among your DNSBL restrictions.

Choosing DNS blacklists

In the beginning, the DNSBLs listed only **open relays**, that is, SMTP servers that accept all messages from all clients to all destinations. Open relays once were the primary source of spam, but this has changed in recent years. Today, a lot of spam is sent from the hijacked home computers of innocent and unknowing people.

Different blacklists have different policies for listing hosts and removing listed hosts. Naturally, the bigger the blacklist, the more legitimate messages you are likely to reject. Before starting to use a particular DNSBL to reject messages, you should examine these policies carefully and preferably also try them out for a while without actually rejecting any messages. The `warn_if_reject` restriction can help you with this.

The blacklists that work great for some people and reject huge amounts of spam but no legitimate messages may have little value for other people and may actually reject more legitimate messages than spam. Take great care when choosing blacklists and avoid blindly copying allegedly good sets of DNSBLs from others. Another good reason for being cautious is that DNSBLs sometimes go out of service because they have been repeatedly attacked by spammers and forced to shut down. This happened to the well-known `relays.ordb.org` DNSBL in 2006. Blacklists that are shut down may, after a while, be reconfigured to always indicate an IP address as listed in the blacklist, that is, you will reject all mail if configured to use that blacklist.

The probably best general-purpose DNSBL out there for use with `reject_rbl_client` is, at the moment, `zen.spamhaus.org`. The false-positive rate, that is the share of incorrectly rejected genuine e-mail, can be expected to be extremely low while the accuracy of catching spam stays high. Unless you have special needs, this may be the only DNSBL that you need to use.

Before implementing any DNSBL at all, make sure you know how to exempt certain clients or domains from rejections. Sooner or later, and no matter which DNSBL you choose to use, you will have cases of legitimate messages being blocked. When that happens, it is too late to start digging in the documentation trying to find out what you can do about it.

The solution to the problem is to have whitelisting access maps before your DNSBL restrictions. Which type of access map you should use depends on the DNSBL type, but in most cases `check_client_access` will be suitable, although `check_sender_access` is more appropriate if you use `reject_rhsbl_sender`.

Continuing the previous example, this is what you can do to exempt certain clients and sender addresses from rejection by any following restrictions:

```
smtpd_recipient_restrictions =
  permit_mynetworks,
  reject_unauth_destination,
  check_client_access hash:/etc/postfix/rbl_client_exceptions,
  check_sender_access hash:/etc/postfix/rhsbl_sender_exceptions,
  reject_rbl_client zen.spamhaus.org,
  reject_rhsbl_sender dsn.rfc-ignorant.org
```

In `/etc/postfix/rbl_client_exceptions`:

```
# Added 2005-01-10 to avoid blocking legitimate mail. /jdoe
1.2.3.4                    OK
example.net                OK
```

In `/etc/postfix/rhsbl_client_exceptions`:

```
mybusinesspartner.com      OK
```

Stopping messages based on content

Often, unwanted messages cannot be spotted without looking at their contents. Postfix provides some unsophisticated but still very useful tools for this purpose. The idea is that the lines in a message are matched against a set of regular expressions that you supply and, if there is a match, an action will be carried out. This is called **header checks** or **body checks**, depending on what part of the message is being inspected. Most often you use header and body checks to reject messages, but messages can also be discarded or redirected to another recipient. Header and body checks can help you solve the following problems, all of which will be discussed in the following sections:

- Reacting to messages containing attachments with forbidden filenames
- Quickly stopping big virus outbreaks

- Custom logging of certain header fields
- Removing certain message headers

An introduction to regular expressions is beyond the scope of this book. If you do not have that knowledge already, there are many regular expression resources and tutorials on the net, for example `http://gnosis.cx/publish/programming/regular_expressions.html` and `http://www.codeproject.com/KB/dotnet/regextutorial.aspx`. If you are looking for a book on the topic, Jeffrey E. F. Friedl's *Mastering Regular Expressions* (O'Reilly, 2006) is quite comprehensive.

Configuring header and body checks

The `main.cf` parameters for header and body checks—`body_checks`, `header_checks`, `mime_header_checks`, and `nested_header_checks`—can contain one or more references to regular expression lookup tables (`regexp` or `pcre`), which will be considered when a message is being received. Technically you could use any other lookup table type for this, but only regular expression tables are really useful. The following parameters are used for different parts of the message:

Parameter	Part of message it applies to
`body_checks`	The body of each message part.
`header_checks`	All non-MIME top-level headers.
`mime_header_checks`	All MIME headers found in any message part. The following headers are considered to be MIME headers: • Content-Description • Content-Disposition • Content-ID • Content-Transfer-Encoding • Content-Type • MIME-Version
`nested_header_checks`	All non-MIME message headers in messages that are attached to the received message.

This means for each header line, a lookup will be made against the lookup tables specified in `header_checks`, each line in the message body will cause a lookup against the lookup tables in `body_checks`, and so on.

The format of regular expression lookup tables is very similar to ordinary indexed ones. One big difference is that they are not indexed and should not be run through the `postmap` program. Postfix will read regular expression lookup tables again when the daemons are restarted, which is often enough in many cases. If you want an immediate update, you must reload Postfix.

Regular expression lookup tables are not exclusively for header and body checks. They can be used wherever Postfix expects a lookup table.

The right-hand side of lookup tables used for header and body checks can contain many of the previously described actions allowed in access maps, but one action, IGNORE, is available only here. The IGNORE action simply removes the matched line from the message.

Message headers such as the ones in the following example that are wrapped to form multiple physical lines, will be joined together before being used as a lookup key.

```
Received: by jeeves.example.com (Postfix, from userid 100)
        id 2BB044302; Sat,  1 Jan 2005 20:29:43 +0100 (CET)
```

Header and body checks examples

Now, let's get concrete and take a look at how header and body checks can be used. Unless otherwise noted, all these examples work with both the regexp and the pcre lookup table type.

Many computer viruses spread by e-mail, and most of them through programs or scripts attached to the messages. Although reacting to messages containing attachments with forbidden filenames is a blunt and inexact tool, it is a simple way to take care of these unwanted messages even before they reach any antivirus scanner. By avoiding large overhead scanning, your server can cope with much larger virus outbreaks. There is no complete list of the filenames that can be banned, but just blocking .exe, .scr, .pif, .bat, and a few more will probably suffice for most people. If your users have a need to send or receive files with these filename extensions, you may need to relax the policy somewhat. To implement this in Postfix, you need to recognize that the filename of an attachment is found in Content-Disposition or Content-Type headers. These are MIME headers, so the expression needs to go in mime_header_checks. In this example, the message is rejected with text that indicates the offending filename. If a legitimate mail is rejected, the sender will hopefully be able to interpret the error message and resend the message.

```
/^Content-(Disposition|Type).*name\s*=\s*"?(.*\.(
    ade|adp|bas|bat|chm|cmd|com|cpl|crt|dll|exe|hlp|hta|
    inf|ins|isp|js|jse|lnk|mdb|mde|mdt|mdw|ms[cipt]|nws|
    ops|pcd|pif|prf|reg|sc[frt]|sh[bsm]|swf|
    vb[esx]?|vxd|ws[cfh]))(\?=)?"?\s*(;|$)/x
    REJECT Attachment not allowed. Filename "$2" may not end with
".$3".
```

Note the indentation on all but the first line. It is needed to have the lines be treated as a single line. Lookup tables work in the same way as the `main.cf` and `master.cf` configuration files in this respect. The `/x` modifier will cause all whitespace to be ignored. This expression, originally constructed by Russell Mosemann and further refined by Noel Jones, requires a `pcre` lookup table, but it is possible to rewrite the expression to use `regexp`.

`body_checks` can be a useful tool in quickly stopping big virus outbreaks. A number of the previous virus outbreaks have had messages with certain characteristics that made them pretty easy to block. If filename blocking is not an option, you can try to find lines that are unique to these messages and construct suitable expressions.

```
/^Hi! How are you=3F$/          REJECT SirCam virus detected.
/^ I don't bite, weah!$/        REJECT Bagle.H virus detected.
```

If you are unsure whether an expression will be too broad and catch legitimate messages, you can use HOLD or WARN instead of REJECT. HOLD will put the messages on hold, allowing you to examine them and either release the messages or delete them. WARN will accept the message but log the incident.

This method of blocking viruses can also be useful when a new virus is just starting to spread and the antivirus software you are using has not yet been updated to catch it.

The WARN action can also be used to get custom logging of certain header fields.

```
/^Subject: /                            WARN
```

Having this expression in `header_checks` will result in all subject headers being logged as a warning message similar to this:

```
Jan  2 00:59:51 jeeves postfix/cleanup[6715]: 6F8184302: warning:
header Subject: Re: Lunch? from local; from=<jack@example.com>
to=<jill@example.com>
```

Sometimes it can be useful to remove certain message headers. For example, some programming libraries that provide SMTP clients add an X-Library header to all messages sent. Apparently, many spammers use these libraries and therefore SpamAssassin gives a pretty high score for messages that contain this header. If you need to use such a library and you cannot or will not modify the source code to avoid having the header added in the first place, Postfix can help you remove it. This `header_checks` expression will remove all X-Library headers in messages passing through Postfix:

```
/^X-Library: /                          IGNORE
```

Caveats

Header and body checks are simple and blunt tools for inspecting message contents. They are useful for a number of things, but do not attempt to overuse use them for general-purpose spam fighting. Many people try to use these tools incorrectly, and this book will try to dispel some common misconceptions.

Header and body checks will inspect only one line at a time, and no state is kept between different lines. This means you cannot reject messages that contain one bad word on one line and another bad word elsewhere in the message. Do not be fooled by the `if...endif` construct allowed in regular expression lookup tables! You cannot use them in this way:

```
if /^From: spammer@example\.com/
/^Subject: Best mortgage rates/          REJECT
endif
```

Remember, lookups are made one line at a time. Obviously, a line that starts with `From` cannot possibly start with `Subject`.

Many spam messages have the mail body in **Base64** encoding. Because of how Base64 works, a word has many possible Base64 representations. Postfix does not perform any decoding before the message content is fed to the header and body checks.

This means that using `body_checks` to block messages containing bad words doesn't work universally. If `body_checks` is your only tool to fight spam, you will spend a couple of hours every day maintaining your regular expressions so they will catch the spam of the day, but you will still not have high accuracy.

Header and body checks apply to all messages. You cannot whitelist a certain sender or a certain client. If you host multiple domains you have the option of using different header and body checks for your hosted domains by running multiple `cleanup` daemons and multiple `smtpd` daemons listening on different IP addresses, or you can run multiple instances of Postfix. The latter means that you have multiple queue directories and multiple copies of Postfix running at the same time. This is required for some complex setups, but can actually simplify setups that are possible with a single instance.

You cannot use header and body checks to check for the nonexistence of something, so you cannot reject messages that have an empty body or messages that do not contain a secret password.

Having a large number of regular expressions in `body_checks` is not only a maintenance nightmare but may also seriously degrades the performance of your server. A reasonable configuration should not need more than, say, 10–20 expressions. If you have too many expressions, Postfix's `cleanup` processes will use a lot of CPU time.

Virtual alias domains and local aliases

In this section, some of Postfix's features for address rewriting to allow hosting multiple domains and implementing group addresses (or distribution lists) will be discussed.

Additionally, this section will take a look at how to find information in MySQL databases using Postfix. The goal of the exercise will be to use MySQL lookups for alias lookups, but the knowledge you can gain will be applicable for all other situations where you might want to use MySQL together with Postfix. It will be assumed that you have basic SQL knowledge and that you are able to set up and operate a MySQL server.

Virtual alias domains

As was explained earlier, even though you can have several local domains (several domains listed in `mydestination`), they will always be equivalent—they share a single localpart namespace. In other words, `joe@localdomain1.com` is `joe@localdomain2.com` is `joe@localdomain3.com`. Obviously, this is not good enough. In order to host multiple domains with distinct localpart namespaces, you need virtual alias domains.

A **virtual alias domain** is a domain where each valid address maps to one or more other e-mail addresses, possibly in other domains. Compare this to local domains where an address typically maps directly to a UNIX system account. `joe@virtualdomain1` and `joe@virtualdomain2` can lead to completely different mailboxes.

Virtual alias domains are sometimes just called virtual domains, but to avoid confusion with virtual mailbox domains, which are also sometimes called virtual domains, the full term will be used.

To show how virtual alias domains work in Postfix, let's return to our friends at Example Inc. for a couple of examples of how they can enhance their mail system by using virtual alias domains.

Many virtual alias domains mapping to one local domain

The directors of Example Inc. have now expanded their business significantly and want to have subdomains for their branch offices to avoid name clashes when two people in different offices share the same name. For their offices in London, Paris, and Berlin they want the domains `gb.example.com`, `fr.example.com`, and `de.example.com` respectively. They have a single Postfix server that receives all messages.

The solution to Example Inc's problem is to let `gb.example.com`, `fr.example.com`, and `de.example.com` all be virtual alias domains. The original `example.com` domain should remain a local domain. Postfix looks for virtual alias domains in the `virtual_alias_domains` parameter.

```
virtual_alias_domains = gb.example.com, fr.example.com, de.example.com
```

Make sure that you do not list any of these domains in `mydestination`. The next step is to tell Postfix which addresses in the virtual alias domains map to which addresses in the `example.com` domain. This is done by specifying one or more lookup tables in the `virtual_alias_maps` parameter. For starters, Example Inc. will just use a simple `hash` type lookup table. When things work as we expect them to, they will create an equivalent configuration that looks up data in a MySQL database.

```
virtual_alias_maps = hash:/etc/postfix/virtual
```

Now, Postfix will use the virtual aliases they put in `/etc/postfix/virtual`. The format of a virtual alias lookup table is very simple; the recipient address is the lookup key and the address/addresses to which the recipient address should be rewritten is the result.

```
joe@gb.example.com        joe1@example.com
joe@de.example.com        joe2@example.com
jane@fr.example.com       jane@example.com
```

After editing the `/etc/postfix/virtual` file, `postmap` must be run in order to transform the file into `/etc/postfix/virtual.db`.

```
$ postmap /etc/postfix/virtual
```

The format of virtual alias lookup tables is described in the `virtual(5)` manual page.

In the above example, all messages to `joe@gb.example.com` will end up in the mailbox of the user "joe1", all messages to `joe@de.example.com` will end up in the mailbox of the user "joe2", and all messages to `jane@fr.example.com` will end up in the mailbox of the user "jane". Note that introducing virtual alias domains does not cause the original local domain to stop accepting messages.

Jane and our two Joes will also receive messages addressed to their actual usernames at `example.com`. (`joe1@example.com`, `joe2@example.com`, and `jane@example.com`). If this is undesirable, you can use `smtpd_recipient_restrictions` and `check_recipient_access` to reject attempts to send messages to these recipients. Add the restriction to the `smtpd_recipient_restrictions` setting (if any) in `main.cf`:

```
smtpd_recipient_restrictions =
    ...
    check_recipient_access hash:/etc/postfix/recipient_access
    ...
```

Then put the following in `/etc/postfix/recipient_access` and run `postmap` on the file:

```
example.com          REJECT Email to this domain prohibited
```

One virtual alias domain mapping to many local domains

After running the previous setup for a while, the staff at Example Inc. decide that they want to return to the old setup with a single domain for all employees. The name clashes can be resolved by including the users' last names in the address. They also want to have one mail server per branch office to avoid latency and network load when the users are accessing their mailboxes. All London users will have their accounts residing on the London server, Paris users on the Paris server, and Berlin users on the Berlin server. This problem is an opportunity to look at a different way of using virtual alias domains.

The idea in this setup is that `example.com` will be the virtual domain and that each Postfix server will have a local domain of its own. The server at the London office will have `gb.example.com` listed as a local domain. Virtual aliasing will be used to map from the `example.com` addresses to the office-specific subdomains. This mapping can either be done exclusively on a master server or on the servers for each of the branch offices. Having a single master server introduces the problem of synchronizing the data between the servers, but that problem can be solved easily by storing the data in a relational database. How to use MySQL for alias lookups will be discussed in the *Introducing MySQL lookups* section later in the chapter.

To implement this, start by removing `example.com` from `mydestination` and add it to `virtual_alias_domains` instead. This needs to be done on all servers. The branch office servers—one of which could easily be the master server—should have their own domain (`gb.example.com`, and so on) listed in `mydestination`. Do not forget to set up the DNS server so that messages to the branch office domains will be routed to the branch office servers. Finally, the virtual alias table should look like this:

```
joe.smith@example.com      joe1@gb.example.com
joe.schmidt@example.com    joe2@de.example.com
jane.doe@example.com       jane@fr.example.com
```

This problem illustrates an important point; the address/addresses in the right-hand side of a virtual alias table do not have to be local. Any domain can be put there. This is what happens when the master server receives a mail to `joe.smith@example.com`:

1. Postfix looks in `virtual_alias_domains` to see if `example.com` is a virtual alias domain, and the result is positive.

2. Next, it looks up `joe.smith@example.com` in `virtual_alias_maps`. The lookup returns `joe1@gb.example.com`.

3. Postfix on the master server decides that `gb.example.com` is not a domain that it hosts, and uses DNS to resolve the destination of the message, and finally delivers it to the London branch office server.

Group addresses

This third and final virtual alias example will do little more than state that the right-hand side of virtual alias tables may contain several addresses, which can be the names of other aliases rather than actual account names.

```
all@example.com        managers@example.com,finance@example.com
managers@example.com   joe.smith@example.com,joe.schmidt@example.com
finance@example.com    jane.doe@example.com,jack.black@example.com
```

In this example, a message sent to `all@example.com` will be sent to all in management and all in finance, which in turn means Joe Smith, Joe Schmidt, Jane Doe, and Jack Black.

It may not be desirable to let anyone send messages to large distribution lists. Luckily, you can use Postfix's SMTP restrictions to restrict the access to the sensitive addresses. If you only want your own users (clients within `mynetworks`) to be allowed to send messages to an address, the solution is very simple. In `main.cf`, use the `check_recipient_access` restriction to disallow access to the address, but use `permit_mynetworks` to exempt your own clients.

```
smtpd_recipient_restrictions =
  permit_mynetworks,
  check_recipient_access hash:/etc/postfix/restricted_recipients,
  reject_unauth_destination
```

If you already use `smtpd_recipient_restrictions` in your `main.cf`, you will have to modify that parameter rather than just adding what is listed in the example above. The key feature is to list the `check_recipient_access` restriction after the `permit_mynetworks` restriction.

Contents of `/etc/postfix/restricted_recipients`:

```
all@example.com                    REJECT
```

In more complex scenarios, like when you want to disallow a recipient address for all but a few sender addresses or clients, you may need to use Postfix's restriction class feature. It is described in `RESTRICTION_CLASS_README` (`http://www.postfix.org/RESTRICTION_CLASS_README.html`) along with an example for this particular case.

Introducing MySQL lookups

If your organization is large, maintaining a flat text file with aliases can be tedious. Storing the data in a real database comes with many advantages—many users can edit the data simultaneously, the users themselves can be allowed to perform some tasks via web interfaces, the data can be easily shared over the network, and so on.

Postfix supports looking up data in a number of *complex* lookup table types. These include MySQL, PostgreSQL, and LDAP. It is *complex* not because it is very difficult to set up, but because there are inherently more things that can go wrong and, yes, simple indexed files (`hash`, `dbm`, `btree`, `cdb`) are easier to get right. If you want to solve a problem with a lookup table, always start with an indexed file. When you get things working and understand why and how they work, try to transform the same idea to the complex lookup table type.

Postfix does not require you to conform to some specific database schema. For each lookup table where you use MySQL, you can use a separate configuration that given whatever schema you have chosen to use (more or less — the current version of Postfix does not quite allow arbitrary MySQL queries), returns the desired result. Each configuration is stored in a separate file that can have restrictive permissions as they contain database passwords. To use MySQL for looking up virtual aliases, the following setting in `main.cf` will do:

```
virtual_alias_maps = mysql:/etc/postfix/mysql-virtual.cf
```

The configuration file follows the same format as `main.cf` and contains all information required to make a lookup — in this case, a virtual alias lookup. The following table describes the parameters that you can put in the configuration file. The parameters will be used to construct the SELECT query. In Postfix 2.1 and later, the format of such configuration files can be found in the `mysql_table(5)` manual page.

Parameter	Description
hosts	A list of the MySQL hosts that Postfix will contact to perform the query. Can contain either IP addresses, hostnames or, when prefixed with `unix:`, the path to a local UNIX domain socket. If you specify multiple hosts, they will be tried in random order. Any UNIX domain socket hosts will be tried first.
user	The username that should be used to log in to the MySQL server.
password	The password that should be used to log in to the MySQL server.
dbname	The name of the database to use.
select_field	The name of the column from which the lookup result will be taken.
table	The table that will be searched for the data.
where_field	The table column with which the lookup key will be compared.
additional_conditions	If you require some additional conditions to be tacked on at the end of the constructed query, you can put them here.
query	The SQL query to perform, with `%s` being a placeholder for the string being looked up. This parameter is mutually exclusive with `select_field`, `table`, `where_field`, and `additional_conditions`. This parameter was introduced in Postfix 2.2 and is the recommended way of configuring the MySQL query.

Let's start with a simple example. You have a table alias with two columns—alias and address. The alias column is the left-hand side of the virtual lookup table (the address with the virtual alias domain) and the address column is the right-hand side (the new address).

```
mysql> SELECT * FROM aliases;

+---------------------+-------------------+
| alias               | address           |
+---------------------+-------------------+
| joe@gb.example.com  | joe1@example.com  |
| joe@de.example.com  | joe2@example.com  |
| jane@fr.example.com | jane@example.com  |
+---------------------+-------------------+
   3 rows in set (0.00 sec)
```

The following simple SQL query is needed to find out whether an address in one of the virtual domains exists and should be rewritten to some other address:

```
SELECT address FROM aliases WHERE alias = 'lookup key'
```

Translating this into a Postfix MySQL lookup table configuration yields the following:

```
hosts = localhost
user = postfix
password = secret
dbname = mail
select_field = address
table = aliases
where_field = alias
additional_conditions =
```

An alternative solution, using the query parameter of Postfix 2.2, would look like this:

```
hosts = localhost
user = postfix
password = secret
dbname = mail
query = SELECT address FROM aliases WHERE alias ='%s'
```

For brevity, the hosts, user, password, and dbname parameters will hereon be omitted from the example configurations.

Sometimes reality is a bit more complicated than this trivial example, so we will move on to something a bit more difficult.

The `select_field`, `table`, `where_field`, and `additional_conditions` parameters are really just inserted directly into the following SELECT query template, together with the lookup string:

```
SELECT select_field FROM table WHERE where_field = 'lookup key'
additional_conditions
```

This means `select_field` does not have to be a single column; it could specify multiple columns combined into one value, and `table` could be multiple tables with the join conditions in `additional_conditions`. For example, consider this slightly more complex query:

```
SELECT CONCAT(aliases.user, '@example.com') FROM aliases, domains
WHERE CONCAT(aliases.name, '@', domains.name) = 'lookup key'
AND aliases.domain = domains.id
```

The following lookup table configuration would be required to execute it:

```
select_field = CONCAT(aliases.user, '@example.com')
table = aliases, domains
where_field = CONCAT(aliases.name, '@', domains.name)
additional_conditions = AND aliases.domain = domains.id
```

Or, using the `query` parameter:

```
query = SELECT CONCAT(aliases.user, '@example.com')
  FROM aliases, domains
  WHERE CONCAT(aliases.name, '@', domains.name) = '%s'
  AND aliases.domain = domains.id
```

Before putting a new MySQL lookup table configuration to work, you should make sure that it returns the desired result for all lookup keys. This can be done with the `postmap` program, the procedure for which is described in the *Troubleshooting lookup tables with postmap* section.

Local aliases

Local aliases are an alternative to virtual aliases. Local aliases pretty much work in the same way, but they apply only to local domains. Local alias tables also provide a couple of extra features. We took a brief look at local aliases even before we started Postfix the first time in the *Error reporting* section.

Lookup tables for local aliases are specified in the `alias_maps` parameter. These lookup tables have a slightly different format than virtual aliases, and the reason is to stay compatible with the file format of the `sendmail` mail transfer agent. Because of this, you should not use the `postmap` command to rebuild the alias file but `postalias` instead. You may also find the `newaliases` command to be convenient.

Many people are confused by the two similar parameters, `alias_maps` and `alias_database`. The difference between the two of them is that `alias_maps` contains the lookup tables that Postfix will use to do local alias rewriting, and `alias_database` contains the lookup tables that the `newaliases` command will rebuild when invoked. Only indexed lookup tables (`hash`, `btree`, `dbm`, `cdb`) need to be rebuilt, so it does not make sense to list MySQL lookup tables there.

Often, you will want `alias_maps` and `alias_database` to refer to the same lookup table(s):

```
alias_maps = hash:/etc/aliases
alias_database = $alias_maps
```

Compared to virtual alias tables, the lookup key in local alias tables does not include the domain part. That information would be useless as all local domains have the same localpart namespaces. When indexed files are used for local aliases, the lookup key must end with a colon, for example see the follwoing:

```
$ cat /etc/aliases

postmaster:        jack, jill
$ postalias /etc/aliases
```

This will send messages addressed to the postmaster address in any local domain to the two users, `jack` and `jill`, assuming that the domain in `myorigin` is local. The next section explains why this assumption is important.

The right-hand side of alias tables does not necessarily have to point to local users. In fact they may point to any valid address in any domain. The format of local alias tables is described in the `aliases(5)` manual page.

Command deliveries

Up until now, everything that could have been done with a local alias could just as well have been done with a virtual alias. So, what is the point of local aliases? One big difference is that local aliases support delivering messages to commands. This is typically required by mailing list manager software. Postfix delivers messages to commands by passing the contents of the messages on the standard input stream.

To run a command when a message is delivered, the following syntax is used:

```
mylist:              |"/usr/local/mailman/bin/wrapper post mylist"
```

The double quotes are necessary only if the command, as in this case, contains spaces.

But what if you want to run a mailing list on a virtual domain? You will have to use virtual aliases to rewrite the addresses in the virtual domain to local aliases. Say you want messages sent to the address `mylist@virtual.example.com` to be posted to the `mylist` mailing list, which accepts messages via command delivery. To enable this you will need a virtual alias such as the following:

```
mylist@virtual.example.com          mylist@localhost
```

Pay attention to what user the programs will run as. Postfix normally uses the owner of the alias file, but not if the owner is the root user. In that case, the user in the `default_privs` parameter (typically "nobody") will be used to run the program.

If you write your own program that you want Postfix to deliver messages to, make sure you return an appropriate exit status when errors occur. Postfix uses the error status constants in `sysexits.h` to determine what to do if the program exits with a non-zero exit status. Depending on the exit status, Postfix will either return the message to the sender or let it remain in the queue and retry delivery later.

Common pitfalls

Virtual aliases not only apply to virtual alias domains but also to all messages that pass through Postfix. Not recognizing this may lead to surprises. For example, if you host many virtual alias domains that all should have some aliases in common—say, `root`, `postmaster`, and `abuse`—you might be tempted to use a regular expression lookup table (`regexp` or `PCRE`) to alias these addresses for all of your virtual alias domains to yourself.

```
# Warning! Does not work!
/^abuse@/                   abuse@example.com
```

Do not do this! As virtual aliases apply to all messages, any messages that you or your users send to, for instance, `abuse@aol.com` or `abuse@mindspring.com` will be sent to you instead of the intended recipient.

A very common pitfall is believing that a non-qualified address on the right-hand side implicitly refers to a local user. For example, `joe` would always mean the local user joe. This is equally untrue for both virtual aliases and local aliases. Recall from the beginning of this chapter when the `myorigin` parameter was discussed. Just as in all other places, Postfix will qualify bare usernames with `myorigin`. If your value of `myorigin` happens to be a local domain listed in `mydestination`, which it probably would be, `joe` will indeed refer to the local user joe. To avoid surprises, if you at some time set `myorigin` to a non-local domain, it is a good idea to always qualify the right-hand side addresses with a local domain. As `localhost.$mydomain` almost always is listed in `mydestination`, a good candidate might be `localhost`.

```
postmaster@example.com        jack@localhost, jill@localhost
```

Other address rewriting mechanisms

Virtual and local aliases are not the only mechanisms for address rewriting that Postfix provides. Most notably, canonical rewriting can be used to rewrite sender and/or recipient addresses in both the envelope and the headers. This type of rewriting is provided by the parameters `canonical_maps`, `sender_canonical_maps`, and `recipient_canonical_maps` and can among other things be useful to rewrite sender addresses such as `joe@example.com` to `Joe.User@example.com` if you do not want to expose the actual usernames of the users.

How Postfix rewrites addresses and in what order rewriting happens is described in *ADDRESS_REWRITING_README* available at `http://www.postfix.org/ADDRESS_REWRITING_README.html`.

Troubleshooting Postfix problems

Postfix provides many tools to simplify problem solving. While implementing new features in your Postfix mail system, do it step by step. The more unsure you are in what you are doing, the smaller should be the steps that you take. If you run into problems, you will discover them early and it will be easier to figure out what went wrong. This is especially true when implementing complex lookup tables using MySQL databases.

If you are even slightly uncomfortable with complex lookup tables, never introduce a new feature and a complex lookup table configuration at the same time. If something breaks, you will have much more trouble figuring out where to start.

When trying out new configurations, it does not hurt to be on the cautious side until the configuration is fully tested. By setting the following feature all permanent errors will be turned into temporary errors:

```
soft_bounce = yes
```

This means the transmission of any messages rejected by your server will be retried, and that Postfix will retry sending any messages that get rejected by a remote server. With this setting in effect, closely monitor the logs and look for rejections that do not seem normal. Do not forget to turn this feature off when you have finished testing!

Reading and interpreting the log files

One key element in troubleshooting Postfix problems is being able to read and interpret the log messages that Postfix produces. Because they are plain text files with one log message per line, they do not require any special programs for inspection. Logs have been looked at a few times before, but this section will explain the messages and give examples of both successful mail deliveries and failures. When reading the examples, refer to the figure in the *Postfix architecture: An overview* section and note how the order of the log entries closely follows the path of the mail through Postfix.

Understanding Postfix's logging is also discussed in Kyle Dent's article *Troubleshooting with Postfix Logs* at http://www.onlamp.com/pub/a/ onlamp/2004/01/22/postfix.html.

Message queue ID

An important property of each message, received and processed, is the queue ID. The **queue ID** is a hexadecimal number of varying lengths that identifies a message. Log messages that have a message context will also log the queue ID. This makes it easy for you to find all log messages that pertain to a message if you have the queue ID (the path to the log file needs to be adjusted for your system).

```
$ grep 92AFD4302 /var/log/maillog
```

The queue ID is assigned when the cleanup daemon creates a queue file in one of the Postfix queue directories. The queue file remains in the system until all recipients have been delivered to or the message expires, after which the qmgr daemon removes the queue file. In recent releases of Postfix, this removal event is logged, as we will see in the examples.

Sometimes you will find that there is no queue ID but instead the word NOQUEUE in the log, as in this example that we have seen before:

```
Dec 31 16:39:31 jeeves postfix/smtpd[28478]: NOQUEUE: reject_warning:
RCPT from unknown[222.101.15.127]: 450 Client host rejected: cannot
find your hostname, [222.101.15.127]; from=<jdoe@example.com> to=<me@
example.com> proto=SMTP helo=<222.101.15.127>
```

The reason is that this message has not yet been given a queue file and thus has not been assigned a queue ID. The queue file is created by the cleanup daemon when the first recipient has been accepted. This helps in performance optimization.

Do not confuse the queue ID with the message ID. The latter is contained in the Message-ID header of each message and is normally added by the mail client before the message is handed over to Postfix. If no such header field is present, the cleanup daemon of Postfix will add one for you. The cleanup daemon will always log the message ID of received messages.

```
Jan  5 23:49:13 jeeves postfix/cleanup[12547]: 92AFD4302:
message-id=<20041214021903.243BE2D4CF@mail.example.com>
```

The Message-ID header contains the hostname of the computer and typically the current date and time, and it will be unique for each message. Do not fall in the trap of thinking that the queue IDs also are unique. Queue IDs can and will be reused for different messages, theoretically as often as every second (but that would have to be on an incredibly busy system).

SMTP submission and local delivery

Let's start by looking at two examples of successful mail transactions. The first one shows a message being received by SMTP and delivered to a local mailbox, and the second example will show a locally submitted message that is delivered to a foreign mailbox via SMTP.

The first example shows what the logs contain after a message has been received via SMTP and delivered to a local user.

```
Jan  5 23:49:13 jeeves postfix/smtpd[12546]:
connect from mail.example.com[1.2.3.4]
```

The smtpd daemon has received a connection from a client.

```
Jan  5 23:49:13 jeeves postfix/smtpd[12546]: 92AFD4302:
client=mail.example.com[1.2.3.4]
```

Postfix has now accepted the first recipient of this message and requested a queue file from the `cleanup` daemon. This is the first log entry for this message that contains the queue ID.

```
Jan  5 23:49:13 jeeves postfix/cleanup[12547]: 92AFD4302:
message-id=<20041214021903.243BE2D4CF@mail.example.com>
```

The `cleanup` daemon has received the whole message from the `smtpd` daemon and logs the message ID.

```
Jan  5 23:49:13 jeeves postfix/smtpd[12546]:
disconnect from mail.example.com[1.2.3.4]
```

The client disconnected from the SMTP server.

```
Jan  5 23:49:13 jeeves postfix/qmgr[22431]: 92AFD4302:
from=<joe@example.com>, size=4258, nrcpt=1 (queue active)
```

The message has entered the active queue and is thus eligible for delivery (unless the queue is congested, delivery will start more or less immediately). The queue manager logs the sender address, the message size in bytes, and the total number of recipients. The reported size will be slightly larger than the actual number of bytes in the message and the size of the message when stored on disk. This is because the reported size is the total size of the message content records in the queue file, and this gives a little overhead.

```
Jan  5 23:49:14 jeeves postfix/local[12653]: 3C21A4305:
to=<jack@example.net>, orig_to=<postmaster@example.net>,
relay=local, delay=0.1, delays=0.04/0.03/0/0.03, dsn=2.0.0,
status=sent (delivered to maildir)
```

The local delivery agent successfully delivered the message to the `maildir` of the local user "jack". The message was originally addressed to `postmaster@example.net`, but some address rewriting mechanism (typically a local or virtual alias) rewrote the recipient address. Finally, the message was delivered about one tenth of a second after it was received (the `delay` keyword).

Note that this message is logged when the delivery is completed. If the delivery agent invokes another program during the delivery and that program logs messages of its own, these will end up in the log before this delivery completion message.

Each recipient delivered to will emit a log message:

```
Jan  5 23:49:26 jeeves postfix/qmgr[22431]: 92AFD4302: removed
```

This final message signals that all recipients have been delivered to so that the queue file is removed.

Local submission and SMTP delivery

Our next example is somewhat the opposite of the previous example. Here, a message submitted via the `sendmail` command is delivered to another host via SMTP:

```
Jan  6 01:41:29 jeeves postfix/pickup[12659]:
CBA844305: uid=100 from=<jack>
```

The submitted message has been taken care of by the `pickup` daemon. The message was submitted by the user having user ID `100`, and the sender was the unqualified address `jack`:

```
Jan  6 01:41:30 jeeves postfix/cleanup[13190]: CBA844305:
message-id=<20050106004129.CBA844305@example.net>
```

Again, the message has been read by the `cleanup` daemon and the message ID is logged:

```
Jan  6 01:41:30 jeeves postfix/qmgr[12661]: CBA844305:
from=<jack@example.net>, size=1309, nrcpt=1 (queue active)
```

Note how the previously unqualified sender address has now been rewritten to a fully qualified address, probably because the `myorigin` parameter is equal to `example.net`.

```
Jan  6 01:41:31 jeeves postfix/smtp[13214]: CBA844305:
to=<joe@example.com>, relay=mail.example.com[1.2.3.4],
delay=1.3, delays=0.03/0.03/0.97/0.22, dsn=2.0.0,
status=sent (250 Ok: queued as DD8F02787)
```

The message was successfully delivered to the recipient `joe@example.com` via the `mail.example.com` SMTP relay. When accepting the message, the remote server said:

250 Ok: queued as DD8F02787

So now we know the queue ID that our message got at the other end. This information may be useful if we need to contact the postmaster at `example.com` regarding this message:

```
Jan  6 01:41:31 jeeves postfix/qmgr[12661]: CBA844305: removed
```

Delivery completed, queue file removed.

Hopefully you are starting to get a grip on the general format of the log entries emitted for a message, so the next example will show only log fragments.

Connection problems upon SMTP delivery

The following example shows what happens when multiple hosts are set up in DNS to receive messages for a domain but some of the hosts are temporarily unreachable causing Postfix to try a few of them before the delivery can be made. We will only look at the logs of the delivery agent:

```
Jan  2 14:19:46 poseidon postfix/smtp[998]: connect to
mx4.hotmail.com[65.54.190.230]: Connection timed out (port 25)

Jan  2 14:20:16 poseidon postfix/smtp[998]: connect to
mx1.hotmail.com[64.4.50.50]: Connection timed out (port 25)

Jan  2 14:20:46 poseidon postfix/smtp[998]: connect to
mx3.hotmail.com[64.4.50.179]: Connection timed out (port 25)

Jan  2 14:20:47 poseidon postfix/smtp[998]: 940C132ECE:
to=<postmaster@hotmail.com>, relay=mx4.hotmail.com[65.54.167.230],
delay=92, delays=92/0/0.27/0.28, dsn=2.0.0,
status=sent (250  <20050102131914.B7C4B32ECF@example.com> Queued mail
for delivery)
```

Clearly, three of the receiving mail hosts for hotmail.com were unreachable when Postfix attempted the delivery. Notice how the connection attempts are evenly spread out at 30-second intervals. This is not a coincidence; the default value of the smtp_connect_timeout parameter that controls how long Postfix will wait for a connection is indeed 30 seconds. These three 30-second timeouts also explain why the delivery delay logged by the last message is 92 seconds. Also do notice that the acceptance message that Hotmail gives us does not contain any queue ID but instead the message ID—the format of the text message following the 250 status code has not been standardized.

Getting more detailed log messages

In most cases, Postfix's default logging is enough to resolve a problem but sometimes more details are needed. For those rare cases, you can ask Postfix's daemon processes to log more detailed messages by making sure they are given at least one -v startup option. This is done by editing master.cf, and adding -v to the end of the line for the daemon from which you want to get more detailed logging. For example, to get verbose logging from the SMTP server, smtpd, change the line:

```
smtp       inet  n        -        n        -        -        smtpd
```

To this:

```
smtp       inet  n        -        n        -        -        smtpd -v
```

Depending on your configuration, the first line may look slightly different, but the important part is what is in the last column, the name of the daemon. In the case of the SMTP server, busy servers may produce insane amounts of logging with this setting. If such is the case, the debug_peer_list parameter can come in handy.

This parameter accepts one or more hostnames or network addresses for which the level of logging will be increased. This makes sense only in contexts where there is a network peer such as in the SMTP server and SMTP client.

If you are having problems sending messages to a particular remote server, say mail.example.com, you can set the following rule:

```
debug_peer_list = mail.example.com
```

You can then watch the increased logging when Postfix connects to that particular host. When using debug_peer_list, there is no reason to touch master.cf.

Troubleshooting lookup tables with Postmap

The postmap command is not only useful for rebuilding indexed lookup tables,you can also use it to query lookup tables in order to check if the lookups work as you expect them to. This is especially useful for regular expression lookup tables and complex lookup table types such as MySQL, LDAP, and PostgreSQL. Before taking new lookup tables into use in Postfix, you should test them with postmap first. To perform lookups with postmap, use the -q option:

```
$ postmap -q postmaster@example.com mysql:/etc/postfix/
mysql-aliases.cf
jack@example.com
```

This will query the MySQL lookup table described by the configuration in /etc/postfix/mysql-aliases.cf for the string postmaster@example.com, simulating a virtual alias lookup by Postfix.

You can also examine the exit status of the command to determine whether the lookup succeeded. As always, a zero exit status indicates success. The UNIX shell stores the exit status of the last process in the $? environment variable. You can use the echo shell command to view the contents of the $? variable after you have run postmap:

```
$ postmap -q badaddress@example.com mysql:/etc/postfix/mysql-aliases.cf
$ echo $?
1
```

If a lookup does not work as you expect, you can (just as with the Postfix daemons) use one or more -v startup options to increase the verbosity of the messages.

Note that postmap performs *raw* queries. For example, if you want to know whether the IP address 1.2.3.4 is matched by the following access map line:

```
1.2.3                       REJECT
```

You cannot test it with the following command:

```
$ postmap -q 1.2.3.4 hash:/etc/postfix/client_access
```

The postmap command does not know about Postfix's rules for how IP addresses are matched in access map context, and even if it did, it has no way of knowing that 1.2.3.4 is an IP address.

Getting help from the Postfix mailing list

The mailing list for Postfix, called Postfix-users, is a very valuable resource when one is stuck with a Postfix problem. Links to the archives of the list as well as instructions for how to subscribe can found at http://www.postfix.org/lists.html.

Although the people on the list are very helpful, they do expect you to do your homework before requesting help. This means that you should search the list archives to see if your question has been asked before, and most importantly, you should read the documentation first.

When asking a question, do not forget to state the bigger goal you are trying to achieve. This is often forgotten, and the question is just too specific. Not only will an understanding of the bigger picture make it easier to help you, but it will also reveal if the solution method you have chosen is completely wrong. However, do not be too verbose in your description! After all, the people reading the Postfix-users list are humans too, and they do get bored with over-long posts.

Because they are humans, they are also not psychic. Therefore, be sure to provide complete configuration and any log messages that may be relevant to your question. Obtain your configuration by running postconf -n. That command will print the values of all parameters that your have set in your main.cf. Do not post the complete contents of your main.cf, or the output of postconf (without the -n). The content of master.cf is rarely needed.

Summary

The time has come to summarize what has been learned in this chapter. We began with a quick look at how the Postfix mail transfer agent works and then looked at how to install the software and prepare the basic configuration.

We then examined various methods to stop spam and other unwanted messages. We introduced virtual alias domains to fully enable your mail server to host many domains. Finally, we took a look at a few structured techniques to help you analyze and solve Postfix problems.

3

Incoming Mail with POP and IMAP

Now that you have a functioning e-mail server, the next stage is to give users access to their e-mail. In this chapter, you will learn the following:

- What POP and IMAP are, and how to choose which of them you should implement

- How to install and configure Courier-IMAP, which can provide both POP and IMAP functionality

- How to configure e-mail servers to be accessible to clients

- How to configure popular e-mail clients to use the services provided by your e-mail server

Choosing between POP and IMAP

Postfix will receive e-mail and deliver it to the user's inbox, but additional software is required to allow users to read their e-mail with ease. There are two standards for retrieval of e-mail from a host. The first is called **Post Office Protocol (POP)**. POP3 is the most commonly used version of POP. This is normally used to download e-mail from the server, store it in a client application, and remove the e-mail from the server. This is often used by Internet Service Providers. The e-mail is subsequently manipulated by the client application, for example, Windows Live Mail or Mozilla Thunderbird.

The second protocol is called **Internet Message Access Protocol (IMAP)**.The IMAP system is usually used when you want a copy of each e-mail to stay on the server. IMAP allows users to create folders for e-mail and to move or copy e-mail between the folders. The client application accesses the e-mail on the server, but does not have to store it on the client machine.The e-mail server must be able to store all of the e-mails for all of its users, and the amount of data will generally grow larger over time. Users rarely delete e-mail. Therefore, IMAP is more frequently used in large organizations with centralized IT facilities.

A program called **e-mail client** handles retrieving mail from a mail server on behalf of a user, and the program that the e-mail client talks to is called an **e-mail server**. There are many POP3 and IMAP servers. Some perform only one of the tasks. The Courier-IMAP suite of software contains both, a POP3 and an IMAP server, and is covered in detail in this chapter.

Courier-IMAP operates by accessing the `maildir` of the user. An overview of the operation is shown in the following image:

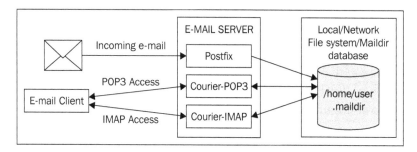

Downloading and installing Courier-IMAP

Courier is a suite of programs and includes a full-fledged MTA. This book assumes that the MTA used is **Postfix**. It is important that only the POP3 and IMAP components of Courier are installed and configured — an e-mail system would be very unstable if there were two MTAs operating at once.

The term "Courier" is often used to refer to the complete suite of Courier software, including the MTA. Courier-IMAP is normally used to refer to the IMAP and POP3 portions of the server. The **Courier Authentication Library** is another Courier module that is required by Courier-IMAP. Ensure that you install only the Courier Authentication Library and Courier-IMAP.

There are a couple of ways to install Courier-IMAP. Courier-IMAP **Redhat Package Managers** (**RPMs**) for several different distributions of Linux are available. These will either be available from the manufacturer of the distribution, or may have been built by a third party, typically an enthusiast or developer of Courier. If your Linux distribution is based on RPM, but a package of Courier-IMAP is not available in RPM, then it has to be built from source.

If your distribution of Linux is based on the Debian software package format, a package of Courier-IMAP will probably be available. If not, then Courier-IMAP will have to be built from source.

Installing Courier-IMAP from a distribution repository

It is best to use a package built by your Linux distributor, if at all possible. Any package they provide should be stable, perform well, and use the default paths and file locations to suit the rest of your software. If your distribution has a package manager, then you should use that as it will install any packages that Courier-IMAP requires automatically.

It is important to get a package that matches the distribution in use. Packages meant for a different distribution may not work correctly and may also make existing software unstable.

Installing Courier-IMAP from RPM

It is important to get an RPM that matches the distribution in use. An RPM meant for another distribution may not work correctly, and may also make existing software unstable.

If your Linux distribution includes a graphical frontend to manage packages (such as gnorpm), it is best to use that because it will manage any dependencies between packages automatically.

To locate an RPM of Courier-IMAP, first check if one is provided by your Linux distributor. If so, then download and use it. If the distributor does not provide a package, it is possible that a suitable package may be provided by another organization or individual. To check this, search the Web. There is a database of RPMs available at `www.rpmfind.net`, and searching for `courier-imap` coupled with the name of the distribution (for example, Fedora or Mandriva) will locate any suitable packages. It is best to use a package designed for a particular version of a distribution. For example, a package for Mandriva Linux 2008.1 should not be used for Mandriva Linux 2009.1. If you are not sure then it is best to install Courier-IMAP from source as described in the next section.

If you are not able to use a frontend to RPM, then to install Courier-IMAP from RPM, firstly download the RPM and change to the directory containing the file using the command prompt. As root, use the `rpm` command to install the RPM.

```
# rpm -ivh courier-imap-4.4.1-1mdv2009.1.i586.rpm
```

The RPM command may fail if all of the prerequisite software is not present. In this case, the output will name the software required. The appropriate package can be downloaded and installed using the `rpm` command as seen earlier. Once all the prerequisite software has been installed, you can install Courier-IMAP using the `rpm` command as explained before.

If the `rpm` command was used to install Courier-IMAP, it can also be used to uninstall it. The command will be as follows:

```
# rpm -e Courier-IMAP
```

Installing Courier-IMAP using the Debian package format

If your Linux distribution includes a graphical frontend to manage packages (such as gnorpm), then you can use that, if you are comfortable doing so.

You can use the following command on any Debian-based system to install Courier-IMAP:

```
# apt-get install courier-imap
```

Installing Courier-IMAP from source

Installing Courier-IMAP from source is not a difficult task on a modern Linux distribution. On older versions of Linux, and on other UNIX platforms such as AIX, Solaris, and HP-UX, problems may arise, particularly if the rest of the system's software is not up to date.

Prerequisites

The following are the prerequisites to install Courier-IMAP:

- **A working C++ compiler**: We recommend the **GNU C++ Compiler**, which is a part of the **GNU Compiler Collection** (**GCC**), which in turn is part of virtually every Linux distribution and is available free for most platforms. If an RPM or other package of GCC is available (and it almost certainly will be), it should be used in preference to building GCC from source.

- A make **utility**: We recommend the GNU make utility, which will be available with most Linux distributions or can be downloaded from `http://gcc.gnu.org/`.

- **The GNU linker**: This is available at `www.gnu.org/software/binutils/`.

- **GNU** Libtool: This is available at `www.gnu.org/software/libtool/`.

- **Berkeley DB library or gdbm library**: These are libraries that allow programs to make databases in files. Again, these should be available in packaged form, but can be downloaded from `www.sleepycat.com/` and `http://www.gnu.org/software/gdbm/gdbm.html` respectively. One or both of these will almost certainly be installed already.

- The Courier-IMAP source code.

To install Courier-IMAP successfully, all these prerequisites must be installed first.

Building the Courier Authentication Library

There are two phases to installing Courier-IMAP. First, the Courier Authentication Library, often called `Courier-authlib`, must be built. Once this is done, Courier-IMAP can be installed.

 Although instructions to install Courier-IMAP are given here, it is always a good idea to read the README, READ.ME or INSTALL files that are supplied with the package. If problems are encountered while installing the software, then always check that the problem is not mentioned in any of the supplied documentation.

The `Courier-authlib` source can be downloaded from `www.courier-mta.org/authlib/`. As with many open source packages, the Courier Authentication Library uses a configuration script to detect system capabilities, then uses the make command to build and install the software.

To build the Courier Authentication Library, enter the following commands. You should see responses similar to the following:

```
$ cd /tmp
$ tar xfj /path/to/courier-authlib-0.62.4.tar.bz2
$ cd  courier-authlib-0.62.4/
$ ./configure
    checking for a BSD-compatible install... /usr/bin/install -c
    checking whether build environment is sane... yes
    checking for a thread-safe mkdir -p... /bin/mkdir -p
    checking for gawk... gawk
```

```
    ... (lots more output appears)
    configure: creating ./config.status
    config.status: creating Makefile
    config.status: creating config.h
    config.status: executing depfiles commands
    config.status: executing libtool commands
```

$

$ make

```
    $ make
    /bin/sh ./config.status --file=authlib.html
    config.status: creating authlib.html
    echo "#define AUTHLDAPRC \"\"" >authldaprc.h
    ...(lots more output)
    /bin/sh ./config.status --file=authlib.3
    config.status: creating authlib.3
    make[2]: Leaving directory `/tmp/courier-authlib-0.62.4'
    make[1]: Leaving directory `/tmp/courier-authlib-0.62.4'
```

$ su -c make install (enter the root password)

 # make install

```
    make  install-recursive
    make[1]: Entering directory `/tmp/courier-authlib-0.62.4'
    Making install in libltdl
    make[2]: Entering directory `/tmp/courier-authlib-0.62.4/libltdl'
    make  install-am
    ...(lots more output)
    make[4]: Leaving directory `/tmp/courier-authlib-0.62.4'
    make[3]: Leaving directory `/tmp/courier-authlib-0.62.4'
    make[2]: Leaving directory `/tmp/courier-authlib-0.62.4'
    make[1]: Leaving directory `/tmp/courier-authlib-0.62.4'
    #
```

After the commands execute successfully, the Courier Authentication Library will be installed. Before it can be started, some configuration is required.

Note that if you are using Red Hat Linux or one of its derivatives such as Fedora Core or CentOS, then the ./configure script detects this and suggests that you use an RPM or the --with-redhat parameter:

$ ./configure

```
    configure: WARNING: === I think you are trying to run this configure
    script
    configure: WARNING: === on Red Hat/Fedora.  You're doing too much
    work!
```

```
configure: WARNING: === It's much faster to create installable binary
RPMs
configure: WARNING: === like this: http://www.courier-mta.org/FAQ.
html#rpm
configure: WARNING: === When you do this you may find that RPM will
tell you
configure: WARNING: === to install some other software first, before
trying to
configure: WARNING: === build this one, and even tell you the name of
RPMs you
configure: WARNING: === build this one, and even tell you the name of
RPMs you
configure: WARNING: === need to install from the distribution CD.
That's much
configure: WARNING: === easier than trying to figure out the same from
some
configure: WARNING: === cryptic error message.
configure: WARNING:
configure: WARNING: === Even if you don't intend to use everything you
need to
configure: WARNING: === have in order to build via RPM, you should
still do as
configure: WARNING: === you're told.  All the extra stuff (LDAP, SQL,
etc...)
configure: WARNING: === goes into RPM sub-packages, which do not need
to be
configure: WARNING: === installed.
configure: WARNING: === But, if you insist, you can simply add '--
with-redhat'
configure: WARNING: === parameter to this configure script and not see
this
configure: WARNING: === error message.  You should also do this when
upgrading
configure: WARNING: === and you didn't use RPM with the older version.
configure: error: ... in either case you better know what you're
doing!
```

In this case, pass the `--with-redhat` parameter to `./configure`:

```
$ ./configure --with-redhat
```

Configuring the Courier Authentication Library

Several decisions need to be made once the authentication library is installed.

The Courier Authentication Library provides the system administrator with flexibility in authenticating users. Authentication is when a user proves his/her identity, typically by providing a valid username and corresponding password. The following authentication methods are available:

Authentication method	Description
authshadow	By default, most Linux distributions hold user passwords in the /etc/shadow system file. Using authshadow for authentication validates passwords against system accounts. This is suitable only when users have system accounts, that is, they can log onto the machine using telnet or ssh.
authpwd	On older systems, passwords were stored in the /etc/passwd file. The authpwd module allows users to be authenticated against their system password. Again, users must have system accounts.
authuserdb	Unlike authshadow where each user needs a system account, authuserdb stores user details separately from the system accounts. This allows a **virtual mailbox** facility, where users can be defined without having real accounts on the machine. A number of scripts are used to administer the database, which is usually held in /etc/userdb. (Many distributions place it in /etc/courier/authlib/userdb.)
authmysql	This is similar to authuserdb, but uses a MySQL database instead of the files used in authuserdb. MySQL is a popular relational database provided by most Linux distributions, and offers both advantages and disadvantages over the other methods. Using a relational database such as MySQL adds complexity to an e-mail server, but it is possible that the authentication will be quicker and a relational database will allow the data to be shared with other applications (if required).
authpam	Authentication is provided by the **Programmable Access Method (PAM)** library. PAM is a commonly used library and is provided by most Linux distributions. PAM is flexible, and can in turn authenticate users from a variety of sources, including the system password database (typically the /etc/passwd file).
authcustom	This allows the system administrators to develop their own custom authentication method.

Choosing an authentication method can be a difficult decision. Here are some guidelines:

- If all users have system accounts, then authshadow, authpwd, or authpam can be used. If PAM is already installed and configured, it should be used in preference to the others.

- If a virtual e-mail system is required, use either authdb or authmysql. For small sites, there is little advantage in choosing authmysql over authdb.

In this book, only simple authentication with authshadow or authpwd is covered. Although if PAM is installed and configured, no additional configuration will be required. authuserdb and authmysql require further configuration, which is described in the documentation for the authentication library.

The /usr/local/etc/courier/authlib directory contains the configuration files for the Courier Authentication Library. For security purposes, it's best to make the whole directory readable only by users who are members of the mail group. The default authdaemonrc file can be copied from the installation directory.

```
# mkdir -p /usr/local/etc/courier/authlib
# chown mail:mail /usr/local/etc/courier/authlib/
# chmod 755 /usr/local/etc/courier/authlib/
# cp /tmp/courier-authlib-0.52/authdaemonrc /usr/local/etc/courier/authlib
```

To complete the configuration as the root user, edit the /usr/local/etc/courier/authlib/authdaemonrc file and alter the following entries:

```
authmodulelist="authshadow"
daemons=3
authdaemonvar=/var/lib/courier/authdaemon
DEBUG_LOGIN=0
DEFAULTOPTIONS=""
```

In the line beginning with authmodulelist, enter the module(s) that you wish to use.

The daemons= line lists how many processes should run, waiting to authenticate users. Unless there are a very high number of users, a value between 3 to 5 should suffice. The larger the number of daemons, the more memory will be used by the authentication library. There will also be less memory available for other processes, which may affect overall system performance.

The `authdaemonvar` line lists where the Courier Authentication Library places its runtime files, in particular the socket used to connect to it. The directory listed here (in this example it is `/var/lib/courier/authdaemon`) should exist and be only readable by the root user. Use the following commands as `root` to create the directory:

```
# mkdir -p /var/lib/courier/authdaemon
```

```
# chmod 750 /var/lib/courier/authdaemon
```

```
# chown mail:mail /var/lib/courier/authdaemon
```

For security purposes, it's best to make the `authdaemonrc` file readable only by certain users.

```
# chown mail:mail /usr/local/etc/courier/authlib/authdaemonrc
```

The authentication daemon needs to be started when the system boots. Typically, a script is placed in `/etc/init.d/` to enable easy starting and stopping of a daemon. A sample script is included with the source of the authentication library in `/courier-authlib.sysvinit`. This file should be placed in `/etc/init.d`.

```
# cd /tmp/courier-authlib-0.52
```

```
# cp courier-authlib.sysvinit /etc/init.d/courier-auth
```

The service can, in future, be started and stopped with the following commands:

```
# /etc/init.d/courier-auth start
```

```
# /etc/init.d/courier-auth stop
```

Initially, the daemon should be run directly from the command line. If there are any errors, they will be displayed.

```
# /usr/local/sbin/authdaemond start
    /usr/local/sbin/authdaemond: line 16: /usr/local/etc/authlib/
    authdaemonrc: No such file or directory
```

In the example just shown, the `/usr/local/etc/authlib/authdaemonrc` file was missing because the default `authdaemonrc` file was not copied from the installation directory.

If the service was started correctly, it can be stopped by passing the `stop` parameter.

```
# /usr/local/sbin/authdaemond stop
```

Consult the documentation for distribution to get the service to start automatically when Linux boots. On Red Hat systems, the `service` command can be used to configure a service to start automatically.

```
# service courier-auth add default
```

For other distributions, the `chkconfig` command might be used.

```
# chkconfig -add imapd
```

Resolving errors

Errors can be generated at each phase of the build. Errors while running the `configure` script will probably relate to a missing dependency. Check the README and INSTALL files supplied with the software and ensure that all dependencies are installed. If the problem is not obvious from the error message generated, an Internet search for the exact error message may find a solution.

An error at build time is unusual, as most errors will be prevented by the `configure` script. Again, the error message should provide a good clue to the source of the error and use of an Internet search engine may pay off.

Runtime errors are generally due to erroneous configuration. There are few configuration options with the Courier Authentication Library, but errors can occur.

If an answer can't be found, there is a Courier mailing list that can be approached for help. As always, first search list archives for your problem and consult the FAQ. For Courier-IMAP, the mailing list is at `http://lists.sourceforge.net/lists/listinfo/courier-imap/`, searchable list archives are available at: `http://sourceforge.net/mailarchive/forum.php?forum_id=7307/`, and the FAQ is available at `http://www.courier-mta.org/FAQ.html`.

Building Courier-IMAP

The Courier-IMAP source code is available in a tarball— a package of all the files, similar to a ZIP file. This can be downloaded from `http://www.courier-mta.org/imap/`, but be careful to download the source for Courier-IMAP and not for the Courier MTA.

 Although details are given here on how to install Courier-IMAP, it is always a good idea to read the README, READ.ME or INSTALL files that are supplied with the package. If problems are encountered when installing the software, always check that the problem is not mentioned in any of the supplied documentation.

To install Courier-IMAP, a few commands must be entered. As with much software provided in source form, a configuration script is run first. The configuration script checks the software installed on our machine and configures the software so that it will build correctly.

When Courier-IMAP is used as an IMAP server, by default it assumes that its clients are going to follow the IMAP standard exactly. Unfortunately this is generally not the case and, if Courier-IMAP expected the clients to conform to the IMAP standard exactly, mail may not be delivered to the e-mail client. The Courier-IMAP developers recognize this, and have built the capability to work with non-standard clients by passing the --enable-workarounds-for-imap-client-bugs flag to the configure script.

Courier-IMAP includes a special check functionality while building it. Unfortunately, using --enable-workarounds-for-imap-client-bugs prevents the check from working successfully. As the check functionality is useful, we will build the software twice. First without the --enable-workarounds-for-imap-client-bugs, then run check, and then build again with the flag, and install the software.

To build Courier-IMAP, enter the following commands. Choose a suitable directory to build the software. In this example, we choose /tmp, and the software unpacks itself into the courier-imap-3.0.8 directory. As noted in the case of the Courier Authentication Library, the configure script will detect when a Red Hat-derived Linux Distribution is being used and the --with-redhat flag can be passed to configure.

```
$ cd /tmp
$ tar xfj /path/to/courier-imap-4.5.1.tar.bz2
$ cd /tmp/courier-imap-4.5.1
$ ./configure --with-redhat
    checking for a BSD-compatible install... /usr/bin/install -c
    checking whether build environment is sane... yes
    checking for a thread-safe mkdir -p... /bin/mkdir -p
    checking for gawk... gawk
    checking whether make sets $(MAKE)... yes
    ... (a lot more output follows)
    config.status: creating config.h
    config.status: executing depfiles commands
    config.status: executing libtool command

$ make check
    Making check in numlib
    make[1]: Entering directory `/tmp/courier-imap-4.5.1/numlib'
    make[1]: Nothing to be done for `check'.
    make[1]: Leaving directory `/tmp/courier-imap-4.5.1/numlib'
    Making check in md5
    ... (a lot more output appears)
    make[2]: Leaving directory `/tmp/courier-imap-4.5.1/imap'
    make[1]: Leaving directory `/tmp/courier-imap-4.5.1/imap'
```

```
make[1]: Entering directory `/tmp/courier-imap-4.5.1'
make[1]: Nothing to be done for `check-am'.
make[1]: Leaving directory `/tmp/courier-imap-4.5.1'
```

$ ./configure --enable-workarounds-for-imap-client-bugs

```
checking for gcc... gcc
checking for C compiler default output file name... a.out
checking whether the C compiler works... yes
checking whether we are cross compiling... no
... (a lot more output follows)
config.status: creating config.h
config.status: executing depfiles commands
config.status: executing libtool command
```

$ make

```
$ make
make  all-recursive
make[1]: Entering directory `/tmp/courier-imap-4.5.1'
make all-gmake-check FOO=BAR
--------------------------------------------------
(lots more output appears)
cp imap/imapd.cnf .
cp imap/pop3d.cnf .
cp -f ./maildir/quotawarnmsg quotawarnmsg.example
make[2]: Leaving directory `/tmp/courier-imap-4.5.1'
make[1]: Leaving directory `/tmp/courier-imap-4.5.1'
```

$ su -c "make install"

Password: (enter password for root)

```
Making install in numlib
make[1]: Entering directory `/tmp/courier-imap-4.5.1/numlib'
make[2]: Entering directory `/tmp/courier-imap-4.5.1/numlib'
make[2]: Nothing to be done for `install-exec-am'.
make[2]: Nothing to be done for `install-data-am'.
(lots more output appears)
Do not forget to run make install-configure
test -z "/usr/lib/courier-imap/share" || /bin/mkdir -p "/usr/lib/
courier-imap/share"
 /usr/bin/install -c mkimapdcert mkpop3dcert '/usr/lib/courier-imap/
share'
make[2]: Leaving directory `/tmp/courier-imap-4.5.1'
make[1]: Leaving directory `/tmp/courier-imap-4.5.1'
```

```
$ su -c "make install-configure"
Password: (enter password for root)
    make[1]: Entering directory `/tmp/courier-imap-4.5.1/numlib'
    make[1]: Leaving directory `/tmp/courier-imap-4.5.1/numlib'
    make[1]: Entering directory `/tmp/courier-imap-4.5.1/md5'
    make[1]: Leaving directory `/tmp/courier-imap-4.5.1/md5'
    (lots more output appears)
    make install-configure-local DESTDIR=
    make[1]: Entering directory `/tmp/courier-imap-4.5.1'
    make[1]: Leaving directory `/tmp/courier-imap-4.5.1'
$
```

If the output appears similar to that shown, Courier-IMAP has been successfully installed and you may skip the next section on error handling.

Handling errors

It is possible that the `configure` command will fail. Configuration attempts to detect existing software, and ensures that Courier-IMAP works with it, but occasionally there are errors.

```
checking whether the shell understands some XSI constructs... yes
checking whether the shell understands "+="... yes
checking for /usr/x86_64-pc-linux-gnu/bin/ld option to reload object files... -r
checking for objdump... objdump
checking how to recognize dependent libraries... pass_all
checking for ar... ar
checking for strip... strip
checking for ranlib... ranlib
checking for getspent... yes
configure: error: /var/vpopmail/etc/lib_deps does not exist - upgrade vpopmail to the
 current version or fix the permissions on this file
configure: error: /bin/sh './configure' failed for authlib
```

In this example, the `configure` command assumed that `vpopmail` was installed, and failed when it couldn't find parts of `vpopmail`. In reality, `vpopmail` was not installed, and could not be detected. We get the following from the INSTALL file:

```
...configure should automatically detect if you use vpopmail, and
compile and install the authvchkpw authentication module.
```

This suggests that the `authvchkpw` is used for `vpopmail`. Further up the INSTALL file we read:

```
    * authvchkpw - this module is compiled by default only if the
vpopmail account is defined.
```

Upon checking the `/etc/passwd` file, we find that there is an account for `vpopmail` which explains the detection. The lack of `vpopmail` files explains the failure of the `configure` script. In the `INSTALL` file, the parameters to the configure script are described.

```
Options to configure:
    . . .
    * --without-module - explicitly specify that the authentication
module named "module" should not be installed. See below for more
details.
        Example: --without-authdaemon.
```

The solution, therefore, is to use the `--without-authvchkpw` option:

$ ./configure –without-authvchkpw

Most problems can be solved in a similar way. It is best not to be put off by terms and names that aren't understood. Without understanding anything about `vpopmail` and just by searching for the term "`vpopmail`" (which was mentioned in the original error message), it is possible to resolve the error by reading the documentation.

If you can't find an answer, there is a Courier mailing list that can be approached for help. Details are given in the *Resolving errors* section.

Using POP3

As mentioned in the introduction, POP3 is typically used when e-mail is to be stored on a client computer. It is most often used when there is an intermittent connection to the e-mail server, for example, while using a dial-up line to access an e-mail account at an ISP. This approach has the advantage that the e-mail is always available to the client, who can work when not connected to the e-mail server. E-mails can be read, and replies created for, when the user is next on line.

The main disadvantage of using POP3 is that e-mail is generally only available on the client PC. If the client PC fails, or is stolen, the e-mail is lost, unless a backup has been made.

POP3 clients can be configured to keep e-mail on the POP3 server for other clients to access, but IMAP is more often used in this situation.

Configuring Courier-IMAP for POP3

The configuration files are located in /usr/lib/courier-imap/etc/courier-imap/, if Courier-IMAP was built from source. If you are using a packaged distribution, they may be located in /etc/courier-imap. The pop3d file contains the settings for the POP3 server.

If you are using a packaged distribution of Courier-IMAP, the configuration files can be found with the following command:

```
# find / -name pop3d 2>/dev/null
    /usr/lib/courier-imap/etc/pop3d
    /usr/lib/courier-imap/bin/pop3d
```

Edit the file and locate and alter the following settings:

Setting	Description
PIDFILE	The pop3d daemon keeps track of the process ID that it uses. It specifies a valid path and a name that suggests the use of the file. Typically, this might be /var/run/pop3d.pid. Ensure that the variable points to an existing directory (such as /var/run) or create the directory specified.
MAXDAEMONS	This specifies the maximum number of pop3d process that can run at one time. This number limits the number of users that can connect at one time. A number higher than the expected number of users may be wasteful, but users attempting to connect are also included in this number. Set this to a number around the maximum number of users who may connect at one time, or a little higher. Note that this is the maximum number of processes started, not the initial number of processes.
MAXPERIP	This specifies the maximum number of connections from each IP address. A low number such as 4 prevents malicious acts such as denial-of-service attacks, where an attempt is made to use up all the connections on the mail server.
POP3AUTH	If the Courier Authentication Library daemon is used, set this to blank, otherwise set it to indicate the type of login authentication performed. For versions prior to 4.0, this should be set to LOGIN.
PORT	This specifies the port that the daemon listens on. The standard port is 110, and a different one should only be chosen if all client software is configured to use the non-standard port.
ADDRESS	This specifies the IP address to listen on. If the machine has multiple network interfaces, Courier-IMAP can be configured to listen only on one of the addresses. A value of 0 indicates that all network interfaces should be used.

Setting	Description
TCPDOPTS	These are options to be used. Typical ones used include `nodnslookup` that prevents the POP3 daemon from attempting to resolve the name of each connection, and `-noidentlookup` that prevents it from attempting an `ident` query for the incoming connection. Specifying both of these settings can decrease the time taken to authenticate a user connection.
MAILDIRPATH	This is the path to a typical user's `maildir`. Specify the appropriate value for your system, for example, `.maildir`.

A sample `pop3d` configuration file is shown here:

```
PIDFILE=/var/run/pop3d.pid
MAXDAEMONS=40
MAXPERIP=4
POP3AUTH=""
PORT=110
ADDRESS=0
TCPDOPTS="-nodnslookup -noidentlookup"
MAILDIRPATH=.maildir
```

Once the POP3 server has been configured, it is time to test it. If you are using a distribution-supplied version of Courier-IMAP, use the distributors' startup script called `/etc/init.d/courier-imap`. This will attempt to start `imapd` as well as `pop3d`, but as most of the configuration will have been done by the distributors, IMAP should start successfully.

 If you are using Courier-IMAP version 4.0 or later, then `courier-authdaemon` must be running before the POP3 or IMAP services. Ensure that you start them as described previously.

To start the POP3 service for testing, run the following command:

```
# /usr/lib/courier-imap/libexec/pop3d.rc start
```

Once the POP3 and IMAP services are configured correctly, they can be started automatically when the machine boots. This is explained in the *Testing the IMAP service* section. The instructions can be followed, even if IMAP is not required.

Testing the POP3 Service

The easiest way to test a service such as POP3 is by using the **telnet** utility and connecting to the appropriate port. This avoids any problems there may be with network connectivity or client configuration. POP3 uses port 110, so connect telnet to port 110 on the local machine.

```
$ telnet localhost 110
    Trying 127.0.0.1...
    Connected to localhost.
    Escape character is '^]'.
    +OK Hello there.
USER username
    +OK Password required.
    PASS password
    +OK logged in.
STAT
    +OK 82 1450826
LIST
    +OK POP3 clients that break here, they violate STD53.
    1 5027
    2 5130
    3 6331
    4 3632
    5 1367
    ... all e-mails are listed, with their sizes in bytes
    82 6427
    .
RETR 1
    +OK 5027 octets follow.
    Return-Path: <user@domain.com>
    X-Original-To: user@localhost
    Delivered-To: user@machine.domain.com
    Received: from isp (isp [255.255.255.255])
    ... e-mail is listed
    .
QUIT
    +OK Bye-bye.
```

Connection closed by foreign host.

The POP3 protocol is based on text commands, and so it is easy to emulate a client with telnet. Initially, use the USER and PASS commands to authenticate a user. If the user is authenticated correctly, the STAT command lists all e-mails and their combined size in bytes. LIST lists each e-mail and its size. The RETR command retrieves (or lists) an e-mail when the e-mail number is specified with the command. The DELE command (not shown in the example) will delete an e-mail from the server.

Now that POP3 is working, it is time to configure an e-mail client to collect e-mails.

Retrieving E-mail via POP3 with Windows Live Mail

Windows Live Mail is a popular e-mail client, available for download for versions of Windows from XP onwards. It includes the ability to connect to POP3-and IMAP-enabled servers. It is available for download at `http://download.live.com/wlmail`.

The following are the steps to configure it:

1. Start Windows Live Mail by locating it in the Start menu hierarchy: **Start | All Programs | Windows Live | Windows Live Mail**. When it is run for the first time, the interface will automatically display the wizard to create new account. Otherwise, click on **Add e-mail account** in the navigation bar.

2. The first page of the new account wizard will be displayed.

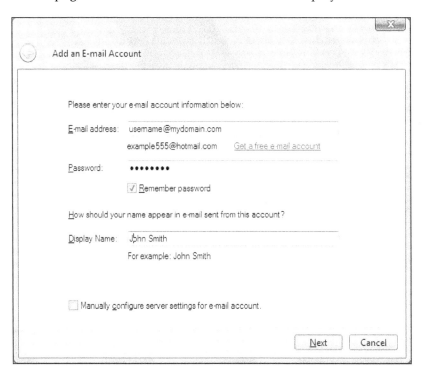

3. Enter the full e-mail address in `username@domain` format. You may decide whether you want to enter the password — if you do not check **Remember password**, you will be prompted for the password every time you start Windows Live Mail. The **Display Name** should be your first and last name — this will appear on outgoing e-mails. There is no need to check the **Manually configure server settings for e-mail account** checkbox.

4. Click on **Next**. The next page of the wizard requires some server details.

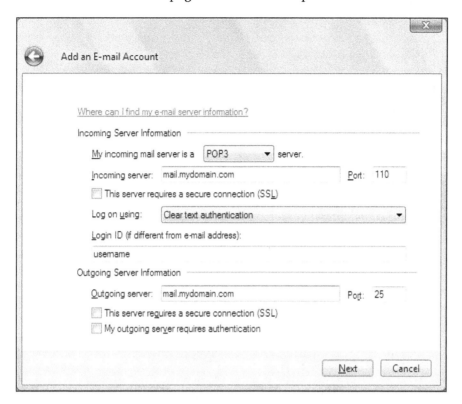

5. The default is for a **POP3** server. The **Incoming server** should be the name (or IP address) of the mail server. The default **Port** of **110** can be kept unchanged. Do not check the box for an SSL connection, and keep the authentication method as **Clear text authentication**. The **Login ID** should be kept as the username part of the e-mail address entered in the first screen. The **Outgoing server** should be as provided for **Incoming server**, and the remainder of the form can be left with the default values.

6. Press **Next**. You will be presented with a confirmation screen.

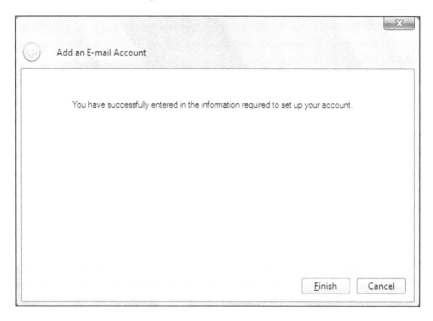

7. When you click on **Finish**, Windows Live Mail will attempt to connect to the e-mail server and download e-mail.

8. If there are any errors, then right-click the account in the navigation pane, and select **Properties**. You can then check and modify any settings.

Now that POP3 has been successfully configured, it is time to move on to IMAP.

Using IMAP

As mentioned in the introduction, with IMAP, the mail is held on the server and might not be held on the client. This makes it ideal for organizations with a central administrative function, as it eases backups and also allows users to change the client computers they work at. However, this also means that the disk storage required to store an entire organizations e-mail will inevitably increase over time. This is particularly true when large attachments are sent or received. If users rely on being able to access their mailbox, they will be inconvenienced if the mail server is unavailable during their working hours. Some e-mail clients can be configured to make copies of e-mails, and so avoid interruption. By using IMAPs ability to create folders and move e-mails between them, this can sometimes be achieved in a relatively straightforward manner.

Configuring Courier for IMAP

After Courier-IMAP has been installed, either from package or from source as described earlier, it needs to be configured before it can be used.

 If you have configured and tested POP3 as described earlier, you should stop the Courier-IMAP daemons while you configure IMAP. If you are using a version of Courier-IMAP greater than 4.0, then you can leave the authentication daemon running.

If Courier-IMAP was built from source, the configuration files are located in `/usr/lib/courier-imap/etc/courier-imap/`. In a packaged distribution, they may be located in `/etc/courier-imap`. The `imapd` file contains the settings for the IMAP server.

If you are using a packaged distribution of Courier-IMAP, the configuration files can be found with this command:

```
# find / -name imapd 2>/dev/null
    /usr/lib/courier-imap/etc/imapd
    /usr/lib/courier-imap/bin/imapd
```

Once the file has been located, it can be modified as appropriate. Here are the main configuration directives:

Setting	Description
PIDFILE	The imapd daemon keeps track of the process ID that it uses. It specifies a valid path and a name, which suggests the use of the file. Typically, this might be /var/run/imapd.pid. Ensure that the setting points to a valid directory.
MAXDAEMONS	This specifies the maximum number of imapd processes that can run at a time. This number limits the number of users that can connect at one time. A number higher than the expected number of users may be wasteful, but users attempting to connect are also included in this number. Set this to a number around the maximum number of users who may connect at one time, or a little higher.
PORT	This specifies the port that the daemon listens on. The standard port is 143, and a different one should only be chosen if all client software is configured to use the non-standard port.
ADDRESS	This specifies the IP address to listen on. If the machine has multiple network interfaces, Courier-IMAP can be configured to listen only on one of the addresses. A value of 0 indicates that all network interfaces should be used.

Setting	Description
TCPDOPTS	These are options to be used. Typical ones include -nodnslookup that prevents the IMAP daemon from attempting to resolve the name of each connection, and -noidentlookup that prevents it from attempting an ident query for the incoming connection. Specifying both of these settings can decrease the time taken to authenticate a user connection.
MAILDIRPATH	This is the path to a typical user's maildir. Specify the appropriate value for your system, for example, .maildir.
MAXPERIP	This specifies the maximum number of connections from each IP address. A low number prevents malicious acts such as denial-of-service attacks, where an attempt is made to use up all the connections on the mail server. Some e-mail clients make multiple connections to a server, and so a low value such as 5 may affect operation of client software.
IMAP_CAPABILITY	This describes the IMAP capabilities that the server reports to clients. It should be left on the default setting.
IMAP_EMPTYTRASH	This specifies how long e-mail messages should be kept in certain folders. Messages older than the date specified are automatically deleted when the user logs in or logs out. This can be used to automatically delete e-mail from the Trash folder after a certain period. This works for all folders, so e-mail in the Sent items folder could be deleted after a longer period has expired.

For example, IMAP_EMPTYTRASH=Trash:7,Sent:30 specifies that e-mails in the Trash folder are deleted after 7 days, and those in the Sent folder will be deleted after 30 days.

If very large numbers of e-mails are present in the folders specified, performance will suffer, as each file will be checked every time the user logs in or logs out of the IMAP server. In this case, it would be better to disable this setting and run a separate script regularly to remove old files. |
IMAP_IDLETIMEOUT	This is the length of time (in seconds) that a client can be idle for (not make any request to the server), before the connection is closed. Values lower than the default of 60 may result in client connections being terminated prematurely, but a well-written client will reconnect without notifying the user. Higher values should be used if users report problems.
IMAP_TRASHFOLDERNAME	This specifies the folder to be used when e-mail is deleted.
SENDMAIL	This specifies the path to sendmail, for sending e-mail. You should ensure that this points to the executable file installed by Postfix in Chapter 2.

Here is a sample `imapd` configuration file:

```
ADDRESS=0
IMAP_CAPABILITY="IMAP4rev1 UIDPLUS CHILDREN NAMESPACE
THREAD=ORDEREDSUBJECT THREAD=REFERENCES SORT QUOTA IDLE"
IMAP_EMPTYTRASH=Trash:7
IMAP_IDLE_TIMEOUT=60
IMAP_TRASHFOLDERNAME=Trash
MAILDIRPATH=.maildir
MAXDAEMONS=40
MAXPERIP=10
PIDFILE=/var/run/imapd.pid
PORT=143
SENDMAIL=/usr/sbin/sendmail
TCPDOPTS="-nodnslookup -noidentlookup"
```

Testing the IMAP service

To start the IMAP service for testing, run the following command:

```
# /usr/lib/courier-imap/libexec/imapd.rc start
```

The easiest way to test a service such as IMAP is by using the telnet utility and connecting to the appropriate port. This avoids any problems with network connectivity or client configuration. IMAP uses port 143, so telnet to port 143 on the local machine:

```
$ telnet localhost 143
    Connected to localhost.
    Escape character is '^]'.
    * OK [CAPABILITY IMAP4rev1 UIDPLUS CHILDREN NAMESPACE
    THREAD=ORDEREDSUBJECT THREAD=REFERENCES SORT QUOTA IDLE ACL ACL2=UNION
    STARTTLS] Courier-IMAP ready. Copyright 1998-2004 Double Precision,
    Inc.  See COPYING for distribution information.

1 capability
    * CAPABILITY IMAP4rev1 UIDPLUS CHILDREN NAMESPACE
    THREAD=ORDEREDSUBJECT THREAD=REFERENCES SORT QUOTA IDLE ACL ACL2=UNION
    STARTTLS
    1 OK CAPABILITY completed
2 login "username" "password"
    2 OK LOGIN Ok.
3 namespace
    * NAMESPACE (("INBOX." ".")) NIL (("#shared." ".")("shared." "."))
    3 OK NAMESPACE completed.
```

Each command is prefixed with an identifier—here we use incremental numbers. The first command asks the IMAP server to list its capabilities. The second command is a user login, and includes the username and password. If this is successful, then the final namespace command shows that the server has accepted the login and the client can determine where in the folder hierarchy the user is placed.

This is enough to confirm that the user can log in and issue commands. The whole IMAP command set is quite large and complex, and does not lend itself to be used by telnet.

Once the POP3 and IMAP services are configured correctly, they can be started automatically when the machine boots. If you have installed from a package, then the distributor will probably have created a suitable startup script in /etc/init.d. Depending on the distribution, this may start when the machine boots. For Red Hat Linux, the command will be:

```
# service courier-imap add default
```

For other distributions, the chkconfig command might be used:

```
# chkconfig -add imapd
```

Now that IMAP is configured correctly, it is time to configure an e-mail client.

Retrieving mail via IMAP with Mozilla Thunderbird

Mozilla Thunderbird is a popular open source e-mail client and can be downloaded from http://www.mozilla.org/. It can be used with a variety of operating systems, including Windows and Linux.

Here are steps to configure it to connect to a Courier-IMAP server:

1. From the main Thunderbird screen, select **Tools | Account Settings**.

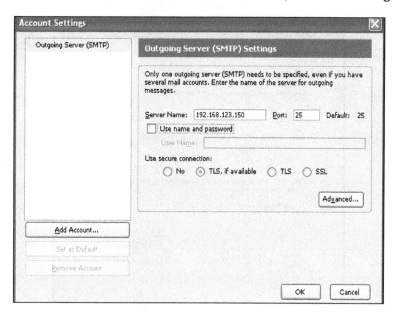

2. Click on the **Add Account...** button. On the next screen, choose **E-mail Account** and then click **Next**. The identity screen opens. Enter your user name and e-mail address, then click **Next**.

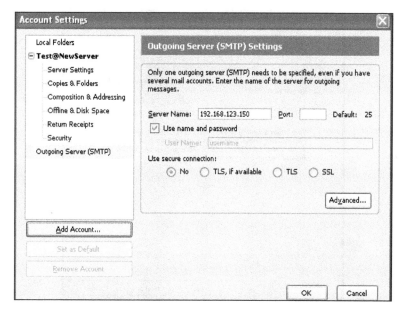

3. On the **Server Information** screen, select **IMAP** as the server type, and enter the name or the IP address of the server for incoming e-mail. Then click the **Next** button.

4. On the next screen, enter the **Incoming User Name**. This will normally be the Linux account name.

5. Finally, provide a useful tag for the e-mail account in the **Account Name** field, in case another account is defined in the future. Click **Next**.

6. On the next screen, the details are summarized. Click **Finish** to save the account details and to exit the **Account Wizard**.

7. Finally, the **Account Settings** screen is shown, listing the account you just defined. Click **OK**.

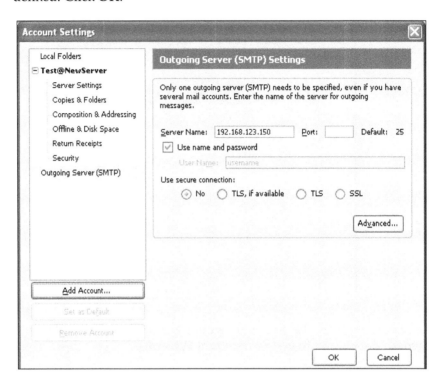

To retrieve messages, click on **File | Get New Messages**, and select the account you just created from the menu.

Thunderbird will prompt you for the password. Enter the correct password and press *Enter*. Thunderbird will then connect to Courier-IMAP and retrieve details of all the e-mail. If you click on an e-mail, Thunderbird will retrieve it using the IMAP protocol.

Summary

In this chapter we saw the two mail protocols for retrieving e-mail, POP3 and IMAP, and explained some strengths and weaknesses. We then covered Courier-IMAP, which can provide both POP3 and IMAP services, and advised you to use a package from your Linux distributor. We also described how to build it from source, should this be required. We then discussed how to configure and test both the POP3 and IMAP services, including configuration of popular e-mail clients.

4
Providing Webmail Access

You learned how to set up and configure an e-mail server in the previous chapters. Now that your e-mail server is ready to serve, how will your users access it? In this chapter, you will learn about the following:

- The benefits and disadvantages of a webmail access solution
- The SquirrelMail webmail package
- Setting up and configuring SquirrelMail
- What SquirrelMail plugins are and what they can do
- How to make SquirrelMail more secure

In the next section, we will introduce the SquirrelMail software package and examine the pros and cons of this and other webmail access solutions. After that, we will follow the installation and configuration of SquirrelMail step by step. Next, we will examine the installation of plugins and include a reference of useful plugins. Finally, we'll include some tips on how to secure SquirrelMail.

The webmail solution

A **webmail solution** is a program or a series of scripts that is run on a server, is accessible over the web, and provides access to e-mail functions similar to a conventional mail client. It is used by Yahoo! Mail, Microsoft Hotmail, Microsoft Outlook Web Access, and Gmail as the primary interface to their e-mail solutions. You may already be familiar with various forms of webmail.

Though we will be examining the SquirrelMail webmail solution specifically, the benefits and drawbacks of SquirrelMail apply to most webmail systems in the market. From this point of view, we will approach the issue from a general perspective, and then in detail for the SquirrelMail package.

The benefits

This section will focus on the advantages offered by installing and maintaining a webmail solution. As with any list, it is not entirely comprehensive. Many benefits will be specific to a particular case; it is important to carefully examine and consider how the following qualities impact your individual situation.

The main benefits we will explore in this section are as follows:

- Easy and quick access with little or no setup
- Easy remote access
- No need to maintain client software or configuration
- Provision of a user interface to configure mail server options
- Possible security benefits

Easy and quick access

Although well suited to certain situations, traditional mail access solutions can often be difficult to set up and maintain. Generally, this involves installing software on a client's local computer and configuring it. This can be difficult, especially in cases where users need to set up the software themselves. Configuration can often be even more problematic as some users may not be competent enough to follow even a very detailed set of instructions. These instructions also need to be provided and maintained for many different mail clients on many different platforms.

However, a webmail solution does not have most of these problems. All of the user's settings can be configured on the server as the application itself resides on the server. This translates to almost zero set up time for the user. Once they have received their login credentials, they can visit the webmail site and instantly have access to all of their mail. The user is able to access the site instantly to send and receive e-mail.

As the Internet is so common now, many users will be familiar with webmail sites such as Google Mail and Windows Live Hotmail, which offer free e-mail services. However, the user interface provided by an open source package may be more primitive and lack some visual features. Squirrelmail provides access to e-mail, including the ability to send and receive attachments, and offers a good user interface.

It is also worth mentioning that a webmail solution can offer what certain traditional mail clients call **groupware** features. These features let groups communicate and coordinate in ways that complement e-mail communication. Examples of groupware components are private calendars, shared calendars, meeting scheduling, To-do lists, and other similar tools.

These applications can be preconfigured so that a user can instantly begin using them without having to configure them on their own. Several SquirrelMail plugins which implement these features are available from the SquirrelMail website.

Easy remote access

Another problem with traditional mail access software is that it is not portable, as an e-mail client needs to be installed and configured on a computer. Once it has been downloaded, installed, and configured on a particular computer, it is accessible only on that computer. Without webmail, users on the road will not be able to access e-mail from friends' computers, mobile devices, or Internet booths at airports.

However, in a webmail solution, e-mail can be accessed from any location with an Internet connection. Employees can access their work e-mail from any computer with an Internet connection and a suitable browser.

As the administrator, you can choose to permit or deny users from accessing e-mail in insecure situations. By requiring the connection to be encrypted, you can ensure that when a user is in a remote location, their communication with the server is secure.

No need to maintain clients

Even if software mail clients have been installed and properly configured, they must be maintained. When a new version is released, all clients must be updated. This is not necessarily an easy task. Software that does not work as expected can result in a large number of support-desk calls.

Updating the software on each client can be a very large administrative burden. In fact, many expensive software packages are designed for the specific purpose of updating software on individual machines automatically. Despite this, problems specific to each local machine often arise and must be solved individually. It may also be difficult to convey instructions or notifications to remote branch locations or remote workers. With a webmail solution, this is not necessary.

In contrast to this, a webmail solution is centrally maintained and administered. The webmail application resides on the server. With webmail, only the web server and the webmail package need to be upgraded. Any exceptions or problems that arise can be dealt with before or during the upgrade. The software upgrade itself can be run through on a test system before it is deployed on a live system. Although changes in settings are rare with SquirrelMail, it is possible to update a user's settings to make them compatible with the changes introduced in an updated version.

Additionally, while upgrading or changing a mail server platform, testing effort can be greatly reduced as only supported browser versions need to be tested. It is advisable to mandate particular browser versions for corporate computers. In contrast with e-mail clients, there is no need to test on all of the possible clients and software platforms.

Configuring mail server interface via the user interface

Many traditional desktop e-mail clients provide only e-mail functionality and nothing more. Often there is no support for other essential tasks (such as changing the access password) that are performed on behalf of a mail user. Certain configuration options that reside on the server may require additional software applications or external solutions to provide for these needs. Examples of mail server options that may need to be configured include each user's password and junk mail filtering settings.

In the case of the SquirrelMail webmail application, many plugins have been developed that provide these features. For example, a user is able to change his/her password directly from the webmail interface. Also, there are plugins and systems that allow users to easily sign up without any direct human intervention. This may be useful if you are interested in providing a service where users can sign up without needing an administrative overhead.

Possible security benefits

This issue can be seen in two different ways—it is for this reason that the title is listed as *"Possible" security benefits*. Nonetheless, this is still an interesting point to examine.

In the software client access model, e-mail is traditionally downloaded onto the local user's computer, being stored in one or more personal folders. From a security perspective, this may be a bad thing. Users of the system may not be as conscientious or knowledgeable about computer security as a trained computer administrator might be. It is often much easier to gain unauthorized access to an end user's computer than a properly configured and secured server. The implication is that someone who stole a company laptop might be able to access all the e-mail stored on that computer.

There is one more disadvantage associated with the client access model. Even if an employee is terminated, he/she may still have access to all of the e-mail that resides on his/her local office computer. It may take a certain amount of time before important information may be secured. A disgruntled worker might easily connect an external storage source to their local office computer and download any data they desire.

It is also worth noting that in a webmail model, all e-mail is centrally stored. If an attacker were to gain access to the central e-mail server, he/she might access all the e-mail stored on that server. However, it is possible that an attacker will gain access to all the e-mail if the central mail server is compromised even if a webmail system is not used.

The disadvantages

This section focuses on the disadvantages resulting from providing and supporting a webmail solution. The warning given in the previous section applies: This list is not entirely comprehensive. Each situation is unique, and may bring its unique disadvantages.

We will go over the following disadvantages of a webmail solution:

- Performance issues
- Compatibility with large e-mail volumes
- Compatibility with e-mail attachments
- Security issues

Performance

The traditional e-mail client is designed in the client-server model. One mail server accepts and delivers e-mail to and from other mail servers. However, a desktop mail client can offer many additional productivity-enhancing features such as message sorting, searching, contact list management, attachment handling, along with more recent ones such as spam filtering and message encryption.

Each of these features may require a certain amount of processing power. The required level of processing power may be negligible when it comes to storing one user's e-mail on a desktop computer, but providing these features may be problematic when applied on a larger scale to a single server.

When examining the performance issue, it is important to consider the number of potential users that will access the webmail application and size a server accordingly. A single server may be able to easily handle something like 300 users, but if the number of users increases significantly, server load may become an issue.

For example, searching through several years' archived mail may take a few seconds on a client's computer. When one user performs this task using webmail, the load will be similar. However, if many clients request this operation at short intervals or concurrently, it may be difficult for the server to process all the requests in a timely manner. This may result in pages being served at a slower rate or, in extreme circumstances, the server failing to respond.

Optimally, load testing in the appropriate conditions should be performed if there is any concern that a server may not be able to handle a particular load of users.

Compatibility with large e-mail volumes

The webmail solution is not well suited to large mail volumes. This disadvantage is related to the previous one, but is more related to the amount of data sent. Even with a relatively low number of users, a large volume of e-mails may be difficult to manage in a webmail application. There are mainly the following two reasons for this:

- Firstly, every e-mail viewed and every folder listed must be sent from the server each time. With a traditional e-mail client, the client software can manage e-mail messages, creating lists and views to suit the user. However, with a webmail solution, this is performed on the server. So, if there are many users, this overhead may use a significant proportion of the server's resources.

- Secondly, each interaction with the webmail application requires a **Hypertext Transfer Protocol (HTTP)** request and response. These messages will typically be larger than those between an e-mail server and a desktop e-mail client. There may also be less parallelism when using a webmail client, in other words, fewer things going on at the same time. A desktop e-mail client may be able to check for new e-mails in several folders at the same time, but a webmail client will typically perform these tasks one after the other, if they occur automatically at all.

Compatibility with e-mail attachments

The webmail solution is not well suited to e-mail attachments. By virtue of the fact that a webmail application resides on a remote server, any and all e-mail attachments must first be uploaded onto that server. For a couple of reasons, it may be difficult or impossible to accomplish this operation with too many attachments or with attachments that are large in size.

Difficulties uploading large attachments may arise due to limited storage space on the webmail server. Large attachments may take a long time to upload over the HTTP protocol and even longer over HTTPS. Additionally, many file size limits may be imposed on uploaded files. PHP, the programming language used with SquirrelMail, imposes a 2MB limit on uploaded files in its default configuration.

The solution to the above problem may lie in the nature of the webmail access solution—e-mail and the mail access software reside on the server. In a traditional mail client, e-mail is often downloaded before the user is aware of the contents or size of the particular e-mail message. As opposed to this, in the case of webmail, the user is able to view e-mail with large attachments without downloading the attachments—a particular benefit to those without high-speed internet connections.

Finally, downloading and uploading large e-mail attachments from the server may cause a performance issue with the user interface. Many users are frustrated by an attachment's upload time in the webmail application, especially as the message cannot be sent until the attachment is uploaded. In a traditional mail client, the attachment is attached instantly, while the message takes time to send.

Security issues

The last issue we will examine is the potential for security shortcomings. One important feature of a webmail access solution also creates a potential problem. The benefit of remote access gives way to the potential insecurity of the local machines upon which the user accesses his/her mail.

A computer that is not directly under your control may be controlled by a third-party intent on accessing your information. Normally, a computer does not record a user's individual keystrokes. Internet cafes and kiosks, and even the home computers of employee's could be running malicious software. This malicious software may monitor keystrokes and websites visited. A user must type in his/her password or login credentials to gain access to the system. When these credentials are captured and stored on the computer with malicious software, they can be intercepted and used by third parties for unauthorized access.

Even if we take malicious intent out of the picture, there are still certain situations that may prove to pose security risks. For example, many modern web browsers offer the option of saving a password whenever it is entered. This password is stored on the local computer where the website is visited. If a user logs in to the webmail application and accidentally saves their password on the local computer, this password may be accessible to any user with access to that local computer.

Finally, users may inadvertently leave themselves logged in to the webmail application. Without logging out, any user with access to that specific computer might be able to gain access to the user's mail account.

The SquirrelMail webmail package

The following screenshot shows the SquirrelMail login screen:

SquirrelMail was chosen based on the combination of the following features it provides:

- It is a proven, stable, and mature webmail platform.

- It has been downloaded over two million times.

- It is standards-based and renders pages in pure HTML 4.0 without requiring the use of JavaScript.

SquirrelMail also includes the following features (and many more, via the flexible plugin system):

- Strong MIME support

- Address book functionality

- A spell checker

- Support for sending and receiving HTML e-mail

- Template and theme support

- Virtual host support

The following screenshot shows an inbox where you can see some of these features:

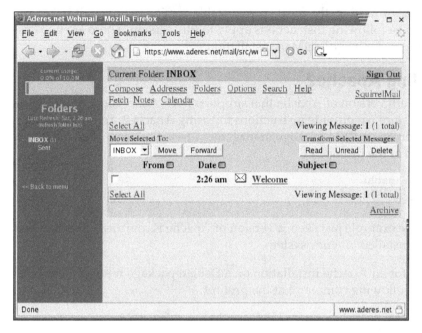

SquirrelMail installation and configuration

SquirrelMail installation and configuration may seem daunting if you are not familiar with installing web applications. But by following the instructions to be discussed next, SquirrelMail can be installed without difficulty.

Prerequisites to installation

SquirrelMail requires both PHP and a web server that supports PHP scripts to be installed before proceeding. In our case, we will be using the Apache2 web server, although others will work as well.

First, we will go over the basic requirements, and what to do if you do not meet them. Then, we will go over some more advanced requirements that may impact on certain features within SquirrelMail.

Basic requirements

At the time of writing, the most current stable version of SquirrelMail available is 1.4.19. The following instructions apply to this version. There are two basic requirements for a SquirrelMail installation.

Installing Apache2

Any modern version of Apache that supports PHP, either the 1.x or 2.x series, will do the trick. Here we provide instructions for using Apache2. To query for an Apache installation on an RPM package management-based system, issue the following command at the prompt:

```
$ rpm -q apache
    apache-1.3.20-16
```

If, as in the example just seen, a version of Apache is returned, then the Apache web server is installed on your system.

To query for an Apache installation on a Debian package management-based system, issue the following command at the prompt:

```
$ apt-cache search --installed apache2 | grep HTTP
    libapache2-mod-evasive - evasive module to minimize HTTP DoS or brute
    force attacks
    libpoe-component-server-http-perl - foundation of a POE HTTP Daemon
    libserf-0-0 - high-performance asynchronous HTTP client library
    libserf-0-0-dbg - high-performance asynchronous HTTP client library
    debugging symbols
    libserf-0-0-dev - high-performance asynchronous HTTP client library
    headers
    nanoweb - HTTP server written in PHP
    php-auth-http - HTTP authentication
    apache2 - Apache HTTP Server metapackage
    apache2-doc - Apache HTTP Server documentation
    apache2-mpm-event - Apache HTTP Server - event driven model
    apache2-mpm-prefork - Apache HTTP Server - traditional non-threaded
    model
    apache2-mpm-worker - Apache HTTP Server - high speed threaded model
    apache2.2-common - Apache HTTP Server common files
```

Similar commands are available for other distributions using other package management systems.

If you do not have an Apache installation present, it is best to first look into your distribution for a copy of Apache—such as on your operating system installation CDs or using an online package repository. Alternatively, you may visit the home page for the Apache foundation at `http://www.apache.org`.

PHP

The PHP programming language (version 4.1.0 or greater, including all PHP 5 versions) is required in order to install SquirrelMail. To check if your system has PHP installed, simply attempt to run it with the following command:

```
$ php -v
```

If the command succeeds, you will see a message describing the version of PHP that is installed. If PHP version 4.1.0 or higher is present, then your system has the required software. Otherwise, you will need to install or upgrade your current installation. As with Apache, it is best to look to your distribution for a copy to install. Alternatively, you may also visit `http://www.php.net`.

Perl

The Perl programming environment is not required for SquirrelMail, but having it available makes configuration of SquirrelMail much simpler. In this chapter, we assume that you will have Perl accessible to enable easy configuration of SquirrelMail.

To query for a Perl installation on an RPM-based system, simply attempt to run it with the following command:

```
$ perl -v
```

If the command succeeds, you will see a message describing the version of Perl that is installed.

If any version of Perl is present, your system has the required software. Otherwise, you will need to install or upgrade your current installation. As with Apache, it is best to look into your distribution for a copy to install. Alternatively, you may also visit `http://www.perl.com/get.html`.

Review configuration

You will need to review the PHP configuration file `php.ini` to ensure that settings are correct. On most Linux systems, this file may be found at `/etc/php.ini`.

`php.ini` is a text file and can be edited with a text editor such as Emacs or vi. Firstly, if you want users to be able to upload attachments, make sure that the option `file_uploads` is set to `On`:

```
; Whether to allow HTTP file uploads.
file_uploads = On
```

The next option within the `php.ini` file you may want to change is `upload_max_filesize`. This setting applies to uploaded attachments and determines the maximum file size of an uploaded file. It may be helpful to change this to something reasonable, such as `10M`.

```
; Maximum allowed size for uploaded files.
upload_max_filesize = 10M
```

Installing SquirrelMail

SquirrelMail may be installed either though a package or directly from source. While no source code compilation takes place in either method, upgrades are made easier using the packages.

Many of the various Linux and Unix distributions include the SquirrelMail package. Install the appropriate package from your distribution to use the binary method. On many Linux distributions, this may be an RPM file that begins with `squirrelmail`....

However, an updated version of SquirrelMail may not be included or available for your specific distribution.

The following are the advantages of using the version of SquirrelMail provided with a Linux distribution:

- It will be very simple to install SquirrelMail.
- It will require much less configuration as it will be configured to use the standard locations chosen by your Linux distributer.
- Updates will be very easy to apply, and migration issues may be dealt with by the package management system.

The following are the disadvantages of using the version of SquirrelMail provided with a Linux distribution:

- It may not be the latest version. For example, a more recent version that may fix a security vulnerability may have been released, but Linux distributors may not have created a new package yet.

- Sometimes Linux distributions alter packages by applying patches. These patches may affect the operation of the package, and may make getting support or help more difficult.

Source installation

If you do not install SquirrelMail through your distribution, you will need to obtain the appropriate tarball. To do so, visit the SquirrelMail website at http://www.squirrelmail.org, and click **download it here**. At the time of writing, this link is http://www.squirrelmail.org/download.php.

There are two versions available for download, a **stable version** and a **development version**. Unless you have specific reasons for choosing otherwise, it is generally best to choose the stable version. Download and save this file to an intermediate location.

```
$ cd /tmp
$ wget http://squirrelmail.org/countdl.php?fileurl=http%3A%2F%2Fprdownloa
ds.sourceforge.net%2Fsquirrelmail%2Fsquirrelmail-1.4.19.tar.gz
```

Next, unpack the tarball (.tar.gz) file. You may use the following command:

```
$ tar xfz squirrelmail-1.4.19.tar.gz
```

Move the folder just created to your web root folder. This is the directory from which Apache serves pages. In this case, we will assume that /var/www/html is your web root. We will also rename the clumsy squirrelmail-1.4.3a folder to a more simple mail folder. You will need to have superuser root privileges in order to do this on most systems.

```
# mv squirrelmail-1.4.19 /var/www/html/mail
# cd /var/www/html/mail
```

Here we have used the name mail, so the URL that users will use will be http://www.sitename.com/mail. You can choose another name, such as webmail, and use that directory name instead of mail in the commands that you enter.

It is also useful and secure to create a data directory for SquirrelMail that is outside the main web root, so that this folder will be inaccessible from the Web.

```
# mv /var/www/html/mail/data /var/www/sqmdata
```

It is important to make this newly created folder writable by the web server. To be able to do this, you must know the user and group that your web server runs under. This may be nobody and nobody, apache and apache, or something else. You will want to verify this; it will be listed in your httpd.conf file as the User and Group entries.

```
# chown -R nobody:nobody /var/www/sqmdata
```

Finally, we will create a directory to store attachments. This directory is special in that, although the web server should have write access to write the attachments, it should not have read access. We create this directory and assign the correct permissions with the following commands:

```
# mkdir /var/www/sqmdata/attachments
# chgrp -R nobody /var/www/sqmdata/attachments
# chmod 730 /var/www/sqmdata/attachments
```

SquirrelMail has now been properly installed. All of the folders have been set up with correct permissions that will secure intermediate files from prying eyes.

If a user aborts a message that contains an uploaded attachment, the attachment file on the web server will not be removed. It is a good practice to create a cron job on the server that erases excess files from the attachment directory. For example, create a file called remove_ orphaned_attachments and place it in the /etc/cron.daily directory. Edit the file to have these lines:

```
#!/bin/sh
```

```
#!/bin/sh
```

```
rm `find /var/www/sqmdata/attachments -atime +2 | grep -v
"\."| grep -v _`
```

This will run daily and search the SquirrelMail attachments directory for files which are orphaned, and delete them.

Configuring SquirrelMail

SquirrelMail is configured through the config.php file. To aid the configuration, a conf.pl Perl script has also been provided. These files are located within the config/ directory in the base installation directory.

```
# cd /var/www/html/mail/config
# ./conf.pl
```

Once you have run this command, you should see the following menu:

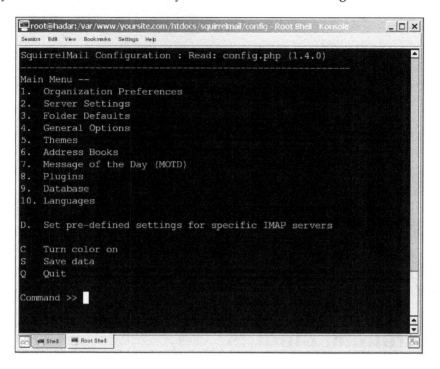

To select an item from the menu, enter the appropriate letter or number, followed by the *Enter* key. As SquirrelMail has been developed, it has been noticed that IMAP servers don't always behave in the same way. To get the most out of your setup, you should tell SquirrelMail which IMAP server you are using. To load a default configuration for your IMAP server, enter the **D** option and type the name of the IMAP server that you have installed. This book covers the Courier IMAP server, so you should choose that. Press *Enter* again, and you will return to the main menu.

We will be moving through the various subsections of the menu and configuring the appropriate options.

Type *1* and then press *Enter* to select the **Organization Preferences**. You will get a list of items you can change. You may wish to edit the **Organization Name**, **Organization Logo**, and **Organization Title** fields. Once you have modified these to your satisfaction, enter *R* to return to the main menu.

After this, type *2* to visit the **Server Settings**. This allows you to set the IMAP server settings. It is important that you update the **Domain** field to the proper value.

In our case, the **Update IMAP Settings** and **Update SMTP Settings** values should be correct. If you would like to use an IMAP or SMTP server that is located on a different machine, you may wish to update these values.

Press *R* followed by the *Enter* key to return to the main menu.

Next, type *4* to visit the **General Options**. You will need to modify two options in this section.

- Data Directory to be `/var/www/sqmdata`.
- Attachment Directory to be `/var/www/sqmdata/attachments`.
- Type in *R* followed by the *Enter* key to return to the main menu. Enter *S* followed by the *Enter* key twice to save the settings to the configuration file. Finally, enter *Q* followed by the *Enter* key to exit the configuration application.

We have finished configuring the SquirrelMail settings needed for basic operation. You may return to this script at any time to update any settings you have set. There are many other options to set, including those regarding themes and plugins.

SquirrelMail plugins

Plugins are pieces of software that extend or add functionality to a software package. SquirrelMail was designed from the ground up to be very extensible, and includes a powerful plugin system. Currently, there are over 200 different plugins available on the SquirrelMail website. They may be obtained at `http://www.squirrelmail.org/plugins.php`.

The functionality they provide includes administration tools, visual additions, user interface tweaks, security enhancements, and even weather forecasts. In the following section, we will first go over how to install and configure a plugin. After that, we'll go over some useful plugins, what they do, how to install them, and more.

Installing plugins

These SquirrelMail additions were designed to be simple to set up and configure. In fact, the majority of them follow exactly the same installation procedure. However, a few require custom setup instructions. For all plugins, the installation process is as follows:

1. Download and unpack the plugin.
2. Perform custom installation if needed.
3. Enable the plugin in `conf.pl`.

Example plugin installation

In this section, we will go over the installation of the **Compatibility plugin**. This plugin is required in order to install plugins created for older versions of SquirrelMail. No matter how bare-bones your installation, the Compatibility plugin will most likely be part of your setup.

Downloading and unpacking the plugin

All available plugins for SquirrelMail are listed on the SquirrelMail website at `http://www.squirrelmail.org/plugins.php`.

Certain plugins may require a specific version of SquirrelMail. Verify that you have this version installed. Once you have located a plugin, download it to the `plugins/` directory within the SquirrelMail root folder.

You may locate the Compatibility plugin by clicking on the **Miscellaneous** category in the plugins page on the SquirrelMail plugins web page. This page has a list of plugins in the **Miscellaneous** category. Locate Compatibility and click on **Details and downloads**, and then download the latest version.

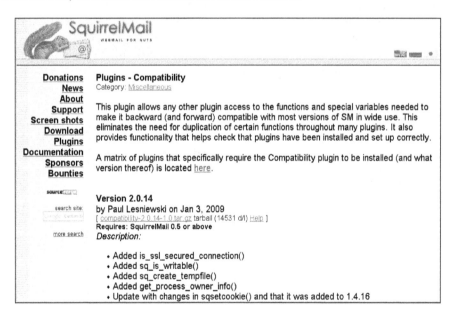

Download tarball to your SquirrelMail plugin directory.

```
# cd /var/www/mail/plugins
# wget http://squirrelmail.org/countdl.php?fileurl=http%3A%2F%2Fwww.
squirrelmail.org%2Fplugins%2Fcompatibility-2.0.14-1.0.tar.gz
```

Once you have downloaded the plugin to the `plugins` directory, unpack it using the following command:

```
# tar zxvf compatibility-2.0.14-1.0.tar.gz
```

 If a plugin of the same name has already been installed, its files may be overwritten. Verify that you either do not have a plugin of the same name, or save the files before you unpack the tarball.

Performing custom installation

The current version of the Compatibility plugin does not require any additional configuration. However, you should always check the documentation for a plugin, as certain other plugins may require custom installation. Once you have unpacked the plugin package, the installation instructions will be listed in the INSTALL file within the newly created `plugin` directory. It is advisable to check the installation instructions before enabling the plugin in the configuration manager, as some plugins may require custom configuration.

Enabling the plugin in conf.pl

Within the main menu of the configuration editor, option number 8 is used to configure and enable plugins. Start `conf.pl` and select option 8.

```
# cd /var/www/mail/plugins
# cd ../config
# ./conf.pl
    SquirrelMail Configuration : Read: config_default.php (1.4.0)
    ---------------------------------------------------------
    Main Menu --
    [...]
    7.   Message of the Day (MOTD)
    8.   Plugins
    9.   Database
    [...]

    Command >>
```

You should get the following display when you select this option for the first time:

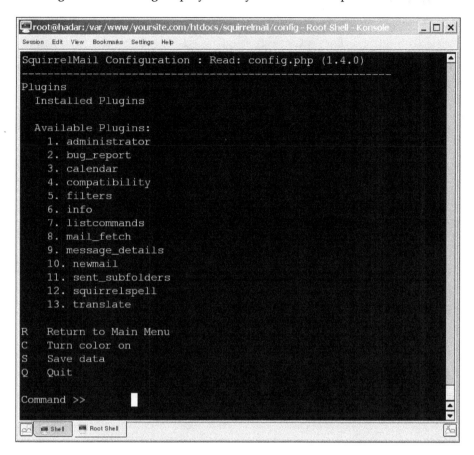

All the plugins that have been installed and enabled are listed under the **Installed Plugins** list. All the plugins that have been installed but not enabled are listed under the **Available Plugins** list.

Once you have unpacked a plugin within the `plugins/` directory, it will show up under **Available Plugins**. As you can see in the previous figure, there are a number of installed plugins, but none of them are enabled. As a malfunctioning or wrongly configured plugin can cause SquirrelMail to stop functioning properly, it is advisable to enable plugins one by one, and verify that SquirrelMail works after each one. To enable the Compatibility plugin, locate it in the list **Available Plugins** (in this case, number **4**) and press the *Enter* key. The Compatibility plugin is now installed. Plugins can be disabled by locating them in the **Installed Plugins** list and entering their number and pressing *Enter*.

Useful plugins

We'll now see some useful SquirrelMail plugins that you may consider installing.

The information has been compiled to provide a helpful reference while deciding whether to install a plugin. Each plugin contains four specific categories:

- **Category**: The category in which the plugin is listed on the SquirrelMail site
- **Authors**: Authors who wrote the plugin, in chronological order
- **Description**: A short description of the plugin's functionality
- **Requirement**: A list of prerequisites for the plugin's successful installation

Plugin name	Category	Author(s)	Description	Requirement
Compatibility plugin	Miscellaneous	Paul Lesneiwski	This plugin allows any other plugin access to the functions and special variables needed to make it backward (and forward) compatible with most versions of SM in wide use. This eliminates the need for duplication of certain functions throughout many plugins. It also provides functionality that helps in checking whether the plugins have been installed and set up correctly.	Nothing
Secure login	Logging in	Graham Norbury, Paul Lesneiwski	This plugin automatically enables a secure HTTPS/SSL-encrypted connection for the SquirrelMail login page if it hasn't already been requested by the referring hyperlink or bookmark. Optionally, the secure connection can be turned off again after successful login.	SquirrelMail version 1.2.8 or above, HTTPS/SSL-capable web server with encryption already working on your SquirrelMail installation.

Plugin name	Category	Author(s)	Description	Requirement
HTTP authentication	Logging in	Tyler Akins, Paul Lesniewski	If you keep SquirrelMail behind a password-protected directory on your web server and if PHP has access to the username and password used by the web server, this plugin will bypass the login screen and use that username/ password pair.	SquirrelMail >= 1.4.0
Password forget	Logging in	Tyler Akins, Paul Lesneiwski	This plugin provides a workaround for the potential vulnerability of browsers, automatically storing usernames and passwords entered into web pages.	SquirrelMail >= 1.0.1
HTML mail	Compose	Paul Lesneiwski	This plugin allows users with IE 5.5 (and up) and newer Mozilla (Gecko-based browsers such as Firefox) browsers to compose and send their e-mail in HTML format.	SquirrelMail >= 1.4.0
Quick save	Compose	Ray Black III, Paul Lesneiwski	This plugin automatically saves messages as they are being composed, in order to prevent accidental loss of message content due to having browsed away from the compose screen or more serious problems such as browser or computer crashes.	SquirrelMail >= 1.2.9, the Compatibility plugin, JavaScript-capable browser

Plugin name	Category	Author(s)	Description	Requirement
Check quota usage (v)	Visual additions	Kerem Erkan	This plugin will check and display users' mail quota status.	SquirrelMail 1.4.0+; Compatibility plugin, version 2.0.7+, UNIX, IMAP or cPanel quotas installed and configured
Sent confirmation	Miscellaneous	Paul Lesneiwski	Displays a confirmation message after a message is successfully sent, as well as other features.	SquirrelMail >= 1.2.0, the Compatibility plugin
Timeout user	Miscellaneous	Ray Black III, Paul Lesneiwski	Automatically logs out a user if they are idle for a specified amount of time.	The Compatibility plugin
E-mail footer	Miscellaneous	Ray Black III, Paul Lesneiwski	This plugin automatically appends a custom footer onto the end of messages sent using SquirrelMail.	SquirrelMail >= 1.4.2
Change password	Change password	Tyler Akins, Seth E. Randall	Allows a user to change their password using PAM or Courier authentication modules.	SquirrelMail >= 1.4.0
Address book import-export	Address book	Lewis Bergman, Dustin Anders, Christian Sauer, Tomas Kuliavas	Allows the importing of address books from a **CSV** (**comma separated values**) file.	SquirrelMail >= 1.4.4
Plugin updates (v0.7)	Administrator's Relief	Jimmy Conner	Checks for updates to your currently running plugins.	SquirrelMail >= 1.4.2

Many other plugins exist that handle vacation messages, calendars, shared calendars, notes, to-do lists, exchange server integration, bookmarks, weather information, and much more. Check the **Plugins** section in the SquirrelMail website for all of the available plugins.

Securing SquirrelMail

The SquirrelMail package, in and of itself, is fairly secure. It is well written and does not require JavaScript to function. However, there are a few precautions that may be taken to allow SquirrelMail to run as a secured mail handling solution.

- **Have an SSL connection**: By using an SSL connection, you may be certain that all communications will be encrypted, and so usernames, passwords, and confidential data cannot be intercepted during transmission. This may be accomplished through the installation of the **Secure Login plugin**. Obviously a web server configured for secure SSL access will also be required; certificates will most likely need to be generated or acquired.

- **Time out inactive users**: Users may leave themselves logged in and neglect to log out once they are finished. To fight this, inactive users should be logged out after a certain amount of time. The **Timeout User plug-in** accomplishes this.

- **Fight "Remembered Passwords"**: Many modern-day browsers offer to remember a user's password. Although a convenience, this may be a large security vulnerability, especially if the user is located at a public terminal. To fight this, install the **Password Forget plugin**. This plugin will change the names in the username and password input fields, to make it more difficult for a browser to suggest them to future users.

- **Do not install security-compromising plugins**: Plugins such as **Quick Save**, **HTML Mail**, and **View As HTML** may compromise security.

Summary

Now that you've finished this chapter, you should have a working SquirrelMail installation as well as a greater understanding of the benefits and disadvantages of a webmail solution. You should be familiar with the benefits and drawbacks of a webmail solution. The benefits include remote access, a single central point to be maintained, and simpler testing; while disadvantages include potential performance problems and the security risk of allowing remote access from potentially compromised computers.

You are now aware of the main features of SquirrelMail, including its flexibility and the availability of plugins, along with what the prerequisites for installing SquirrelMail are, and how to identify if they are already installed.

You also have learned how to configure SquirrelMail, including locating, installing, and configuring plugins. You have been walked through the installation of a key plugin; the Compatibility plugin. Several other useful plugins have also been introduced. Finally, you have learned about some ways to improve the security of SquirrelMail, including web server configuration and some appropriate plugins.

5
Securing Your Installation

Of all the things that can happen to your SMTP server, probably the worst is having it abused as an open relay—a server that relays mail to third parties without your permission. This will consume a lot of bandwidth (which can be costly), eat up server resources (possibly slowing down or stopping other services), and can be expensive in both time and money. A more serious consequence is that your e-mail server will probably end up on one or more blacklists, and any e-mail server that refers to those lists will refuse to accept any mail from your server until you have proven it to be relay safe. If you need to use e-mail in order to carry out business, you will have a big problem.

This chapter will explain how to:

- Protect Postfix from relay abuse

- Differentiate between statically and dynamically assigned IP addresses

- Configure relay permissions using Postfix for static IP addresses

- Use Cyrus SASL for authentication from unpredictable and dynamic IP addresses

- Use the Secure Sockets Layer to prevent usernames and passwords from being sent in plaintext

- Configure Postfix to defeat or at least slow down dictionary attacks, where e-mails are sent to many e-mail addresses within a domain, in the hope that a few will reach a valid recipient

Configuring Postfix network maps

When the Internet was mainly used by academics, no one had to protect their mail servers from relay abuse. In fact, not many people had a mail server, and so permitting others who did not have an e-mail server to relay e-mail using your server was considered a service to them.

This changed with the advent of people who soon became known as spammers. They would abuse open relays to send advertisements to large numbers of remote recipients leaving the owner of the mail server to pay for the traffic.

This is when postmasters started to handle relay permissions restrictively. They used to permit relaying only for trusted IP addresses, refusing messages from other IP addresses. A trusted IP address in this context was an IP address that could be associated statically (refer the *Static IP Ranges* section) with a host that belonged to a known user, or a range of IP addresses known to belong to a trusted network. It worked well as most computers would have static IP addresses (the IP address wouldn't change over time).

However a new approach had to be found when users became mobile and would use dial-up providers to access the Internet and wanted to use a mail server in an unknown location. Access providers would give these users dynamic IP addresses, that is, their IP address would change every time they dialed in.

Suddenly the criteria used to distinguish good users from bad users were gone. Postmasters would either have to loosen their relay permissions to permit a whole network of potentially untrusted IPs to use the relay, or would have to find another way to handle relaying for dynamic IP addresses. Over time, several approaches to handle relaying for dynamic IP addresses emerged, such as:

- SMTP-after-POP
- Virtual Private Networks
- SMTP Authentication

All of the three approaches differ in their requirements and how they work. The following sections provide more detail on each approach.

SMTP-after-POP

Historically, many internet connections were dial up; if one wished to send an e-mail, he/she would have to compose it offline, start the dial-up connection, and then tell the e-mail client to "send and receive" mails. In this case, the mail client first sends mail (via SMTP) and then checks the server (via POP) to see if there is any new mail—the SMTP part happens before the POP part.

This makes it impossible for the SMTP server to find out if the sender should be permitted to relay, because the dynamic IP is in no relation with any other criteria that would make the sender's one a trusted host. ISP's would be able to recognize the IP address of the dial-up connection as one of their own, and permit relaying. Any connection from outside their own network would typically be rejected. For a small organization with users outside the corporate network, it is impossible to keep track of all potential valid source IP addresses.

However, the transactions can be turned on their head, and the checking for mail can be performed before sending mail. Checking for mail requires a password, which means that the user can be authenticated. Popular e-mail clients can now check for e-mail as soon as they are started, and check for new e-mails periodically. If the SMTP server can be told that the user at a particular IP address is authenticated by the POP server, it can allow relaying. This is the essence of SMTP-after-POP. The SMTP server needs to know if a particular IP address has an authentic POP user connected to it.

There has to be a time limit on how long the user connection is valid after the last connection to the POP server, otherwise a traveling salesman might leave a hundred different IP addresses as valid relay hosts a week, one of which might later be occupied by a spammer. These days e-mails are often composed while the user is online and sent between periodic, automatic checks for new mail. Therefore, any composed e-mails sent to the SMTP server will normally be sent within a few minutes of a POP3 request, so the time period can be short, typically tens of minutes.

The disadvantages of SMTP-after-POP are that you need a POP server even if you only want to allow relaying of messages. A POP server will complicate the setup on a server if you don't need it. It might also bind updates of your SMTP server to your POP server to keep compatibility. And POP is not a secure method of authentication, as it can be spoofed.

Virtual Private Networks

Virtual Private Networks (**VPNs**) assign the client another private IP address if authentication to the VPN succeeds. The VPN server will allocate IP addresses in a known block. The SMTP server can be configured to permit relaying for a mail client coming from a VPN-allocated IP address.

Again, running a VPN just for the sake of relaying mails involves a lot of effort. It only pays off if additional resources and services are provided via the VPN, for example access to shared storage, databases, intranet sites, or applications.

SMTP Authentication

SMTP Authentication, also known as **SMTP AUTH**, uses a different method to identify valid relay users. It requires mail clients to send a username and password to the SMTP server during the SMTP dialogue, and if the authentication succeeds, they may relay.

It is less complex than running a full-blown POP server or a VPN, and it solves the problem where it arises—in the SMTP server. You will learn what it takes to offer SMTP AUTH, after you've learned how to configure your server to handle a range of trusted static IP addresses.

Static IP ranges

By default, Postfix will allow only hosts from its own network(s) to relay messages. Trustworthy networks are those you configured for your network interfaces. Run `ifconfig -a` to get a list of what has been configured on your system.

If you want to change the default, you can either use some generic values using the `mynetworks_style` parameter or provide explicit ranges of IP addresses noted as values for the `mynetworks` parameter in `main.cf`.

Generic relay rules

To configure generic relay rules, you need to add one of the following values to the `mynetworks_style` parameter in `main.cf`:

- `host`: If you configure `mynetworks_style = host`, Postfix will permit only the IP addresses of the host it runs on to send messages to remote destinations. If you provide only a webmail interface, this may be acceptable, but no desktop clients would be able to connect.

- `class`: If you configure `mynetworks_style = class`, Postfix will allow every host in the network class (Network class A/B/C) it serves to relay. A network class specifies a range of IP addresses, either approximately 255 (class C), 65,000 (class B), or 16,000,000 (class A) addresses.

Explicit relay rules

Explicit relay rules allow for finer-grained relay permissions. To use this, you need to understand the notation used to specify network address ranges. If your network spans the range from 192.168.1.0 to 192.168.1.255, then this can be specified as 192.168.1.0/24. The 24 is used as the first 24 bits of the 32-bit network address are the same for each client. If you use a DHCP server (for example, in your Linux server or a firewall serving a DSL connection), your network address range will probably be defined by that device, and you should use appropriate values in your Postfix settings. If you allocate IP addresses manually and hard-code them, you can either specify each IP address individually as a /32 range, or you can ensure that each IP address falls in an easily identifiable range once you allocate them. The class A network 10.0.0.0/8, the 16 class B networks in the range 172.16.0.0 to 172.31.255.255 and the 256 class C networks in the range 192.168.0.0 to 192.168.255.255. These are all available for private network addresses and can be used for internal network addresses.

You can add a list of remote and local hosts and/or networks to the `mynetworks` parameter in `main.cf`. If you want to permit localhost, all hosts in your LAN (in the following example the IP addresses `10.0.0.0` to `10.0.0.254`), and your static IP from home (here `192.0.34.166`) should be noted as a list in CIDR notation as shown in this example:

```
mynetworks = 127.0.0.0/8, 10.0.0.0/24, 192.0.34.166/32
```

Once you reload Postfix, the new settings will take effect.

Dynamic IP ranges

In the previous section, you saw how to permit relaying for static IP addresses. This section will show how you can configure Postfix to permit relaying for dynamic IP addresses.

Although, as mentioned in this chapter's introduction, there are several ways to achieve this, we are only going to describe the method of SMTP authentication. It provides a simple and stable mechanism, but the setup is not trivial. The reason for this is that SMTP AUTH isn't processed by Postfix on its own. Another software module, Cyrus SASL, is required to offer and process SMTP AUTH to mail clients. You will need to configure Cyrus SASL, Postfix, and how they interoperate.

Cyrus SASL

Cyrus SASL (`http://cyrusimap.web.cmu.edu/`) is Carnegie Mellon University's implementation of SASL. **SASL (Simple Authentication and Security Layer)**, is an authentication framework described in RFC 2222 (`http://www.ietf.org/rfc/rfc2222.txt`).

SASL was written to provide an application-independent authentication framework for any application that needs to use or offer authentication services.

Cyrus SASL isn't the only SASL available today, but was the first to emerge and is used in various applications such as Postfix, Sendmail, Mutt, and OpenLDAP. In order to use Cyrus SASL, you need to understand its architecture, how the various layers are made to work together, and how the layers' functionalities are configured.

SASL layers

SASL consists of three layers—**authentication interface**, **mechanism**, and **method**. Each of these takes care of a distinct job when an authentication request is being processed.

An authentication process usually goes through the following steps:

1. A client connects to an SASL server.
2. The server announces its capabilities.
3. The client recognizes the option to authenticate among the listed capabilities. It also recognizes a list of mechanisms it can choose to process authentication.
4. The client chooses one of the mechanisms and computes a coded message. The exact content of the message depends on the mechanism used.
5. The client sends the command AUTH <mechanism> <coded message> to the server.
6. The server receives the authentication request and hands it over to SASL.
7. SASL recognizes the mechanism and decodes the coded message. The decoding depends on the mechanism chosen.
8. SASL contacts an authentication backend in order to verify the information given by the client. What it exactly looks for, depends on the mechanism used.
9. If it can verify the information it will tell the server and the server should permit the client to relay a message. If it can't verify the information, it will tell the server and the server may reject the client's wish to relay a message. In both cases, the server will tell the client whether authentication was successful or it failed.

Let's take a closer look at the three SASL layers in the following sections.

Authentication interface

In steps 1 to 5 and step 9 that we just discussed, you can see client and server exchange data to process authentication. This part of communication takes place in the authentication interface.

Though SASL defines what data must be exchanged, it does not specify how it must be communicated between the client and the server. It leaves this to their specific communication protocol, which is why SASL can be used by various services such as SMTP, IMAP, or LDAP.

 SASL is not as old as the SMTP protocol (see: RFC 821). It was added later in RFC 2554 (`http://www.ietf.org/rfc/rfc2554.txt`), which describes the **SMTP Service Extension for Authentication**.

An SMTP conversation where the server offers SMTP authentication among its other capabilities looks like this:

```
$ telnet mail.example.com 25
    220 mail.example.com ESMTP Postfix
EHLO client.example.com
    250-mail.example.com
    250-PIPELINING
    250-SIZE 10240000
    250-VRFY
    250-ETRN
    250-ENHANCEDSTATUSCODES
    250-AUTH PLAIN LOGIN CRAM-MD5 DIGEST-MD5 1)
    250-AUTH=PLAIN LOGIN CRAM-MD5 DIGEST-MD5 2)
    250 8BITMIME
QUIT
```

- `250-AUTH PLAIN LOGIN CRAM-MD5 DIGEST-MD5 1)`: This line tells the client that the server offers `SMTP AUTH`. It consists of two logical parts. The first part, `250-AUTH`, announces `SMTP AUTH` capability and the rest of the line is a list of available mechanisms from which the client may choose the one it prefers.

- `250-AUTH=PLAIN LOGIN CRAM-MD5 DIGEST-MD5 2)`: This line repeats the line above, but differs in the way it announces SMTP authentication. Instead of whitespace after `250-AUTH`, it adds an equal sign like this `250-AUTH=`. This is for broken clients that do not follow the final specification of SASL.

Mechanism

Mechanisms (as described in steps 4 through 7) represent the second layer of SASL. They determine the verification strategy used during authentication. There are several mechanisms known to SASL. They differ in how they transmit data and their level of security during transmission. The most commonly used mechanisms can be grouped into **plaintext** and **shared secret** mechanisms.

One mechanism you should never have Postfix offer to clients is the **anonymous** mechanism. We will have a look at this first.

- anonymous: The anonymous mechanism requires a client to send any string it wants to. It was designed to allow anonymous access to, say, global IMAP folders, but not for SMTP. An SMTP server offering ANONYMOUS in the AUTH line will eventually be abused. You should never offer this in an SMTP server! Postfix does not offer anonymous access in out of the box configuration.

- plaintext: Cyrus SASL knows the **PLAIN** and **LOGIN** plaintext mechanisms. LOGIN is pretty much the same as PLAIN, but is used for mail clients that don't follow the final SASL RFC by the books, such as Outlook and Outlook Express. Both mechanisms require the client to calculate a Base64 encoded string of the username and password and transmit it to the sever for authentication. The great thing about plaintext mechanisms is that they are supported by nearly every mail client in use today. The bad news is that plaintext mechanisms are not secure if used without **Transport Layer Security** (**TLS**). This is because a Base64 encoded string is merely encoded, but not encrypted — it can easily be decoded. It is safe though to use plaintext mechanisms to transmit one during a Transport Layer encrypted session. However, if you use TLS, it will protect the Base64 encoded string from eavesdroppers.

- shared secret: The shared secret mechanisms available in Cyrus SASL are **CRAM-MD5** and **DIGEST-MD5**. Shared secret based authentication has a totally different strategy to verify a client. It is based upon the assumption that client and server both share a secret. A client choosing a shared secret mechanism will only tell the server the name of the specific shared secret mechanism. The server will then generate a challenge, based on their secret and send it to the client. The client then generates a response, proving that it knows the secret. During the whole authentication process neither a username nor a password is sent over the wire. That's why shared secret mechanisms are a lot more secure than the ones mentioned before. However, the most popular mail clients Outlook and Outlook Express do not support shared secret mechanisms.

 On a heterogeneous network, you will probably end up offering plaintext and shared secret mechanisms side by side.

Now that the mechanisms have been covered, there's only one layer left — the method layer. This is where lookups to data stores that hold credentials are configured and processed. The next section will tell you more about methods.

Method

The last layer SASL refers to is the method layer. Methods are represented by libraries in the Cyrus SASL install directory. They serve to access data stores, which Cyrus SASL not only refers to as methods but also as authentication backends. Out of the number of methods SASL has, the most commonly used are:

- `rimap`: The `rimap` method stands for **remote IMAP** and enables SASL to log in to an IMAP server. It uses the username and password given by the client. A successful IMAP login is a successful SASL authentication.

- `ldap`: The `ldap` method queries an LDAP server to verify a username and password. If the query succeeds the authentication succeeds.

- `kerberos`: The `kerberos` method uses the popular Kerberos method, and checks a Kerberos ticket.

- `Getpwent/shadow`: The `getpwent` and `shadow` methods access your system's local user password databases to verify an authentication request.

- `pam`: The `pam` method accesses any PAM module you configure in your PAM settings to verify an authentication request.

- `sasldb`: The `sasldb` method reads and even writes to Cyrus SASL's own database called sasldb2. Usually this database is used in conjunction with Cyrus IMAP, but you can use it without the IMAP server.

- `sql`: This method uses SQL queries to access various SQL servers. Currently these are MySQL, PostgreSQL, and SQLite.

Now that you know about the three layers of the SASL architecture, it's time to take a look at the SASL service that handles all the requests between them. It is called the **password verification service** and will be described in the following section.

Password verification service

A password verification service handles an incoming authentication request from a server, does mechanism-specific calculations, calls a method to query an authentication backend, and finally returns the result to the server that sent the authentication request.

> In the case of Postfix, the server that hands over the authentication request is the `smtpd` daemon. In the *Postfix SMTP AUTH configuration* section you will learn how you can configure the `smtpd` daemon to choose the right password verification service.

Cyrus SASL version 2.1.23, the latest version at the moment, provides us with three different password verification services:

- `saslauthd`
- `auxprop`
- `authdaemond`

Mechanisms that your mail clients may use successfully and the methods that Cyrus SASL can access during authentication depend on the password verification service you tell Postfix to use.

- `saslauthd`: `saslauthd` is a standalone daemon. It can be run as root, which gives it the privileges needed to access sources accessible to root only. However, `saslauthd` is limited in the range of mechanisms it supports; it can handle only plaintext mechanisms.

- `auxprop`: `auxprop` is the short name for **auxiliary property plugins**, a term used in the Project Cyrus mail server architecture. `auxprop` represents a library that is used by the server offering authentication. It accesses sources with the privileges of the server that uses it. Unlike `saslauthd`, `auxprop` can handle every mechanism available within the Cyrus SASL authentication framework.

- `authdaemond`: `authdaemond` is a password verification service written especially to use Courier's `authdaemond` as password verifier. This way you can access any authentication backend that Courier can deal with. This `auxprop` plugin can deal only with plaintext mechanisms.

The following table gives you an overview of the mechanisms the password verification services (methods) can handle:

Method/mechanisms	PLAIN	LOGIN	CRAM-MD5	DIGEST-MD5
saslauthd	yes	yes	no	no
auxprop	yes	yes	yes	yes
authdaemond	yes	yes	no	no

Only the `auxprop` password verification service is able to handle the more secure mechanisms; `saslauthd` and `authdaemond` can process only plaintext mechanisms.

Now we have covered some of the Cyrus SASL theory, it is about time to install it. This is exactly what we do in the next sections.

Installing Cyrus SASL

The chances are that you already have Cyrus SASL on your system. However, various Linux distributions have begun to install Cyrus SASL in a different location from the typical default one of `/usr/lib/sasl2`. To check if Cyrus SASL is installed on your server, either run your package manager and query for `cyrus-sasl` or run `find`. A query to the Red Hat package manager (on Fedora Core 11) would return something like this if SASL is installed:

```
$ rpm -qa | grep sasl
   cyrus-sasl-2.1.18-2.2
   cyrus-sasl-devel-2.1.18-2.2
   cyrus-sasl-plain-2.1.18-2.2
   cyrus-sasl-md5-2.1.18-2.2
```

A query to `dpkg` (on Ubuntu) would return something like this if SASL is installed:

```
$ dpkg -l | grep sasl
   ii  libsasl2-2                      2.1.22.dfsg1-23ubuntu3
         Cyrus SASL - authentication abstraction libr
   ii  libsasl2-modules                2.1.22.dfsg1-23ubuntu3
         Cyrus SASL - pluggable authentication module2
```

A `find` looking for `libsasl*.*` looks like this:

```
$ find /usr -name 'libsasl*.*'
   /usr/lib/libsasl.so.7.1.11
   /usr/lib/libsasl2.so
   /usr/lib/libsasl.la
   /usr/lib/libsasl2.so.2.0.18
   /usr/lib/libsasl.a
   /usr/lib/libsasl2.a
   /usr/lib/libsasl2.la
   /usr/lib/sasl2/libsasldb.so.2.0.18
   /usr/lib/sasl2/libsasldb.so.2
   /usr/lib/sasl2/libsasldb.so
   /usr/lib/sasl2/libsasldb.la
   /usr/lib/libsasl.so.7
   /usr/lib/libsasl.so
   /usr/lib/libsasl2.so.2
```

This proves that you have SASL installed on your system. To verify the location of the SASL libraries simply do an `ls` like this:

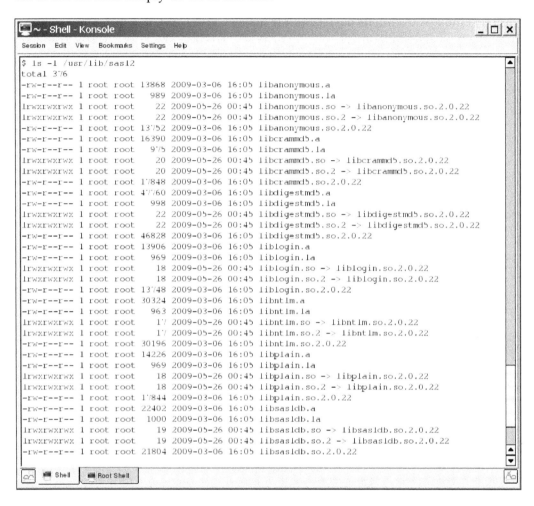

As mentioned earlier, your distribution might put them somewhere else. In this case, the `find` method will locate the correct location, or your distribution's documentation should give you this information.

If you don't have Cyrus SASL installed, you will have to either use your package manager to get it, or install it manually.

The latest version of Cyrus is normally available to download from
`http://cyrusimap.web.cmu.edu/downloads.html`. To download version 2.1.23
(always choose the latest stable release, not a developer release), issue these commands:

```
$ cd /tmp
$ wget ftp://ftp.andrew.cmu.edu/pub/cyrus-mail/cyrus-sasl-2.1.23.tar.gz
$ tar xfz cyrus-sasl-2.1.23.tar.gz
$ cd cyrus-sasl-2.1.23
```

After you have downloaded and unpacked the source files, change into the source
directory and run `configure`. A typical configuration of the sources goes like this:

```
$ ./configure \
    --with-plugindir=/usr/lib/sasl2 \
    --disable-java \
    --disable-krb4 \
    --with-dblib=berkeley \
    --with-saslauthd=/var/state/saslauthd \
    --without-pwcheck \
    --with-devrandom=/dev/urandom \
    --enable-cram \
    --enable-digest \
    --enable-plain \
    --enable-login \
    --disable-otp \
    --enable-sql \
    --with-ldap=/usr \
    --with-mysql=/usr \
    --with-pgsql=/usr/lib/pgsql
```

This will configure Cyrus SASL to give you plaintext and shared secret mechanisms,
and will build `saslauthd` and give you the SQL method including support for
MySQL and PostgreSQL.

After the `configure` script has finished, run `make`, become `root`, and then run
`make install`.

```
$ make
$ su -c "make install"
    Password:
```

Cyrus SASL will install itself to `/usr/local/lib/sasl2`, but it will expect to find the libraries in `/usr/lib/sasl2`. You need to create a symbolic link like this:

```
$ su -c "ln -s /usr/local/lib/sasl2 /usr/lib/sasl2"
Password:
```

Finally you need to check if SASL log messages will be caught and written to a log file by `syslogd`. Cyrus SASL logs to the `syslog auth` facility. Check your `syslogd` configuration, usually `/etc/syslog.conf`, to see if it contains a line that catches auth messages.

```
$ grep auth /etc/syslog.conf
    auth,authpriv.*                    /var/log/auth.log
    *.*;auth,authpriv.none            -/var/log/syslog
            auth,authpriv.none;\
            auth,authpriv.none;\
```

If you don't find an entry, add the following, save the file, and restart `syslogd`:

```
    auth.*                             /var/log/auth.log
```

Once you've got all this done, you are ready to configure SASL.

Configuring Cyrus SASL

It is vital that you always configure and test Cyrus SASL before you return to Postfix and work on Postfix-specific SMTP AUTH settings.

The reason to follow this procedure is quite simple. An authentication framework that cannot authenticate will be of no assistance to any other application using it. It's quite possible that you will end up debugging Postfix for hours when the problem is Cyrus SASL-related.

To understand how and where you must configure SASL, recall that it is an authentication framework and was designed to offer its service to many applications. These applications might have totally different requirements for not only the password verification service to be used but also the mechanisms to be offered, along with the method used to access an authentication backend.

Cyrus is configured using application-specific files. The configuration for each client application is in a separate file. When an application connects to the SASL server, it sends its application name. Cyrus uses this name to look for the correct configuration file to use.

In our scenario, the application requiring SMTP AUTH is the smtpd daemon within Postfix. When it contacts SASL, it not only sends authentication data but also its application name, smtpd.

 The application name smtpd is a default value that is sent to Cyrus SASL from Postfix. You can change it using the smtpd_sasl_application_name, but usually this is not required. You need it only if you run different Postfix daemons that need different Cyrus SASL configurations.

When Cyrus SASL receives the application name, it will append a .conf and start to look for a configuration file containing configuration settings.

By default, the location for smtpd.conf is /usr/lib/sasl2/smtpd.conf but for various reasons some Linux distributions have started to put it in other locations. On Debian Linux you will have to create the configuration at /etc/postfix/sasl/smtpd.conf. Mandrake Linux expects the file to be located at /var/lib/sasl2/smtpd.conf. All others are known to expect it at /usr/lib/sasl2/smtpd.conf.

Check your system and find out if smtpd.conf has already been created. If not, a simple touch command (as root) will create it:

```
# touch /usr/lib/sasl2/smtpd.conf
```

All of the configuration that follows now will center on smtpd.conf. Here's a quick rundown of what we will put in there:

- The name of the password verification service we want to use
- The log level at which SASL should send log messages to the log output
- A list of mechanisms Postfix should advertise when offering SMTP AUTH to clients
- Configuration settings specific to the password verification service chosen

Finally we will configure how the password verification service should access the authentication backend. How this needs to be done depends on the password verification service we choose and will be explained when we get there.

Selecting a password verification service

The first configuration step is to choose the password verification service that SASL should use during authentication. The parameter that tells SASL which password verification service should handle authentication is `pwcheck_method`. The values you may provide are:

- `saslauthd`
- `auxprop`
- `authdaemond`

Depending on the password verification service you've chosen, you will have to add the correct value. The names should speak for themselves and tell you which password verification service will be called. A configuration that would use `saslauthd` would add the following line to `smtpd.conf`:

```
pwcheck_method: saslauthd
```

Choosing a log level

Cyrus SASL does not handle logging consistently. What Cyrus SASL will log depends on the password verification service and the method that is being used. The parameter to define a log level is `log_level`. A reasonable setting during setup would be log level 3.

```
log_level: 3
```

This line should be added to `smtpd.conf`.

Here is a list of all the log levels Cyrus SASL knows:

log_level value	Description
0	No logging
1	Log unusual errors; this is the default
2	Log all authentication failures
3	Log non-fatal warnings
4	More verbose than 3
5	More verbose than 4
6	Log traces of internal protocols
7	Log traces of internal protocols, including passwords

Choosing valid mechanisms

Your next step will be to choose the mechanisms that Postfix may offer when it advertises SMTP authentication to clients. The parameter in Cyrus SASL to configure a list of valid mechanisms is `mech_list`. The names of the mechanisms are exactly like the ones we used when we introduced them in the *Mechanism* section.

It is important to set the `mech_list` parameter and list only the mechanisms your password verification service can handle. If you don't do it, Postfix will offer all mechanisms SASL provides and authentication will fail if your mail client chooses a mechanism that the SASL password verification service cannot handle.

Recall that the password verification services `saslauthd` and `authdaemond` can handle only two plaintext mechanisms— PLAIN and LOGIN. Consequently a `mech_list` for those password verification services must hold only the values PLAIN and LOGIN. Any mail client capable of stronger mechanisms will always prefer the stronger over the weaker ones. It will do its calculation and send the result to the server. The server will fail to authenticate because neither `saslauthd` nor `authdaemond` is capable of handling non-plaintext mechanisms.

The following example would define valid mechanisms for `saslauthd` in `smtpd.conf`:

```
mech_list: PLAIN LOGIN
```

A list of valid mechanisms for any of the `auxprop` password verification services could go further and list the following mechanisms:

```
mech_list: PLAIN LOGIN CRAM-MD5 DIGEST-MD5
```

The order of mechanisms in this list has no influence on the mechanism the client will choose. Which mechanism is selected depends on the client; it will usually choose the one that provides the strongest cryptography.

In the sections that follow, we will take a look at how you configure the password verification service to choose an authentication backend and how to provide additional information to pick the relevant data. As mentioned before, this is handled differently by the three password verification services. We will have a look at each password verification service separately.

saslauthd

Before you can use `saslauthd`, you need to check whether it is able to establish a socket in a directory that `saslauthd` refers to as `state dir`. Check this carefully because there are two common problems related to the socket:

- **The directory does not exist**: In this case, `saslauthd` will quit running and you will find a log message indicating the missing directory.

- **The directory is not accessible to applications other than** `saslauthd`: In this case, you will find log messages in the mail log indicating that `smtpd` was unable to connect to the socket.

To get around these problems, you first need to find out where `saslauthd` would like to establish the socket. Just fire it up as root, like in the example (shown next) and look out for the line that has `run_path` in it:

```
# saslauthd -a shadow -d
    saslauthd[3610] :main              : num_procs  : 5
    saslauthd[3610] :main              : mech_option: NULL
    saslauthd[3610] :main              : run_path   : /var/run/saslauthd
    saslauthd[3610] :main              : auth_mech  : shadow
    saslauthd[3610] :main              : could not chdir to: /var/run/
    saslauthd
    saslauthd[3610] :main              : chdir: No such file or directory
    saslauthd[3610] :main              : Check to make sure the directory
    exists and is
    saslauthd[3610] :main                 : writeable by the user, this
    process runs as—If you get no errors, the daemon will start, but the
    -d flag means that it will not start in the background; it will tie
    up your terminal session. In this case, press Ctrl+C to terminate the
    process.
```

As you can see in the previous example, `saslauthd` would want to access `/var/run/saslauthd` as `run_path`. As it cannot access the directory, it quits immediately. Now there are two ways to deal with this. It depends whether you acquired `saslauthd` from a package or installed it from the source.

In the first case, it is quite likely that the package maintainer built `saslauthd` with the default settings; choose a different location as `state dir` and configure the `init-script` to override the default path by giving the `-m /path/to/state_dir` option.

On Debian systems, you would typically find command-line options in /etc/
default/saslauthd. On Red Hat systems, you would typically find command-line
options passed to saslauthd in /etc/sysconfig/saslauthd. The following listing
gives you an overview of the settings for Fedora Core 2:

```
# Directory in which to place saslauthd's listening socket, pid file,
and so
# on.  This directory must already exist.
SOCKETDIR=/var/run/saslauthd
# Mechanism to use when checking passwords.  Run "saslauthd -v" to get
a list
# of which mechanism your installation was compiled to use.
MECH=shadow

# Additional flags to pass to saslauthd on the command line.  See
saslauthd(8)
# for the list of accepted flags.
FLAGS=
```

Speaking for most Linux distributions, typical locations for the state dir would be
either /var/state/saslauthd or /var/run/saslauthd.

Now consider the case where you built saslauthd manually. You should then create
a directory that matches the value of the --with-saslauthd parameter you used
when you executed the configure script.

In the SASL configuration example, the value for --with-saslauthd was
/var/state/saslauthd. Create this directory and make it accessible to user
root and group postfix like this:

```
# mkdir /var/state/saslauthd
# chmod 750 /var/state/saslauthd
# chgrp postfix /var/state/saslauthd
```

Once you have verified saslauthd can create a socket and pid file in your
state dir, you can start configuring saslauthd to access the authentication
backend of your choice.

The following examples presume that you don't have to provide an
extra run path to saslauthd. If you need to do so, just add it to the
examples given.

Using an IMAP server as authentication backend

Specify the -a option together with the value rimap to have Cyrus SASL log in to an IMAP server with the credentials given by the mail client. Additionally you must use the -O option to tell saslauthd which IMAP server it should turn to, like this:

```
# saslauthd -a rimap -O mail.example.com
```

Upon successful login into an IMAP server, saslauthd will report an authentication success to Postfix and Postfix may permit the mail client to hand over the credentials to the relay.

Using an LDAP server as authentication backend

Verifying credentials with an LDAP server is a little more complex than with an IMAP server. It requires far more configuration and that's why you don't give all the options to saslauthd on the command line but put them into a configuration file instead. By default, saslauthd expects the LDAP configuration to be located at /usr/local/etc/saslauthd.conf. If you choose a different location, you need to state it on the command line.

```
# saslauthd -a ldap -O /etc/cyrussasl/saslauthd.conf
```

In the previous example, the value ldap tells saslauthd to turn to an LDAP server and the -O option provides the path to the configuration file. Your configuration file might hold the following parameters:

```
ldap_servers: ldap://127.0.0.1/ ldap://172.16.10.7/
ldap_bind_dn: cn=saslauthd,dc=example,dc=com
ldap_bind_pw: Oy6k0qyR
ldap_timeout: 10
ldap_time_limit: 10
ldap_scope: sub
ldap_search_base: dc=people,dc=example,dc=com
ldap_auth_method: bind
ldap_filter: (|(&(cn=%u)(&(uid=%u@%r)(smtpAuth=Y))))
ldap_debug: 0
ldap_verbose: off
ldap_ssl: no
ldap_start_tls: no
ldap_referrals: yes
```

As you might have expected, you will have to accommodate the settings to suit your LDAP tree and other settings specific to your LDAP server. For a complete list of all LDAP-related parameters (there are many more than listed here), take a look at the LDAP_SASLAUTHD readme that comes with the Cyrus SASL sources and is located in the saslauthd subdirectory.

Using the local user accounts

This is the configuration that most people use `saslauthd` for. You can either configure `saslauthd` to read from the local password file or the local shadow password file on systems that support shadow passwords.

To have it read from `/etc/passwd`, use the `-a getpwent` option like this:

```
# saslauthd -a getpwent
```

Most modern Linux distributions do not store passwords in `/etc/passwd`, but in `/etc/shadow`. If you want `saslauthd` to read from `/etc/shadow`, run it as root like this:

```
# saslauthd -a shadow
```

Using PAM

It is also possible to use **PAM (Pluggable Authentication Modules)** as the authentication backend, which in turn has to be configured to access other authentication backends. Start by running `saslauthd` like this:

```
# saslauthd -a pam
```

Then create a `/etc/pam.d/smtp` file or a section in `/etc/pam.conf` and add PAM-specific settings to it. If you installed Cyrus SASL from a package, the chances are that you already have such a file. For example, on Red Hat it looks like this:

```
#%PAM-1.0
auth        required       pam_stack.so service=system-auth
account     required       pam_stack.so service=system-auth
```

 The name of the configuration file must be `smtp`. This has been defined in RFC 2554, which says that the service name for SASL over SMTP is `smtp`. The postfix `smtpd` daemon passes the value `smtp` as the service name to Cyrus SASL. `saslauthd` in turn passes it to PAM, which then looks in the `smtp` file for authentication instructions.

auxprop

Auxiliary Property Plugins (or **auxprop**) are configured differently from `saslauthd`. Instead of passing command-line options, you simply add auxprop-specific settings to your `smtpd.conf`. Any auxprop configuration that you set up in your `smtpd.conf` should begin with these three lines:

```
log_level: 3
pwcheck_method: auxprop
mech_list: PLAIN LOGIN CRAM-MD5 DIGEST-MD5
```

To tell Cyrus SASL which plugin you want to use, you need to add an additional parameter to the configuration. The parameter is called `auxprop_plugin` and we will examine its use in the following sections.

Configuring the sasldb plugin

The auxprop plugin `sasldb` is the default plugin that Cyrus SASL will use even if you don't set the `auxprop_plugin` parameter. `sasldb` is SASL's own database that is manipulated with the `saslpasswd2` utility.

> This tends to irritate people who try to set up a different plugin and have something wrong in their configuration. Cyrus SASL will fail if it uses the default configuration instead of the desired one. When you get an error message that says Cyrus SASL can't locate `sasldb`, it is probably an error in your configuration (unless you chose to configure `sasldb` deliberately), and the first step should be to check your configuration files.

To use `sasldb`, first of all you need to create an `sasldb` database. Use the following command as root to create an `sasldb2` file and add a user.

```
# saslpasswd2 -c -u example.com username
```

This command will create an `sasldb2` file and will add a user username with the realm of `example.com`. It is important that you pay special attention to the realm you add, as it will be part of the username the mail client will have to send later.

> The realm is part of the concept of Kerberose infrastructure. Kerberose is a distributed, encrypted authentication protocol. By adding a realm you can define a context (for example, a domain or host) in which the user may do something. If you don't add a realm, `saslpasswd2` will add the hostname of your server by default.

Now that you have created the database and added a user, you need to change access permissions on `sasldb` to have Postfix access the database as well. Simply give access to the group `postfix` to `sasldb2` like this:

```
# chgrp postfix /etc/sasldb2
```

Don't get confused because the `sasldb` is called `sasldb2`. The format of `sasldb` changed when Cyrus SASL major version 2.x came out. For reasons of compatibility, the new `sasldb` file is called `sasldb2`. Once you've created the database, you need to tell Cyrus SASL to use it. Add the `auxprop_plugin` parameter to `smtpd.conf` like this:

```
auxprop_plugin: sasldb
```

That's all you need to do and you should be ready to start testing (see the *Testing Cyrus SASL authentication* section). If, for any reason, you need to put `sasldb` in a location that differs from the default, you can use the following additional parameter:

```
sasldb_path: /path/to/sasldb2
```

Configuring the sql plugin

The **sql auxprop** plugin is a generic plugin that gives you access to MySQL, PostgreSQL, and SQLite. As an example we will show you how to configure the sql plugin to access a MySQL database. Configuring access to the other two databases is pretty much the same, with one exception that we will note.

First of all, you need to create a database. This, of course, is specific to the database you use. Connect to MySQL and create a database if you don't have one already.

```
mysql> CREATE DATABASE `mail`;
```

Then add a table that holds everything you need to SASL-authenticate users. It will look similar to this:

```
CREATE TABLE `users` (
    `id` int(11) unsigned NOT NULL auto_increment,
    `username` varchar(255) NOT NULL default '0',
    `userrealm` varchar(255) NOT NULL default 'example.com',
    `userpassword` varchar(255) NOT NULL default 't1GRateY',
    `auth` tinyint(1) default '1',
    PRIMARY KEY (`id`),
    UNIQUE KEY `id` (`id`)
) TYPE=MyISAM COMMENT='Users';
```

The table has fields for username, userrealm, userpassword, and an additional field `auth` that we will use later to determine if a user may relay or not. This way we can use the table for other authentication purposes as well—for example, for granting access to specific folders over `httpd` in conjunction with the `mysql` module for Apache.

 Don't forget to set a default value for the `userpassword`, as shown in the previous example, or all that would be required to get relay permissions would be sending a valid username.

Once you've created the table, add a user like this for testing purposes:

```
INSERT INTO `users` VALUES (1,'test','example.com','testpass',0);
```

Then add a user for Postfix to access the database to the user database of MySQL like this:

```
mysql> CONNECT mysql;
mysql> INSERT INTO user VALUES ('localhost','postfix','','Y','Y','Y','
Y','Y','Y','Y','Y','Y','Y','Y','Y','Y','Y');
mysql> UPDATE mysql.user SET password=PASSWORD("bu0tt^v") WHERE
user='postfix' AND host='localhost';
mysql> GRANT SELECT, UPDATE ON mail.users TO 'postfix'@'localhost';
mysql> FLUSH PRIVILEGES;
```

Once you're done setting up MySQL, you need to add `sql auxprop`-specific parameters to your `smtpd.conf`. The following parameters are available:

- `sql_engine`: Specifies the database type. You can pick `mysql`, `pgsql`, or `sqlite`. We use `mysql` in this example. If you choose a different database, you will need to change this value as appropriate.

- `sql_hostnames`: Specifies the database server name. You can specify one or more FQDNs or IP addresses separated by commas. Even if you pick `localhost`, the SQL engine tries to communicate over a socket.

- `sql_database`: Tells Cyrus SASL the name of the database to connect to.

- `sql_user`: The value you set here must match the name of the user that connects to the database.

- `sql_passwd`: The value you set here must match the password of the user that connects to the database. It must be a plaintext password.

- `sql_select`: The `sql_select` parameter defines the SELECT statement to authenticate a user.

- `sql_insert`: The `sql_insert` parameter defines an INSERT statement that would allow Cyrus SASL to create users in the SQL database. You would use the `saslpasswd2` program to do so.

- `sql_update`: The `sql_update` parameter defines the UPDATE statement that would allow Cyrus SASL to modify existing entries in your database. If you choose to configure this you will have to use it in combination with the `sql_insert` parameter.

- `sql_usessl`: You can set either `yes`, `1`, `on`, or `true` to enable SSL to access the MySQL over an encrypted connection. By default this option is `off`.

A straightforward configuration bringing all parameters together would look like this:

```
# Global parameters
log_level: 3
pwcheck_method: auxprop
mech_list: PLAIN LOGIN CRAM-MD5 DIGEST-MD5
# auxiliary Plugin parameters
auxprop_plugin: sql
sql_engine: mysql
sql_hostnames: localhost
sql_database: mail
sql_user: postfix
sql_passwd: bu0tt^v
sql_select: SELECT %p FROM users WHERE username = '%u' AND userrealm =
'%r' AND auth = '1'
sql_usessl: no
```

As you can see, macros have been used in the `sql_select` statement. Their meaning is:

- `%u`: This macro is a placeholder for the username that is to be queried for during authentication.
- `%p`: This macro is a placeholder for the password.
- `%r`: The `r` stands for realm and whatever was given as realm by the client will be inserted at `%r`.
- `%v`: This macro is only used in combination with the `sql_update` or `sql_insert` statement. It represents the submitted value that should replace an existing value.

 Take special notice of the notations. Macros must be quoted using single quotation marks (`'`).

That completes the configuration. If you are using `auxprop` and followed the instructions to this point, you are ready to start testing and can skip the next section on `authdaemond`.

authdaemond

authdaemond was created especially to work together with Courier IMAP. If you configure Cyrus SASL to use authdaemond, it will connect to Courier authlib's authdaemond socket asking Courier authlib to verify the credentials of the mail client sent in. On one hand Cyrus SASL benefits from the various backends Courier authlib can turn to for user verification, but on the other hand Cyrus SASL's authdaemond password verification service is limited to plaintext mechanisms, which doesn't give you the mileage you get when you use auxprop plugins.

Setting up the authdaemond password verification service is pretty straightforward. We will take a look at it in the following sections.

Setting the authdaemond password verification service

Your first step is to configure Postfix to use the authdaemond password verification service. Just as with saslauthd or auxprop, you add the pwcheck_method parameter to your smtpd.conf and choose it to be authdaemond.

```
log_level: 3
pwcheck_method: authdaemond
mech_list: PLAIN LOGIN
```

Due to the limitations of authdaemond, you must also limit the list of mechanisms to PLAIN and LOGIN — the only plaintext mechanisms available.

Configuring the authdaemond socket path

You need to tell Cyrus SASL where it can find the socket that has been created by Courier authlib's authdaemond.

Use the authdaemond_path parameter to provide the full path including the socket name.

```
authdaemond-path:        /var/spool/authdaemon/socket
```

Finally check the permissions of the authdaemond directory and verify that at least the user postfix may access the directory. Once this is done you are ready to start testing.

Testing Cyrus SASL authentication

There are no testing utilities, but you can use the sample applications `sample-server` and `sample-client` to test authentication without any other application (example Postfix) interfering with the test. If you built Cyrus SASL from source, you can find them in the `sample` subdirectory of the Cyrus SASL sources. Fedora-based Linux distributions include the samples as part of the `cyrus-sasl-devel` package, so if available, you should install that package. Debian-based Linux distributions do not have a similar package, so you will now have to build them yourself.

To build just the samples, locate, download, and extract the release of Cyrus SASL that matches your installation from your package manager. To locate and install the source, follow the instructions as described in the *Cyrus SASL installation* section. Then instead of issuing the `make install` command, issue these commands:

```
# cd sample
```

```
# make
```

We will use these samples to test the Cyrus SASL configuration we've created in `smtpd.conf`. However, the programs don't expect to find their configuration in `smtpd.conf`, but in `sample.conf`. We will simply create a symbolic link from `sample.conf` to `smtpd.conf` to meet the requirements:

```
# ln -s /usr/lib/sasl2/smtpd.conf /usr/lib/sasl2/sample.conf
```

Next we need to start the server application to have it listen for incoming connections. Start the server like this:

```
$ ./server -s rcmd -p 8000
    trying 2, 1, 6
    trying 10, 1, 6
    bind: Address already in use
```

Do not be concerned about the message `bind: Address already in use`. The fact that the server has continued to run indicates that it has managed to listen on the specified port. The message is because the application is IPv6 enabled and the underlying system does not support IPv6.

If you receive an error such as `./server: No such file or directory`, check that you have installed the `cyrus-sasl-devel` package from your distribution, or that your build from source worked correctly and that you are in the correct directory.

The server will listen on port 8000 for incoming connections. Next open a new terminal and start the client using the same port and the mechanism PLAIN and point to localhost where your server utility should be listening. When prompted, enter test, test, and testpass, which are valid values provided by the test server. A successful authentication looks like this:

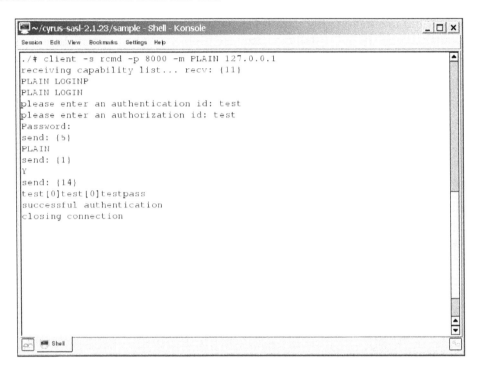

You should be able to see some logging in the auth log. If you are going to use saslauthd, start it on a separate terminal in debug mode and you will be able to follow the authentication like this:

```
# saslauthd -m /var/run/saslauthd -a shadow -d
    saslauthd[4547] :main : num_procs : 5
    saslauthd[4547] :main : mech_option: NULL
    saslauthd[4547] :main : run_path : /var/run/saslauthd
    saslauthd[4547] :main : auth_mech : shadow
    saslauthd[4547] :ipc_init : using accept lock file: /var/run/
    saslauthd/mux.accept
    saslauthd[4547] :detach_tty : master pid is: 0
    saslauthd[4547] :ipc_init : listening on socket: /var/run/saslauthd/
    mux
    saslauthd[4547] :main : using process model
    saslauthd[4548] :get_accept_lock : acquired accept lock
```

```
saslauthd[4547] :have_baby : forked child: 4548
saslauthd[4547] :have_baby : forked child: 4549
saslauthd[4547] :have_baby : forked child: 4550
saslauthd[4547] :have_baby : forked child: 4551
saslauthd[4548] :rel_accept_lock : released accept lock
saslauthd[4548] :do_auth : auth success: [user=test] [service=rcmd]
[realm=] [mech=shadow]
saslauthd[4548] :do_request : response: OK
```

saslauthd[4548] :get_accept_lock : acquired accept lock

If you were able to authenticate successfully, proceed to configure SMTP AUTH in Postfix. If your authentication fails, follow the log and iterate through the instructions on how to set up and configure SASL as discussed earlier.

Configuring Postfix SMTP AUTH

Configuring SMTP AUTH in Postfix is pretty straightforward now that you have managed to set up and configure Cyrus SASL. The first thing you need to do is to check if Postfix was built to support SMTP authentication. Use the ldd utility to check if the Postfix smtpd daemon has been linked to libsasl:

```
# ldd /usr/libexec/postfix/smtpd | grep libsasl
        libsasl2.so.2 => /usr/lib/libsasl2.so.2 (0x00002aaaabb6a000)
```

If you don't get any output, you will probably have to rebuild Postfix. Read the SASL_README from the Postfix README_FILES directory to get detailed information on what you must include in the CCARGS and AUXLIBS statements.

Preparing the configuration

Once you've verified that Postfix supports SMTP AUTH, you need to verify that the smtpd daemon does not run chrooted while you configure SMTP AUTH. Many people spend hours with a chrooted Postfix that cannot access the saslauthd socket before they realize that the reason is the chroot jail. A Postfix smtpd daemon that does not run chrooted has an n in the chroot column in /etc/postfix/master.cf:

```
# ====================================================================
# service type  private unpriv  chroot  wakeup  maxproc command + args
#               (yes)   (yes)   (yes)   (never) (100)
# ====================================================================
smtp      inet  n       -       n       -       -       smtpd
```

Reload Postfix if it was running chrooted after you changed the chroot settings for smtpd and turn to main.cf.

Enabling SMTP AUTH

The first thing you will do is enable SMTP AUTH by adding the smtpd_sasl_auth_
enable parameter and setting it to yes:

```
smtpd_sasl_auth_enable = yes
```

This will make Postfix offer SMTP AUTH to clients that use ESMTP, but you still need to
configure a few settings before you can start testing.

Setting the security policy

You will have to decide which mechanisms Postfix should offer using the smtpd_
sasl_security_options parameter. This parameter takes a list of one or more of
the following values:

- noanonymous: You should always set this value or Postfix will offer
  anonymous authentication to mail clients. Allowing anonymous
  authentication makes you an open relay and should not be used for
  SMTP servers.

- noplaintext: The noplaintext value will prevent Postfix from offering the
  plaintext mechanisms PLAIN and LOGIN. Usually you don't want that because
  the most widespread clients support only LOGIN. If you set this option, we
  won't be able to authenticate some clients.

- noactive: This setting excludes SASL mechanisms that are susceptible to
  active (non-dictionary) attacks.

- nodictionary: This keyword excludes all mechanisms that can be broken by
  means of a dictionary attack.

- mutual_auth: This form of authentication requires the server to authenticate
  itself to the client as well as the other way around. If you set it, only servers
  and clients capable of doing this form or authentication will be able to
  authenticate. This option is hardly ever used.

A common setting for the smtpd_sasl_security_options parameter adds the
following line to main.cf:

```
smtpd_sasl_security_options = noanonymous
```

This prevents anonymous authentication and permits all others.

Including broken clients

Next you have to decide if Postfix should offer SMTP AUTH to broken clients. Broken clients, in the context of SMTP AUTH, are clients that will not recognize a server's SMTP AUTH capability if authentication has been offered the way RFC 2222 requires. Instead they adhere to a draft of the RFC that had an additional = in the line that shows SMTP AUTH capability during SMTP communication. Among the clients that are broken are several versions of Microsoft Outlook Express and Microsoft Outlook. To get around this problem, just add the broken_sasl_auth_clients parameter to main.cf like this:

```
broken_sasl_auth_clients = yes
```

Postfix will print an additional AUTH line when it lists its capabilities to the mail client. This line will have the extra = in it and the broken clients will notice the SMTP AUTH capability.

Finally, if you want to limit the users that may relay to a group with the same realm, add the smtpd_sasl_local_domain parameter and provide the realm as value like this:

```
smtpd_sasl_local_domain = example.com
```

Postfix will append the value to all usernames that get sent by mail clients successfully limiting relaying to those users whose username contains the smtpd_sasl_local_domain value in their username.

Once you're done with all the configuration steps, reload Postfix to let the settings become active and start testing. As root, issue the command:

```
# postfix reload
```

Testing SMTP AUTH

When you test SMTP authentication, don't use a regular mail client as the mail client may introduce some problems. Instead use the Telnet client program and connect to Postfix in an SMTP communication. You will need to send the username and password of your test user in a Base64-encoded form so the first step will be to create such a string. Use the following command to create a Base64 encoded string for the user test using the password testpass:

```
$ perl -MMIME::Base64 -e 'print encode_base64("test\0test\0testpass");'
dGVzdAB0ZXN0AHRlc3RwYXNz
```

Note that the \0 separates the username from the password, and the username will have to be repeated twice. This is because SASL expects two, possibly different usernames (userid, authid) to support additional functionality that isn't used for SMTP authentication.

Also keep in mind that if your username or password contains the @ or $ characters you will need to escape them with a prepended \, or Perl will interpret them and this will result in a non-functional Base64 encoded string.

Once you have the Base64 encoded string at hand, use the Telnet program to connect to port 25 on your server like this:

```
$ telnet mail.example.com 25
    220 mail.example.com ESMTP Postfix

EHLO client.example.com
    250-mail.example.com
    250-PIPELINING
    250-SIZE 10240000
    250-VRFY
    250-ETRN
    250-STARTTLS
    250-AUTH LOGIN PLAIN DIGEST-MD5 CRAM-MD5
    250-AUTH=LOGIN PLAIN DIGEST-MD5 CRAM-MD5
    250-XVERP
    250 8BITMIME

AUTH PLAIN dGVzdAB0ZXN0AHRlc3RwYXNz
    235 Authentication successful

QUIT
    221 Bye
```

You can see that in the previous example the authentication was successful. First the mail client sent an EHLO during the introduction and Postfix responded with a list of capabilities. If you set the broken_sasl_auth_clients parameter to yes as we did in our example, you will also have noted the additional AUTH line containing the =.

Authentication took place when the client sent the AUTH string along with the mechanism it wanted to use and, in the case of plain mechanism, appended the Base64 encoded string. If your authentication did not succeed, but you were able to authenticate during the SASL testing, take a look at the parameters in main.cf and double-check the chroot status of smtpd in master.cf.

Enabling relaying for authenticated clients

If authentication has been successful, we just have to tell Postfix to allow relaying of messages for those who have been authenticated. This is done by editing `main.cf` and adding the `permit_sasl_authenticated` option to your list of restrictions in `smtpd_recipient_restrictions` like this:

```
smtpd_recipient_restrictions =
  ...
  permit_sasl_authenticated
  permit_mynetworks
  reject_unauth_destination
  ...
```

Reload Postfix and start testing with a real mail client. If possible, ensure that its IP address is not part of `mynetworks`, as Postfix might be allowed to relay for that reason and not because SMTP AUTH worked out. You might want to limit relaying to the server only during the test. Change the `mynetwork_classes = host` setting so that clients from other machines automatically will not be a part of the Postfix network.

If you still experience problems with SMTP AUTH, take a look at `saslfinger` (`http://postfix.state-of-mind.de/patrick.koetter/saslfinger/`). It's a script that gathers all kinds of useful information about SMTP AUTH configuration and gives you output that you can append to your mail when you ask on the Postfix mailing list.

Securing plaintext mechanisms

We already noted that SMTP AUTH using plaintext mechanisms isn't really safe because the string that is sent during authentication is merely encoded and not encrypted. This is where **Transport Layer Security (TLS)** comes in handy because it can shield the transmission of the encoded string from curious eyes.

Enabling Transport Layer Security

To enable TLS you must generate a key pair and a certificate, and then alter the postfix configuration to recognize them.

To generate an SSL certificate, and to use SSL, you need to have the OpenSSL package installed. This will be installed in many cases, otherwise use your distribution's package manager to install it.

To create a certificate, issue the following commands (as root):

```
root@hadar: /etc/postfix/certs - Root Shell - Konsole          _ □ x
Session  Edit  View  Bookmarks  Settings  Help

# mkdir -p /etc/postfix/certs
# cd /etc/postfix/certs
# openssl req -new -x509 -nodes -out smtpd.pem -keyout smtpd.pem -days 3650
Generating a 1024 bit RSA private key
...++++++
.............++++++
writing new private key to 'smtpd.pem'
-----
You are about to be asked to enter information that will be incorporated
into your certificate request.
What you are about to enter is what is called a Distinguished Name or a DN.
There are quite a few fields but you can leave some blank
For some fields there will be a default value,
If you enter '.', the field will be left blank.
-----
Country Name (2 letter code) [AU]:GB
State or Province Name (full name) [Some-State]:Greater London
Locality Name (eg, city) []:London
Organization Name (eg, company) [Internet Widgits Pty Ltd]:General Products
, Inc
.
Organizational Unit Name (eg, section) []:Hull Manufacture
Common Name (eg, YOUR name) []:Beowulf Shaeffer
Email Address []:beofulf@an_invalid_domain.com




   Shell     Root Shell
```

This will create certificates in /etc/postfix/certs called smtpd.key and
smtpd.crt. Add the smtpd_use_tls parameter to main.cf and set it to yes:

```
smtpd_use_tls = yes
```

Then you will need to tell smtpd where it can find the key and the certificate by
adding the smtpd_tls_key_file and smtpd_tls_cert_file parameters:

```
smtpd_tls_key_file = /etc/postfix/certs/smtpd.key
smtpd_tls_cert_file = /etc/postfix/certs/smtpd.crt
```

A mail server that sends a certificate to prove its identity must also keep a copy of
the certification authority's public certificate on hand. Presuming that you've already
added it to your server's local CA root store in /usr/share/ssl/certs, use the
following parameter:

```
smtpd_tls_CAfile = /usr/share/ssl/certs/ca-bundle.crt
```

If the CA certificates aren't all in one file, but in separate files in the same directory, for example `/usr/share/ssl/certs`, use the following parameter instead:

```
smtpd_tls_CApath = /usr/share/ssl/certs/
```

Once you have all this configured, you're done with the basic TLS configuration and you can take care of securing plaintext authentication.

Configuring security policy

There are several ways you can secure plaintext authentication using TLS. The most radical approach is to use `smtpd_tls_auth_only` parameter and set it to `yes`. If you use it, `SMTP AUTH` will be announced only once the mail client and mail server have established an encrypted communication layer. By doing this, all username/ password combinations will be encrypted and not vulnerable to eavesdropping.

However, this punishes all the other mail clients that are capable of using other safer mechanisms such as shared secret mechanisms. If you want to handle this a little more selectively you should go for the following approach that disables plaintext authentication over an unencrypted wire, but permits it as soon as an encrypted communication has been established.

First of all you need to reconfigure your `smtpd_sasl_security_options` parameter to exclude plaintext mechanisms from being offered to mail clients:

```
smtpd_sasl_security_options = noanonymous, noplaintext
```

Then you set the additional `smtpd_sasl_tls_security_options` parameter that controls the same settings, but applies to TLS sessions only:

```
smtpd_sasl_tls_security_options = noanonymous
```

As you can see, the `smtpd_sasl_tls_security_options` parameter will not exclude plaintext mechanisms. This way clients that can use other non-plaintext mechanisms don't have to go for TLS and those that can only do plaintext mechanisms can do it safely once they have established an encrypted session.

Once you've reloaded Postfix, you are ready to test.

 Don't forget to add the certificate of the certification authority that signed your server's certificate request to your mail client's CA root store, or it will at the very minimum complain that it cannot verify the server's identity when it presents its server certificate.

Dictionary attacks

Dictionary attacks are attacks where clients try to send mail to countless potential recipients, whose e-mail addresses are derived from words or names in a dictionary:

```
anton@example.com
bertha@example.com
...
zebediah@example.com
```

If your server doesn't have a list of valid recipient addresses, it must accept these mails regardless whether the recipient actually exists. Then, this onslaught of e-mails needs to be processed as usual (virus check, spam check, local delivery) until, at some stage, the system realizes that the recipient does not even exist!
Then a non-delivery report will be generated and sent back to the sender.

So, for every non-existing recipient, one mail is being accepted and processed, and additionally another e-mail (the bounce) is generated, and is subject to delivery attempts.

As you can see, this course of action wastes precious resources on your servers. Because the server is busy trying to deliver mail that it should never have accepted in the first place, legitimate mail is falling behind in the flood of spam. Spammers can also use the bounce messages to determine legitimate e-mail addresses for further attacks. Bounce messages can also give a hint at which SMTP server is used, allowing them to target any known vulnerabilities in particular versions.

Recipient maps

Postfix is able to verify recipient addresses before it accepts a message. It can run checks for local domains (listed in `mydestination`) and for relay domains (listed in `relay_domains`).

Checking local domain recipients

The `local_recipient_maps` parameter controls which recipients Postfix will hold to be valid local recipients. It defaults to the following:

```
local_recipient_maps = proxy:unix:passwd.byname, $alias_maps
```

With this setting, Postfix will check the local `/etc/passwd` file for recipient names as well as any map that has been assigned to the `alias_maps` parameter in `main.cf`. Adding virtual users is beyond the scope of this book, but if you needed to expand this list, you would create a database with the users and add the path to the map that holds additional local recipients.

Checking relay domain recipients

The `relay_recipient_maps` parameter controls which recipients are valid for relay domains. It is empty by default, and in order to have Postfix get more control, you need to build a map where Postfix can look up valid recipients.

Let's say your server relays mail to and from `example.com`, then you would create the following configuration:

```
relay_domains = example.com
relay_recipient_maps = hash:/etc/postfix/relay_recipients
```

The `relay_domain` parameter tells Postfix to relay mail for recipients in the `example.com` domain and the `relay_recipient_maps` parameter points to a map that holds valid recipients. In the map you would create a list like this:

```
adam@example.com        OK
eve@example.com         OK
```

Then run the `postmap` command to create an indexed map like this:

 # postmap /etc/postfix/relay_recipients

To get postfix to recognize the new database, reload it:

 # postfix reload

```
postfix/postfix-script: refreshing the Postfix mail system
```

This will allow only `adam@example.com` and `eve@example.com` as recipients for the domain `example.com`. Mail to `snake@example.com` would be rejected with a **User unknown in relay recipient table** error message.

Rate-limiting connections

Rejecting mail for non-existing recipients helps a lot, but when your server is subject to a dictionary attack, it will still accept all the client's connections and produce an appropriate error message (or accept the mail, should a valid recipient address have been hit by chance).

Postfix's anvil server maintains short-term statistics to defend your system against clients that hammer your server with either of the following cases within a configurable period of time:

- Too many simultaneous sessions
- Too many successive requests

As the hardware and the software you use limit the number of mails your server is able to process per given time unit, it makes sense not to accept more mail than your server can handle.

```
anvil_rate_time_unit = 60s
```

The previous line specifies the time interval used for all the following limits:

- `smtpd_client_connection_rate_limit = 40`: This specifies the number of connections a client can make during the period specified by `anvil_rate_time_unit`. In this case, it's 40 connections per 60s.

- `smtpd_client_connection_count_limit = 16`: This gives the maximum number of simultaneous connections any client is allowed to make to this service per `anvil_rate_time_unit`.

- `smtpd_client_message_rate_limit = 100`: This is an important limit, as a client could reuse an established connection and send many mails using just this single connection.

- `smtpd_client_recipient_rate_limit = 32`: This gives the maximum number of recipient addresses that any client is allowed to send to this service per `anvil_rate_time_unit` regardless of whether or not Postfix actually accepts those recipients.

- `smtpd_client_event_limit_exceptions = $mynetworks`: This can be used to exempt certain networks or machines from the rate limiting. You may want to exempt your mailing list server from the rate limiting, as it will undoubtedly send lots of mails to many recipients during a short period.

The `anvil` will emit detailed log data about the maximum connection rate (here: `5/60s`) and which client reached that maximum rate (`212.227.51.110`) and when (`Dec 28 13:19:23`)

```
Dec 28 13:25:03 mail postfix/anvil[4176]: statistics: max connection
rate 5/60s for (smtp:212.227.51.110) at Dec 28 13:19:23
```

This second log entry shows which client established the most concurrent connections and when:

```
Dec 28 13:25:03 mail postfix/anvil[4176]: statistics: max connection
count 5 for (smtp:62.219.130.25) at Dec 28 13:20:19
```

If any limit is being exceeded, `anvil` will log this as well:

```
Dec 28 11:33:24 mail postfix/smtpd[19507]: warning: Connection rate
limit exceeded: 54 from pD9E83AD0.dip.t-dialin.net[217.232.58.208] for
service smtp

Dec 28 12:14:17 mail postfix/smtpd[24642]: warning: Connection
concurrency limit exceeded: 17 from hqm-smrly01.meti.
go.jp[219.101.211.110] for service smtp
```

Any client that exceeds these limits will be given a temporary error code, thus signaling it to retry at a later time. Legitimate clients will honor that and retry. Open proxies and trojaned machines will most likely not retry.

Summary

In this chapter, we discussed how to secure your installation. There were several different topics covered, firstly, the configuration of Postfix to only accept e-mail from certain IP addresses, which is useful if all your users are office based. Next, the chapter covered using SASL to authenticate users who might connect from any IP address. Then, we looked at using TLS to encrypt the authentication between client and server. Finally, we looked at limiting clients which behave badly, using the `anvil` daemon to limit clients that connect too often within a certain time period, and clients that open too many connections at one time.

The measures shown in this chapter will make your life as a postmaster easier, and also help to limit the amount of spam that your users endure, and if you had inadvertently configured an open relay, limit the amount of spam passed on to other Internet users too. For more details on limiting spam, move on to Chapter 8 that describes using the open source spam filtering tool SpamAssassin. Or read on to Chapter 6 that covers using Procmail to manipulate e-mail messages as they arrive.

6
Getting Started with Procmail

Procmail is a versatile e-mail filter that is typically used to process messages before they are delivered to a user's inbox.

This chapter includes the following topics:

- A brief introduction to Procmail
- The typical filtering tasks that can be performed by Procmail
- How a mail filtering system can be installed and set up on the server to handle the repetitive sorting and storing tasks that you would rather not spend your time on every day
- The basic structure of the rules and actions within a Procmail recipe
- How to create and test the rules within our recipe
- Finally, some example recipes to perform filtering

By the end of the chapter, you will understand the basics of the filtering process — how to set up the system to perform filtering and how to perform a number of very simple but extremely useful filtering operations on your own mail. All of which will help you keep on top of all the mail you have already or will soon be receiving.

Introduction to Procmail

Procmail is a mail filter that is executed after messages have arrived on the mail server but before final delivery to the intended recipient. The behavior of Procmail is controlled by a number of user written recipes (or scripts). Each recipe can contain a number of pattern matching rules to select messages based on at least, the recipient, the subject, and the message content. If the match criteria in a rule selects the message as a candidate, the recipe may perform a number of actions to move the message to a folder, reply to the sender, or even discard the message before delivery. As with the rules, actions are user written in the recipe and can perform almost any operation on a message.

The Procmail home page is located at `http://www.procmail.org`.

Who wrote it and when

Version 1.0 was released in the late 1990's and has evolved to represent one of the best and most commonly used mail filtering solutions for UNIX-based mail systems. Procmail was originally designed and developed by Stephen R. van den Berg (`srb@cuci.nl`). In the fall of 1998, recognizing that he didn't have the time to maintain Procmail on his own, Stephen created a mailing list for discussion of future development and deputized Philip Guenther (`guenther@sendmail.com`) as a maintainer.

Procmail has been stable since Version 3.22, which was released in September 2001, so most recent installations will have this latest version installed, and this is the version we will be using throughout this book.

How can a filtering system help me?

By now you should have an e-mail system up and running, and sending and receiving e-mails. You have probably registered with a number of useful mailing lists with messages arriving at varying intervals. You should also be receiving messages informing you of the status of the system. All this extra, low priority information can easily distract and get in the way of the important e-mails that you need to read ahead of others.

How you organize your mail is up to your own personal taste; if you are very organized you may have already set up some folders in your e-mail client and move messages into appropriate locations when you have read them. Nevertheless, one thing you have probably realized is that it would be very useful to be able to have some messages stored automatically by the system in a different location than your important e-mail.

What you will need to think about while setting up an automatic process, is how you identify what the mail item is about. The most important indicators are to whom it was sent, the title or subject line, and also the sender details. If you take a few minutes now to make a few notes on how you already handle your mail, the types of messages that arrive and what you do with them, you will have a clearer idea of what automatic processes you may want to set up.

In general terms there are several different classes of messages that you might receive.

- **Membership of mailing lists**: Mail arriving from a mail group, or mailing list, is normally easy to identify from the sender information or possibly from the subject line. A number of groups send messages every few minutes while others may only send a couple of messages a month. Typically different mail group items are identified by different pieces of information. For example, some groups send messages with the "From" address being that of the real sender while others add a fake or system-generated "From" address. Some groups may, for example, automatically add a prefix to the "Subject" field.

- **Automated system messages**: Your server generates a number of messages each day. Although normally they are sent only to the system administrator or root user, one of the first things to do is to make sure that you receive a copy of the mail so that you are kept informed of the system status and events. This you would do by editing the default destinations in the `/etc/mail/aliases` or `/etc/aliases` file depending on how your system is set up. These system-generated messages are nearly always identifiable as originating from a small number of specific system user IDs. These are typically `root` and `cron`.

- **Unsolicited bulk e-mail**: Messages identified as spam would normally be considered unimportant. As such you may choose to move these items to a separate folder for later review or even discard them completely. Discarding spam automatically is not advised, as any mail misidentified would be lost forever.

- **Individual messages**: Mail arriving from clients, colleagues, or friends would generally be considered as important. As such it would normally be delivered to your Inbox giving you the opportunity to provide a more timely response. Individual messages are more difficult to identify with a filter, especially those from new clients or colleagues, so messages that do not fit into one of the categories just discussed should be delivered normally.

After completing the work in this chapter, you should have the tools and knowledge to start to examining mail in more detail and set up some basic filtering operations.

Potential uses of mail filtering

The basic mail system you have already set up has some inbuilt abilities of its own to process incoming mail according to a user setup. The default operation would be for messages to go to your Inbox; other options are to automatically forward all your mail to another user. Consider you have multiple mail accounts on different systems and want all your mail to end up in one particular mail account. You can then have that mail sent to a particular file, or have it passed to a program or application to allow it to do its own work.

The downside of this setup is that all your mail has to follow one particular route, so over time a number of options have been created to intelligently filter mail. One of the most powerful and popular of these is Procmail.

Filtering and sorting mail

Procmail is designed to handle a wide variety of processing and filtering tasks on mail being received by users within the system. Filtering only applies to users who have an account on the system—not to virtual users—and may be applied system wide to all users or individual users may add their own filters.

For system administrators, Procmail offers a range of facilities for applying rules and operations to all the mail being received by users of the system. Such actions may include making a copy of all mail for historical purposes or in businesses where the content of e-mail messages may be used in some form of legal or business situation.

Elsewhere in this book, we will be discussing ways of identifying e-mail-borne viruses and spam. Procmail can take the information provided by these processes and perform actions based on the information added by these processes, such as storing all mail items containing a virus in a secure mail folder that is checked by system administrators.

For a system user, the most common operation to perform on incoming mail is to sort it into some organized layout so that you can easily find the items you are looking for, based on the topic area that you are interested in. A typical organizational layout could be a hierarchical one similar to the following:

```
/mailgroups/Procmail
/mailgroups/postfix
/mailgroups/linux
/system/cron
/system/warnings
/system/status
/inbox
```

If you plan on keeping mail in store for long periods of time for historical reference, it may be worth adding an extra layer or two to separate the mail into years and months. This makes it easier in the future to archive or purge older e-mail, and it also means that searching and sorting will be quicker.

Forwarding mail

Sometimes you may get lots of e-mail that is easily identified as needing to be sent to another user at another e-mail address. In this case, rather than storing the file on the system, you may set up a rule that will forward the e-mail to one or more other e-mail addresses. Of course you need to be careful to make sure that the forwarding does not end up coming back to you, creating a never-ending loop.

Forwarding of mail in this way has a big advantage over the manual forwarding of mail from within your mail client software, quite apart from not needing any manual intervention. Mail forwarded by Procmail is transparent, it appears to the recipient as if the mail has arrived directly from the original sender. Whereas, if it was forwarded using a mail client, it would appear as though it had been sent by the person or account doing the forwarding.

Where all mail items for a single address need forwarding to a single other address, a more efficient way to achieve this is using the aliasing mechanism of the Postfix mailing system. Procmail should only be used where an intelligent filtering of the mail is required dependent upon factors that can only be determined at the time of receipt of the message.

Processing the mail in an application

Some mail items could be suitable for passing through to an application where the application program does some work on the e-mail. Perhaps it could read the contents and then store the information in a bug-tracking database or update the company history log for a client activity. These are more advanced topics that are briefly covered in the following chapter.

Acknowledgements and out of office/vacation replies

If you wanted to send an automatic reply to certain messages, a filter or rule could be set up to send such a message. When you are away from the office for a prolonged period of time on holiday, vacation, or perhaps illness, it is possible to set up a reply service to inform the sender that it will be some time before you are able to respond to their mail and perhaps give them alternative contact details or ask them to contact another person.

It is important that you organize such a feature carefully. You shouldn't send such a reply to a mailing group or keep sending repeated replies to people who already know that you are away but need to send you information for after your return. This requires that a log of the addresses that the message is sent to is kept to avoid repeat messages being sent. We will investigate the setting up of such a service in the next chapter.

File locking and integrity

An important concept to keep in mind during all your work with Procmail is that it is always possible for multiple mail messages to be arriving at the same time, all vying to be processed. Therefore, it is quite possible that two or more messages are going to be stored in the same location at the same time—a recipe for disaster exists. Assume the simple example of two items arriving at the same time. The first mail opens the storage location and starts to write the contents of the message, and then the second process does the same. A variety of possible results could occur from this, ranging from one message being lost totally through, to both messages being stored intertwined and totally illegible.

To make sure that this doesn't happen, a strict locking protocol needs to be observed to ensure that only one process can write at a time and all other applications need to wait patiently for their turn. Procmail itself has the ability to enforce a locking protocol appropriate to the type of process being applied and will, by default, lock the physical file in which a mail is being stored.

In some cases, the mail is being processed by an application and Procmail can be instructed by the use of flags within the rule to use an appropriate locking mechanism. This is covered more completely in Chapter 7.

What Procmail is not suitable for

There are some very specific mail filtering and processing requirements for which Procmail may be considered to be suitable. In most cases, it is flexible and capable enough to perform the task at least at a rudimentary level. Such tasks could be filtering of spam-related e-mails or filtering out viruses or running a mailing list operation. For each of these, there are a number of solutions available that go beyond the capabilities of using just Procmail filters. We will be looking at SpamAssassin for performing spam filtering and a virus filtering solution later in Chapter 8.

We have already mentioned that Procmail is suitable only for users having accounts on the system that Procmail runs on. Nevertheless, it is worth reinforcing that Procmail is unable to process mail that is being delivered to a virtual user and such mails will end up on another system. If it is necessary to process mail for such a user, it is possible to create a real user account on the system and then use Procmail to perform the final forwarding as part of its filtering processes. This is not an ideal use as the Postfix system is much more efficient if it is allowed to do this work rather than using Procmail.

Downloading and installing Procmail

As the software is now reasonably mature, Procmail is usually available for installation on most Linux distributions and can be installed by using the package manager. This is the recommended way to install Procmail. If it is not available via a package manager in your Linux distribution, it can also be installed from the source code.

Installing via a package manager

For Fedora users, the simple way to install Procmail if it isn't already installed is to use the yum command as follows:

```
yum install procmail
```

For Debian-based users you could use the following command:

```
apt-get install procmail
```

This will ensure that the binary of Procmail is correctly installed on your system and you can then decide how you want it to integrate into your Postfix system.

Installing from source

Procmail may be obtained from a number of sources but the official distribution is maintained and available from www.procmail.org. There you will find links to a number of mirror services from which you can download the source files. The version used in this book can be downloaded from http://www.procmail.org/procmail-3.22.tar.gz.

It can be downloaded by using the wget command as follows:

```
wget http://www.procmail.org/procmail-3.22.tar.gz
```

Once you have downloaded and unpacked the archive, cd to the directory, example procmail-3.22. Before starting to build and install the software, it is well worthwhile reading through the INSTALL and README documents.

For most Linux systems, the simplest installation method can be reduced by following the steps listed here:

1. Run the `configure` utility to create the right build environment by running the `configure` command:

   `$ ./configure`

2. After the configuration script is completed, you can run the `make` command to build the software executables:

   `$ make`

3. The final step, as `root`, is to copy the executables into the correct position for operation on the system:

   `# make install`

In the last step, the software is installed into the `/usr/local` directory.

At all stages, you should check the processes output for any significant errors or warnings.

Installation options/considerations

For most people following the instructions, throughout this book you will be the system administrator of the machine or machines you are managing and will probably be applying the installation to process all mail for all users on the system. If you are not an administrator, or you wish only a limited number of people on the system to take advantage of the features of Procmail, you can install Procmail for individual users.

Individual installation

If you are installing Procmail for your own use or for only a few people on your server, the most common method is to call the Procmail program directly from the `.forward` file in your home directory on the server (this file needs to be world-readable).

The entry in `.forward` when using Postfix as an MTA should be like this:

```
"|IFS=' ' && exec /usr/bin/procmail -f- || exit 75 #username"
```

The quotes are required and the username should be substituted for your username. The syntax for other MTAs may be different so consult the MTA documentation.

You will also need to install a `.procmailrc` file in the home directory — this is the file that holds the rules that Procmail will use to filter and deliver your e-mail.

System-wide installation

If you are a system administrator, you can decide to install Procmail globally. This has the advantage that users do not need to have a `.forward` file anymore. Simply having a `.procmailrc` file in each user's HOME directory will suffice. The operation is transparent in this case—if no `.procmailrc` file is present in the HOME directory, the mail will be delivered as usual.

A global `.procmailrc` file can be created that takes effect before the user's own file. In this case, you need to be careful to ensure that the configuration has the following instruction included so that messages are stored with the end user's privileges rather than the root user's privileges.

```
DROPPRIVS=yes
```

This also helps protect against weaknesses in your system security. This file is normally stored in the `/etc` directory as `/etc/procmailrc` where it is intended to provide a default set of personal rules for all users as they are added to the system. It will be worth configuring a `.procmailrc` file in the skeleton account that is used by the add user capabilities of your system. Consult your Linux documentation for information on how this can be set up.

Integration with Postfix for system-wide delivery

To integrate Procmail into the Postfix system is simple but, as with any other configuration change, care must be taken. Postfix runs all external commands such as Procmail with the user ID of nobody. So it would be unable to deliver mail to the user root. To ensure that important system messages are still received, you should make sure that an alias is configured so that all mail intended for the root user is forwarded to a real user who will read the mailbox.

Creating an alias for system accounts

To create an alias for the root user, you must edit the appropriate `alias` file, normally found in `/etc/aliases or /etc/mail/aliases`.

If you are unable to find the file, use the following command:

```
postconf alias_maps
```

The entry in the alias file should be as follows with just a single tab character between the colon (`:`) and the start of the e-mail address and no trailing spaces:

```
root:  user@domain.com
```

After creating the text entry, you should run the `newaliases` command to convert the text file into a database file ready for Postfix to read.

It is worthwhile to add additional aliases for any other system accounts that may receive mail. For example you may end up with an `aliases` file similar to the following:

```
# /etc/aliases
postmaster: root
nobody: root
hostmaster: root
usenet: root
news: root
webmaster: root
www: root
ftp: root
abuse: root
noc: root
security: root
root: user@example.com
clamav: root
```

Adding Procmail to the Postfix configuration

For system-wide delivery of mail by Procmail, it is necessary to modify the Postfix `main.cf` file to specify the application that will be responsible for the actual delivery.

Edit the `/etc/postfix/main.cf` file and add the following line:

```
mailbox_command = /path/to/procmail
```

When the change has been made, you need to instruct Postfix that the file has changed using the following command:

```
postfix reload
```

Postfix-provided environment variables

Postfix exports information regarding the mail package by use of a number of environment variables. The variables are modified to avoid any shell expansion issues by replacing all characters that may have special meaning to the shell, including whitespace with the underscore character. The following is a list of variables that are exported and their meaning:

Variable	Meaning
DOMAIN	The text to the right-hand side of the @ in the recipient address
EXTENSION	Optional address-extension part
HOME	The recipient's home directory
LOCAL	The text to the left-hand side of the @ in the recipient address, for example, $USER+$EXTENSION
LOGNAME	The recipient username
RECIPIENT	The entire recipient address, $LOCAL@$DOMAIN
SENDER	The complete sender address
SHELL	The recipient's login shell

Basic operations

When a mail item arrives and is passed to the Procmail program, the sequence of operations follows a set format. It starts by loading the various configuration files to obtain the rules that have been set up for that particular user. The message is then tested by each of these rules in turn and when a suitable match is made, the rule is applied. Some rules terminate when they have completed, while others return control so that the message can be assessed against remaining rules for potential processing.

Configuration file

The system-wide configuration is normally made in /etc/procmailrc, while personal configuration files are normally stored in the user's home directory and called .procmailrc. Individual rules can be stored in separate files or grouped together into a number of files and then included as part of the mail filtering process by the main .procmailrc file. Typically these files would be stored in the Procmail subdirectory of your home directory.

File format

Entries in the configuration file are made in a simple text format according to a basic layout. Comments are allowed and are formed by the text following a # character; empty lines are simply ignored. Rules themselves do not have to be laid out in any particular format, though for ease of maintenance and readability, it is well worth writing the rules in a consistent and simple format.

Configuration file dissection

The Procmail configuration file contents can be classified into three main sections:

- **Variables**: Information necessary for Procmail to do its work may be assigned to variables within the configuration file in a manner similar to how they are used in shell programming. Some of the variables are obtained from the shell environment that Procmail is running in, others are created by Procmail itself for use within the scripts, while other variables can be assigned within the script itself. An additional use for variables is to set flags as to how Procmail itself should operate.

  A few useful variables can be set in most scripts:

  ```
  PATH=/usr/bin: /usr/local/bin:.
  MAILDIR=$HOME/Maildir              # Make sure it exists
  DEFAULT=$MAILDIR/                  # Trailing / indicates maildir
  format mailbox
  LOGFILE=$HOME/procmail.log
  LOG="
  "
  VERBOSE=yes
  ```

  - The VERBOSE variable is used to affect the level of logging that is performed, while the NEWLINE embedded in the LOG variable is deliberate and intended to make log files easier to read.

  - Chapter 7 also includes a short script that displays all the variables assigned within Procmail.

- **Comments**: A # character and all the following characters up to a NEWLINE are ignored. This does not apply to condition lines that cannot be commented. Blank lines are ignored and may be used in conjunction with comments to document your configuration and to aid readability. You should comment your rules as what makes obvious sense today as you are writing your rules may well defy explanation in six months time without checking the manual.

- **Rules or recipes**: Recipe is a common name for rules we create. A line starting with a colon (:) marks the beginning of a recipe. A recipe has the following format:

  ```
  :0 [flags] [ : [locallockfile] ]
  <zero or more conditions (one per line)>
  <exactly one action line>
  ```

The :0 is a hangover from earlier versions of Procmail. The number following the : was originally intended to indicate the number of actions contained within the rule, this is now calculated automatically by the Procmail parser. However, the :0 is required for compatibility purposes.

Analyzing a simple rule

Let us assume that we are receiving large amounts of mail from a particular mail group that we subscribed to. The mail is interesting, but isn't important and we would prefer to read it at our leisure. The subject is "mythical monsters" and all e-mail arriving from this mailing list has a "To" address of mythical@monsters.com. We have decided that we will create a special folder just for these items of mail, and copy all the mail into this folder. This is a simple rule that you will be able to easily copy and modify to process your own mail in the future.

The rule structure

The following is an example copy of a very simple .procmail file taken from a user's home directory and is intended to explain some of the basic features of a Procmail configuration. The rule itself is designed to store all mail sent to a certain e-mail address, mythical@monsters.com, in a special folder called monsters. Most mail will be sent to multiple people including yourself and the "To" address can hold a useful indication of the mail contents. For example, mail may be sent to a distribution list at info@yourcompany.com and you need to prioritize this e-mail.

Take a few moments to read the contents of the file and then we will break down each section in turn and analyze what its function is.

```
#
#   Here we assign variables
#
PATH=/usr/bin: /usr/local/bin:.
MAILDIR=$HOME/Maildir                    # Make sure it exists
DEFAULT=$MAILDIR/                        # Trailing / indicates maildir
format mailbox
LOGFILE=$HOME/procmail.log
LOG="
"
VERBOSE=yes

#
#   This is the only rule within the file
#
```

```
:0:                              # Anything to mythical@monsters.com
* ^TO_ mythical@monsters.com
monsters/                        # will go to monsters folder. Note the
trailing /
```

Variable analysis

To examine this file in detail, we can start with the definition statements where the variables are assigned with specific values. These values will override any values that Procmail has already assigned. By doing this manual assignment, we can ensure that paths are optimized for the script operation and that we are certain of what values are being used rather than assuming the values that Procmail may assign.

```
PATH=/usr/bin: /usr/local/bin:.
MAILDIR=$HOME/Maildir
DEFAULT=$MAILDIR/
LOGFILE=$HOME/procmail.log
LOG="
"
VERBOSE=yes
```

These set up instructions to Procmail to define some basic parameters:

- The PATH instruction specifies where Procmail can find any programs it may need to execute as part of the processing.

- MAILDIR specifies the directory that all the mail items will be stored in. This directory should exist.

- DEFAULT defines where mail will be stored if a specific location is not defined for the individual rule. Following the recommendation in the chapter on Postfix about selecting the mailbox format, the trailing /(slash) indicates to Procmail that it should deliver mail in Maildir format.

- LOGFILE is the file where all tracking information will be stored so that we can see what is happening.

Rule analysis

Next we have the recipe instructions beginning with :0. The second : instructs Procmail to create a lock file to ensure only one mail message is written to the file at a time, in order to avoid corruption of the message store. The single line rule may be broken down as follows:

- ***:** All rule lines begin with an *. This is the way Procmail knows that they are rules. There may be one or more rules per recipe.
- **^TO_:** This is a special Procmail built-in macro that searches most headers that can carry your address in them, such as `To:`, `Apparently-To:`, `Cc:`, `Resent-To:`, and so on, and will match if it finds the address `mythical@monsters.com`.

The final line is the action line and by default specifies a mail folder in the directory specified by the `MAILDIR` variable.

The trailing slash is required on folder names for Maildir format mailboxes, otherwise mail is delivered in unix mbox format which is not supported by Courier-IMAP. If you are using IMAP, folder names should also be prefixed with a . (period) because the period character is designated as a hierarchy separator.

Creating and testing a rule

Procmail allows you to organize your rules and recipes into multiple files and then process each file in turn. This makes it much easier to manage the rules and also to switch rules on and off as the needs change. For this first test case, we will create a special rule set for testing and organize all our rules in a subdirectory of our home directory. Typically, the subdirectory is called `Procmail` but you are free to use your own name.

We will start off by looking at a simple personal rule and testing it for a single user. Later in the chapter, when we have covered all of the basics and you are comfortable with the process of creating and setting up rules, we will show how to start applying rules to all system users.

A "hello world" example

Almost all books on programming start off with a very simple "hello world" example to show the basics of the programming language. In this case, we will create a simple personal rule that processes all e-mails received by a user and checks to see if the subject contains the words "hello world". If the mail subject contains these particular words, the mail message will be stored in a special folder. If it does not contain these magic words, the mail will be stored in the user's normal inbox.

Creating rc.testing

When you are working in a production environment, it is important to make sure that the rules being written and tested do not interfere with your normal day-to-day mail activities. One way of controlling this is to create a special file specifically for testing new rules and only include it in the Procmail processing when you are actually doing the testing work. When you are happy with the rule operation, you can move it to a specific file of its own, or add it to other similar or related rules. In this example, we will create a new file for testing rules called rc.testing. In the $HOME/Procmail directory, use your favorite editor to create the file rc.testing and enter the following lines:

```
# LOGFILE should be specified early in the file so
# everything after it is logged
LOGFILE=$PMDIR/pmlog

# To insert a blank line between each message's log entry,
# Use the following LOG entry
LOG="
"
# Set to yes when debugging; VERBOSE default is no
VERBOSE=yes

#
#   Simple test recipes
#
:0:
* ^Subject:.*hello world
TEST-HelloWorld
```

By now, you are hopefully beginning to recognize the structure of the rules. This one is broken down as follows.

The first few lines set up variables that are applicable to our testing environment. As they are assigned within the testing script, they will only apply while the script is being included in the processing. As soon as we exclude the test script, the testing settings will, of course, not be applied.

Match all lines that begin (^) with the string Subject: and containing the string hello world. We have deliberately not used a string such as test, as a small number of systems can strip out messages that appear to be test messages. Remember that default operation of Procmail is to be case independent so we don't need to test for all variations such as Hello World.

The last line directs Procmail to store the output in the TEST-HelloWorld file.

Create `testmail.txt` in the `$HOME/Procmail` directory, use your favorite editor to create the file `testmail.txt` and enter the following lines:

```
From: me@example.com
To: me@example.com (self test)
Subject: My Hello World Test

BODY OF TEST MESSAGE SEPARATED BY EMPTY LINE
```

The subject line is mixed case compared to our rule in `rc.testing` that contains the candidate string in order to demonstrate case-insensitive matching.

Performing static testing of the script

Running the following command from the `Procmail` directory will generate the debugging output:

```
formail -s procmail -m PMDIR=. rc.testing < testmail.txt
```

 During static testing, we have defined the variable PMDIR in the previous command to be our current directory.

After running the command, you can look at the log file for error messages. If everything worked fine, you would see the creation of the file TEST-HelloWorld with the contents of `testmail.txt` and following output in the log.

```
procmail: [9060] Mon Jun  8 17:52:31 2009
procmail: Match on "^Subject:.*hello world"
procmail: Locking "TEST-HelloWorld.lock"
procmail: Assigning "LASTFOLDER=TEST-HelloWorld"
procmail: Opening "TEST-HelloWorld"
procmail: Acquiring kernel-lock
procmail: Unlocking "TEST-HelloWorld.lock"
From me@example.com  Mon Jun  8 17:52:31 2009
 Subject: My Hello World Test
   Folder: TEST-HelloWorld                                      194
```

If the `Subject` line had not contained the relevant matching phrase, you might have seen the following output in the log:

```
procmail: [9073] Mon Jun  8 17:53:47 2009
procmail: No match on "^Subject:.*hello world"
From me@example.com  Mon Jun  8 17:53:47 2009
 Subject: My Goodbye World Test
   Folder: **Bounced**                                            0
```

Configuring Procmail to process rc.testing

You will need to edit your `.procmailrc` configuration file. There may well be some entries in there already, so it is worth making a backup of the file before you make any changes. Ensure that the following lines are included in the file:

```
# Directory for storing procmail configuration and log files
PMDIR=$HOME/Procmail

# Load specific rule sets
INCLUDERC=$PMDIR/rc.testing
```

Some lines are deliberately commented out using #. These may be required if we need to do some more detailed debugging later.

Testing the setup

Using the following command, send yourself two messages:

```
echo "test message" | mail -s "hello world" $USER
```

One should include the string `hello world` in the subject line and one should not include this particular string.

When you check your mail, you should find that the message with the key word in the subject has been stored in the `TEST-HelloWorld` mail folder, while the other message was left in the normal mail inbox.

Configuration debugging

If this has all worked correctly — congratulations! You are well on the way to organizing your mail.

If it didn't quite work as expected, there are a number of simple things we can do to find out what the problem is.

Checking for typos in the scripts

As with any programming process, if at first it doesn't work, check the code to make sure that there were no obvious typos introduced during the editing phase.

Looking at the log file for error messages

If that doesn't highlight anything, you can look at the log file created by Procmail. In this case, the log file is called `pmlog` in the `~/Procmail` directory. To look at just the last few lines, use the following command:

`tail ~/Procmail/pmlog`

In the following example there is a missing `:0` so that the rule lines are being skipped:

```
* ^Subject:.*hello world

TEST-HelloWorld
```

This would give the following errors:

```
procmail: [10311] Mon Jun  8 18:21:34 2009
procmail: Skipped "* ^Subject:.* hello world"
procmail: Skipped "TEST"
procmail: Skipped "-HelloWorld"
```

Here there is no storage instruction to follow the rule `:0`:

```
:0:

* ^Subject:.*hello world
```

This would give the following errors:

```
procmail: [10356] Mon Jun  8 18:23:36 2009
procmail: Match on "^Subject:.* hello world"
procmail: Incomplete recipe
```

Checking file and directory permissions

Use the `ls` command to check the permissions on the `~/.procmailrc` and `~/Procmail/*` files and the `~/` home directory. The rules files should be writable by users other than the owner and should have permissions similar to the following:

`rw-r--r—`

The home directory should have permissions such as the following where the `?` may be either `r` or `-`:

`drwx?-x?-x`

Turning on Full Logging

When you are creating more complex rules, or if you still have a problem, you need to enable the **Full Logging** capability of Procmail. To do this, you need to remove the comment # from the lines in the ~/.procmailrc file so that they are enabled as follows:

```
# Directory for storing procmail configuration and log files
PMDIR=$HOME/Procmail

# LOGFILE should be specified early in the file so
# everything after it is logged
LOGFILE=$PMDIR/pmlog

# To insert a blank line between each message's log entry,
# add a return between the quotes (this is helpful for debugging)
LOG="
"

# Set to yes when debugging; VERBOSE default is no
VERBOSE=yes

# Load specific rule sets
INCLUDERC=$PMDIR/rc.testing
```

Now resend the two sample messages and check the log file for the output information. The log file should indicate some areas of problems for you to investigate.

Taking steps to avoid disasters

The following recipe inserted early in the .procmailrc file will ensure that the last 32 messages received are each stored in the backup directory, ensuring that valuable mail is not lost in cases where a recipe contains a fault or has an unexpected side effect.

```
# Create a backup cache of 32 most recent messages in case of
mistakes.
# For this to work, you must first create the directory
# ${MAILDIR}/backup.
:0 c
backup

:0 ic
| cd backup && rm -f dummy `ls -t msg.* | sed -e 1,32d`
```

For now we will assume that this works, and in the next chapter we will analyze the recipe in detail to see how exactly it works and what it does.

Understanding e-mail structure

In order to make full use of the capabilities of Procmail, it is worth taking some time to understand the basic structure of a typical e-mail message. Over time, the structure has grown in complexity, but it can still be broken down into two discrete blocks.

Message body

The message body is separated from the headers by a single blank line (all the headers must be on consecutive lines, as any headers following a blank line will be assumed to be part of the message body).

The message body itself may be either a simple text message composed normally of simple ASCII characters or it may be a complex combination of parts encoded using something known as **MIME**. This has allowed e-mail to be able to transfer all forms of data ranging from simple text, HTML, or other formatted pages, and to include information such as attachments or embedded objects such as images. Discussion of MIME encoding is beyond the scope of this book, and is not necessary for most processes that you are likely to come across in mail filtering.

If you decide to try to process the data held in the message body, it is important to remember that what you see as the output of the mail program, may be very different from the actual data transmitted in the raw mail message.

E-mail headers

The headers are the tags that an e-mail contains that permit the various mailing components to send and process messages. The typical format of a mail header is a simple two-part construction composed of a keyword terminated by a : and followed by the information assigned to the keyword. The headers provide a lot of information about how the e-mail was created, what form of mail program created the message, from whom it came, to whom it should go, and how it reached your mailbox.

The following mail headers relate to an e-mail received from one of a number of mailing lists at `freelancers.net`. The most useful identifying feature of the e-mail is the subject line as most of the other mail groups use the same values for the other headers discussed.

```
Return-Path: <do-not-reply@freelancers.net>
Received: from fnmail.co.uk (evls-207-44-214-84.evlservers.net [207.44.214.84] (may be forged))
        by delta.adepteo.net (8.12.5/8.12.5) with SMTP id iA3LGkGD002068
        for <projects@adepteo.net>; Wed, 3 Nov 2004 21:16:46 GMT
Received: (qmail 4477 invoked by uid 0); 3 Nov 2004 18:30:47 -0000
Date: 3 Nov 2004 18:30:47 -0000
Message-ID: <20041103183047.4476.qmail@fnmail.co.uk>
To: projects@adepteo.net
Subject: FN-PROJECTS Freelance Web Designers
From: Do Not Reply <do-not-reply@freelancers.net>
X-Mailer: http://www.phpclasses.org/mimemessage $Revision: 1.29 $
MIME-Version: 1.0
Content-Type: text/plain
X-Spam-Checker-Version: SpamAssassin 3.0.0 (2004-09-13) on delta.adepteo.net
X-Spam-Level:
X-Spam-Status: No, score=-2.3 required=5.0 tests=AWL,BAYES_00,COMBINED_FROM    autolearn=no version=3.0.0
```

Header structure

The previous example contains a large number of headers inserted by a number of processes that the mail has been through on its journey from sender to recipient. There is, however, a small number of key headers that are very useful for processing e-mail and are used in a significant number of recipes.

Official definitions for headers

All headers that do not begin with x- are assigned specific functions by the relevant standards authority. More information about them may be found in the **RFC (Request for Comment) Document 822** at `http://www.ietf.org/rfc/rfc0822.txt`.

Headers beginning with x- are user defined and are applicable to a specific application only. However, some applications may use the same header tag as other applications, but for different reasons and with a different format for the information provided.

Example rule sets

In order to help you understand the way Procmail rules work, we will go through the design and setup of several simple but very useful rule sets. This should help to get you into the swing of designing your own rule sets as you find more specific needs to filter your incoming mail items.

All these examples are based on the mail messages received from the Freelancers Mailing List from which the previous example headers were taken. They all achieve the same result and once again prove that there is no one correct solution to a programming problem.

From header

This header explains who the originator of the e-mail was. There are a variety of formats that may be used and are formed of various combinations of human-readable and computer-readable items of information. When you have looked at a few e-mails, you will begin to see the various patterns that can be used by differing mail systems and software. The actual formatting of this header is not necessarily important, as you are looking to generate rules to match specific e-mails.

```
From: Do Not Reply <do-not-reply@freelancers.net>
```

Return-Path Header

This field is added by the final transport system that delivers the message to its recipient. The field is intended to contain definitive information about the address and route back to the message's originator.

Return-Path: <do-not-reply@freelancers.net>

Filtering by Return-Path

The majority of mailing lists use the `Return-Path` header:

```
:0:
* ^Return-Path: <do-not-reply@freelancers.net>
freelancers//
```

This is a useful way of easily filtering mailing list items. Here, the ^ character performs a special function that instructs Procmail to start the match process at the beginning of a new line. This means that lines that contain the phrase embedded in the middle of the line are not matched. The default operation for Procmail is to return a match if the string is found anywhere within the header or anywhere within the mail body, depending on where the script has been set to search.

To and Cc headers

Messages are normally sent to one or more people who are listed in the To: or Cc: headers of the e-mail. Like the From: header, these addresses may be formatted in several ways. These headers are visible to all mail recipients and allow you to see all the public recipients listed.

To: `projects@adepteo.net`

There is a third recipient header that is not quite as common as the To: and Cc: but is used quite a lot in bulk mailings. This is the Bcc: (Blind Carbon Copy). Unfortunately, as the name implies, this is a blind header and so the information is not included in the actual header information and hence not available for processing.

Filtering by To or Cc

Procmail has a number of special built-in macros that can be used to identify mail items. The special rule `^TO_` is intended to search all the destination headers available. The rule must be written as exactly four characters with no spaces and with both `T` and `O` in capitals. The phrase being matched must follow immediately after the _ again without a space.

```
:0:
* ^TO_do-not-reply@freelancers.net
freelancers/
```

Subject header

The subject line is usually included in the e-mail headers unless the sender has decided not to include a subject line at all.

Subject: FN-PROJECTS Freelance Web Designers

In this example, all the mail items sent to this particular list start with the phrase "FN-PROJECTS" and so are sometimes suitable for filtering.

Filtering by subject

When mailing lists add a prefix to subject lines, this prefix may be suitable for filtering:

```
:0:
* ^Subject: FN-PROJECTS
freelancers//
```

System-wide rules

Now that we have covered all the basics of setting up rules, analyzing e-mails, and generally seeing how all of the processing operations interact, we will look through a couple of examples for system-wide filtering, testing, and operations.

Removing executables

In Chapter 9, we will see how to integrate a complete virus checking system into the Postfix mail architecture. This will perform accurate virus signature recognition and add suitable flags to the mail headers to indicate if a virus is present in the mail. However, if it is not possible to set up such a system, this rule will provide an alternative but more brutal approach to block all e-mails with executable attachments.

If you place the following in /etc/procmailrc, it will affect all mail traveling through the system that contains certain types of documents as attachments.

```
# Note: The whitespace in the [ ] in the code comprises a space and a
tab character
:0
* < 256000
* ! ^Content-Type: text/plain
{
    :0B
    * ^(Content-(Type|Disposition):.*|[      ]*(file)?)name=("[^"]*|[^
]*)\.(bat|cmd|com|exe|js|pif|scr)
    /dev/null
}
```

The rule starts with the customary :0 instruction.

The conditions are applied as follows:

Firstly, ensure that we are only going to filter messages less than 256 KB in size. This is primarily for efficiency and most spam is smaller than this size. You could obviously increase it if you are getting viruses that are bigger, but there could be a higher load on your system.

The next line says that we also only look at those messages that are MIME types (that is, not plain text), as attachments, by definition, cannot be included in a plain text message.

We have a subfilter between the curly braces. The `:0B` says we are processing the body of the message, rather than the headers. We have to do this because attachments come in the body, not the headers. We then look for lines that have the signature of being a MIME heading for an executable file. You can amend the filename extensions if you wish; these are simply the ones that are commonly used to transmit viruses.

The action in this case is to send this message to `/dev/null` if it matches. Note that this means no message bounce or error message to the sender; the message is simply dropped, never to be seen again. You may of course store the messages in a secure location and nominate someone to monitor the account for valid messages that do not contain viruses. For a more elegant solution to this problem, remember to check Chapter 9.

Large e-mails

With the ever increasing use of high speed, always-on Internet connections, people are starting to send larger and larger e-mail messages. Once upon a time, it was considered rude to have more than four lines in your signature file, nowadays people happily include images and wallpapers, and send both HTML and text versions of the e-mail all without realizing the size of message they are sending.

Storing such large messages in your Inbox adds considerably to the processing overhead to search through your mail messages. One simple solution is to move all messages over a certain size into an oversize folder. This can be achieved very simply by using the following rule that looks for messages over 100,000 bytes in size and stores them in the `largemail` folder.

```
:0:
* >100000
largemail/
```

The downside of this rule is that your users need to remember to check on a regular basis both their Inbox and the `largemail` folder. A more elegant solution will allow you to copy the first few lines of the message together with the headers and subject line, and store that in the Inbox and inform you that the complete version needs to be checked for. Such a solution can be seen in the examples at the end of the next chapter.

Summary

In this chapter, we have discovered some of the basics of Procmail. By now you should be familiar with the various files that Procmail uses to load recipes, the core principles of filtering, and the options available. We have also analyzed e-mails, set up individual and system wide filters, and looked at some of the simple testing, logging, and debugging options that will help us manage a company's mail more effectively.

We have just scratched the surface of what is possible, but hopefully this little taste has already provided you with a whole load of ideas about how you could go about processing and filtering your daily overload of e-mail. It may well have given you ideas for more advanced filters and the next chapter will provide more advice and explanations of how to go about setting these up.

7
Advanced Procmail

Now that we have got the basics of Procmail under our belt, we can move on and start putting together a more complete mail-handling system. The advanced techniques in this chapter are required only if you need a very specialized handling for your mail and are not needed for setting up a basic e-mail server. You may wish to skip this chapter and return to it once your server is fully configured and operational.

We will be using a number of more advanced Procmail capabilities in this chapter. This chapter will cover:

- The differences between delivering and non-delivering recipes
- The usage of variables, substitutions, and pseudo-variables in advanced recipes
- Locking and the use of various flags to control execution
- How conditions can be applied to test various parts of a message
- Advanced actions to forward, save, or pass a message on to an external program for processing
- An introduction to regular expressions
- Using Procmail macros to simplify e-mail header analysis
- Detailed analysis of some advanced recipes with a number of example recipes

By the end of this chapter, you should have a useful tool chest of routines for putting together your own set of Procmail recipes and getting your mail under control.

Delivering and non-delivering recipes

So far we have covered only those recipes that either do a final delivery of the mail to a program or a file, or forward a message to another mail user. There is another option available, and to quote from the Procmail documentation:

> *There are two kinds of recipes – delivering and non-delivering recipes. If a delivering recipe is found to match, Procmail considers the mail (you guessed it) delivered and will cease processing the* .procmailrc *file after having successfully executed the action line of the recipe. If a non-delivering recipe is found to match, processing of the* .procmailrc *file will continue after the action line of this recipe has been executed.*

Non-delivering example

We introduced an example in the previous chapter that was intended to make backups of mail items, in case a recipe that is being tested deletes all mails. This is a very useful non-delivering recipe example and may be found in the Procmail manual page procmailex.

If you are fairly new to Procmail and plan to experiment a little, it often helps to have a safety net of some sort. Inserting the two recipes mentioned before, all other recipes will make sure that the last 32 arriving mail messages will always be preserved. In order to make this work as intended, we have to create a directory named backup in $MAILDIR prior to inserting these two recipes:

```
:0 c
backup
:0 ic
cd backup && rm -f dummy `ls -t msg.* | sed -e 1,32d`
```

The second recipe uses several features of Procmail, which we will be exploring in more detail in later sections of this chapter.

If we work step by step through this recipe, we will end up with a useful archive utility that records the last 32 mail items to be received and allows us to manually recover mail if we ever create a recipe that ends up destroying mail rather than storing it. On a busy mail server, it might be prudent to increase this number to keep a larger archive of messages.

The first recipe performs a simple backup operation by delivering a copy or clone of the mail into the backup directory:

```
:0 c
backup
```

Before adding the second recipe, create the above recipe in the `.procmailrc` file and send a couple of mail messages to yourself. We can see that each mail item is stored in the backup directory (provided it exists and has the correct permissions).

The second recipe is just as simple, but uses some more complex features of Linux system commands to delete all but the mail items in the `backup` directory, except the most recent 32 items.

```
:0 ic
| cd backup && rm -f dummy `ls -t msg.* | sed -e 1,32d`
```

Let's look at how this recipe works. Firstly, we will see the rule flags and their meanings:

Flag	Meaning
i	Ignore the return code of the subsequent pipeline command
c	Clone or copy the incoming data so that the original data is not affected

The | instructs Procmail to pass the data matched to the following pipeline command. Each of these commands performs a specific action.

Command	Action
cd backup	Moves to the backup directory.
ls -t msg.*	Obtains a list of files beginning with msg and sorts them in to time order.
sed -e 1,32d	Deletes all but the last 32 lines — that is, the 32 most recent mail items.
rm -f dummy...	The parameter dummy is to stop error messages in case there are no files to be deleted, and then the rm command continues to remove the files listed by the sed filter.

These two recipes are examples of unconditional recipes that are run on every incoming mail message. The fact that there are no conditional lines, that is, the lines beginning with an asterisk symbol (*), infers that the recipes are unconditional. As both the recipes include a c flag in the recipe, they are also defined as non-delivering recipes.

Once we have collected a number of Procmail recipes, we will find that the order in which the recipes are processed can be important. By setting the order of processing correctly, we can improve performance and reduce the time taken to process incoming mails. We can also make sure that more critical rules are applied to important messages before the more general rules that are intended to act on bulk messages.

A typical scenario could be to apply rules in the following order:

1. Process daemon or server messages first.

2. Mailing lists should be handled as early as possible, but after the server messages, as we want our services handled first.

3. Apply `kill file` to block any known spammers.

4. Do not send vacation replies before we have handled mailing lists to prevent annoying vacation replies to mailing lists.

5. Save private messages.

6. Check for **Unsolicited Bulk E-Mail (UBE)** — spam. This avoids the high overhead of processing spam checks on known valid e-mail.

Formail

Formail is an external utility program (from Procmail) that is nearly always available on systems where Procmail is installed. Its function is to process mail messages and extract information from within the headers of the messages. It acts as a filter that can be used to force mail into a format suitable for storing in a Linux mail system. It can also perform a number of other useful functions such as 'From' escaping, generating auto-replying headers, simple header extracting, or splitting up a mailbox/digest/ articles file.

The input data mail/mailbox/article contents need to be provided using the standard input. Therefore, `formail` is ideally suited for use in pipeline command chains. Output data is provided on the standard output.

We are not going to go into the subtleties of `formail` in this chapter, but as it is a useful tool, we will make reference to some of its functionality in some of our examples. More information can be obtained from the system manual pages.

Advanced recipe analysis

Here we have a much more complicated recipe that implements a form of vacation service to inform senders that you are away and unable to reply to e-mails. At first thought this could be a simple non-delivering recipe to send a message back to all messages received. However, this is not ideal as some people may end up receiving multiple delivery confirmation messages and you may also end up sending messages back to system utilities that have no way of understanding your well-meant reply.

The example is based on the "vacation example" from the Procmail `procmailex` manual page.

The `vacation.cache` file is maintained by Formail. It maintains a vacation database by extracting the name of the sender and inserting it in the `vacation.cache` file. This ensures that it always contains the most recent names. The size of the file is limited to a maximum of approximately 8192 bytes. If the name of the sender is new, an auto reply will be sent.

The following recipe implements a vacation auto reply:

```
SHELL=/bin/sh # for other shells, this might need adjustment

:0 Whc: vacation.lock
# Perform a quick check to see if the mail was addressed to us
$TO_:.*\<$\LOGNAME\>

# Filter out the mail senders we don't want to send replies to - Ever
* !^FROM_DAEMON

# Make sure that we do not create an endless loop that keeps
# replying to the reply by checking to see if we have already
processed
# this message and inserted a loop detection header
* !^X-Loop: your@own.mail.address
| formail -rD 8192 vacation.cache


:0 ehc
# We are pretty certain it's OK to send a reply to the sender of this
message
|   (
    formail -rA"Precedence: junk" \
    -A"X-Loop: your@own.mail.address" ; \
    echo "Hi, Your message was delivered to my mailbox,"; \
    echo "but I won't be back until Monday."; \
    echo "-- "; cat $HOME/.signature \
    ) | $SENDMAIL -oi -t
```

We will come back to this recipe at the end of this section and work through creating a slightly updated version using some of the things we have learned about Procmail. For now, the example will help as a reference to understand some of the concepts we explore in the following breakdown of a general recipe structure.

Adding comments

Documentation or adding comments to our rules and recipes is always an important task. All comments begin with a # character and continue till the end of the line. In most cases, it is useful to place comments at the beginning of a line or with one or two tabs after a single line that we wish to document.

However, there is one section of the rule file where comments *must* be included on their own lines and that is in the *Conditions* section.

```
# Here is a full line comment
MAILDIR=${HOME}/Maildir              # This comment spans multiple
                                     # lines for clarity.
:0:                                  # Comment OK here
* condition                          # BAD comment. NOT allowed.
# Old versions of Procmail don't understand this.
* condition
{                                    # Comment OK
                                     # Comment OK
   do_something                      # Comment OK
}
```

Assigning variables

In order to keep track of settings, results from tests, default values, and so on, we can store this information in variables. The assignment operation is simple and follows the same format as other Linux scripting languages. The basic format is VARIABLENAME=VALUE.

 There must be no spaces within the variable name. If there are spaces within the value being assigned, the whole of the variable should be stored between double quotes.

The correct way to access a variable is by enclosing the VARIABLENAME within braces {}, and prefixing it all with a dollar ($) sign. It is quite acceptable to use variables within other assignments. Some examples are as follows:

```
MAILDIR=${HOME}/Maildir       # Set the value of the MAILDIR
LOGFILE=${MAILDIR}/log        # Store logfiles in the MAILDIR
```

Notice in the previous example that ${HOME} takes the value of the shell environment setting as it was set when the process was started.

Careful use of variables and their naming can make a recipe much easier to read and also to maintain.

Performing substitutions

Sometimes it will be necessary or useful to be able to replace a literal element with a variable that can be calculated or evaluated only at run time. Procmail allows the author to replace most literal elements with variable substitutions or command substitutions in most places. The simplest way to use a variable is to make use of the `$varname` format, which is common to a number of scripting languages.

Variable/Command	Substitution
`$VAR`	Wherever `$VAR` occurs in the recipe, replace it with the value held by this variable.
`${VAR}iable *`	When we need to concatenate a variable with literal text, use `{ }` to enforce the fact that the name is `${VAR}` and not `$VARiable`.

 If it is necessary to combine variables with fixed text or values, the `{ }` elements allow absolute definition of the variable name to be established. Notice that this will not happen in condition lines unless we include the `$` modifier.

Assigning variable with default values

Procmail borrows some standard shell syntax for variable initialization.

If we wish to be able to assign a default value to a variable to be used in cases where the variable has not been set or could not be calculated for some reason, it is possible to use the `-` or `:-` separator. If we wish to apply an alternative value where the variable has been set or is non null, use the `+` or `:+` separator.

Separator	Action
`${VAR:-value}`	If `VAR` is unset or null, the expansion of `value` is substituted; otherwise, the value of `VAR` is substituted.
`${VAR-value}`	If `VAR` is unset, the expansion of `value` is substituted; otherwise, the value of `VAR` is substituted.
`${VAR:+value}`	If `VAR` is set or non-null, the expansion of `value` is substituted; otherwise, the value of `VAR` is substituted.
`${VAR+value}`	If `VAR` is set, the expansion of `value` is substituted; otherwise, the value of `VAR` is substituted.

Some examples are as follows:

```
VAR = ""                    # Set VAR to null
VAR = ${VAR:-"val1"}   # VAR = "val1"
VAR = ""
VAR = ${VAR-"val2"}    # VAR = ""

VAR = ""
VAR = ${VAR:+"val3"}   # VAR = ""
VAR = ""
VAR = ${VAR+"val4"}    # VAR = "val4"

VAR = "val"
VAR = ${VAR:+"val3"}   # VAR = "val3"
VAR = "val"
VAR = ${VAR+"val4"}    # VAR = "val4"

VAR                         # unset VAR
VAR = ${VAR:-"val1"}   # VAR = "val1"
VAR
VAR = ${VAR-"val2"}    # VAR = "val2"

VAR
VAR = ${VAR:+"val3"}   # no action
VAR
VAR = ${VAR+"val4"}    # no action
```

Assigning command output to variables

It is possible to assign the output of a command to a variable by use of the (back tick) ` operator—the back tick (`) is ASCII value 96 and not a normal apostrophe ('), which has the ASCII value 39.

```
`cmd1 | cmd2`
```

This example will assign the output from the pipeline between the two back ticks to the variable or inline in the code as applicable.

Pseudo-variables

There are a number of special variables or pseudo-variables assigned directly by Procmail. Changing some of these values can actually change the way Procmail operates.

Mailbox variables

The following variables are used by Procmail to determine where it will store any delivered mail.

Name	Action
MAILDIR	The default value for MAILDIR is taken from the value of the $HOME environment variable. It is also the value used for the current working directory for Procmail during execution. Unless the output file names include a path component, they will be created in this default directory.
MSGPREFIX	This option is used when we want files to be written sequentially to a directory. The MSGPREFIX is prefixed to the name of the file created using this option. The default prefix is msg., so the file will be named msg.xyz. The option is not used when delivering to a maildir or an MH directory.
DEFAULT	This is the location of the default mail storage area on our system. Normally we would not modify this variable.
ORGMAIL	This is used as a disaster recovery location for cases where DEFAULT is unavailable for any reason. This should definitely not be modified.

Program variables

Procmail has reasonable defaults written in at the compile time. Mostly these do not need to be changed.

Name	Action
SHELL	This is a standard environment variable that specifies the shell environment within which Procmail needs to invoke sub-processes. The value assigned to it should be Bourne shell-compatible such as /bin/sh.
SHELLFLAGS	This specifies any optional flags that should be passed to the SHELL when starting it.
SENDMAIL	This instructs Procmail where to find the sendmail program used for sending mail on to other users. (Usually not to be fiddled with).
SENDMAILFLAGS	Like SHELLFLAGS, this specifies any flags or command-line arguments that should be passed to the SENDMAIL program when it is executed.

System interaction variables

During the execution of recipes, Procmail may need to run external commands, handle errors, or create files. These variables control how Procmail interacts with the shell.

Name	Action
UMASK	This gives the file permissions mode used when creating any files. See man umask for details.
SHELLMETAS	The shell pipeline is compared with the contents of SHELLMETAS before execution. If any characters from SHELLMETAS are found in the pipeline command, the command is considered too complicated for Procmail to manage itself and a sub-shell process is spawned. If we know that a particular pipeline will always be simple enough for Procmail to manage itself but contains characters held in SHELLMETAS, we can temporarily assign an empty string to SHELLMETAS while processing the pipeline and then restore SHELLMETAS. This will avoid the overhead of spawning a sub-shell.
TRAP	Here we can assign a code segment to be executed at the end of execution of Procmail. A use of it, for example, could be to delete temporary files created during execution of the recipes.
	`TEMPORARY=$HOME/tmp/pmail.$$` `TRAP="/bin/rm -f $TEMPORARY"`
EXITCODE	This value is given back to the process that started Procmail, when Procmail exits. Typically the value of 0 is returned for success and non-zero values indicate some form of failure. By modifying the EXITCODE value, we can return specific information about the processing performed.
	The exit code of a program started by Procmail is stored in the variable $?.

Logging variables

The verbosity and location of any log output required during recipe execution is controlled by the following variables:

Name	Action
LOGFILE	This specifies the location to which Procmail should write all its logging and debugging information. If this value is empty, output is sent to the **standard error output**, which means it will be lost unless the program is running interactively or stderr is redirected somewhere.
LOG	If we wish to write something directly to the log file ourselves, we can assign a value to the LOG variable, and it will be appended to LOGFILE. If we want to format the output and include a blank line after our log message, we must remember to include a blank line in the message that is output. `LOG="Procmail is great"`
VERBOSE	This allows the output to be the basic default or provide detailed information. Setting VERBOSE=1 will include detailed logging information that will aid in debugging our recipes. To reduce the amount of output information, remember to set VERBOSE=0 after the recipe has been run.
LOGABSTRACT	If LOGABSTRACT is set to all, all the deliveries will have information regarding the sender, subject, and size of the mail delivered. If you wish to stop this logging, set LOGABSTRACT=no.
COMSAT	If set to yes, Procmail will generate comsat/biff notifications. For more information, see the comsat and biff manual pages.

Procmail's state variables

During the processing of a recipe, Procmail updates the following variables with the current state of the recipe:

Name	Action
PROCMAIL_OVERFLOW	If Procmail finds any lines in the Procmail recipe file that are longer than the buffer size while reading the file at startup, it will set the value of PROCMAIL_OVERFLOW as yes. If the line being read is a condition or action line, the action will be considered to have failed. However, if it is a variable assignment or recipe start, Procmail will stop reading the file and exit with an abnormal termination.
HOST	This holds the name of the host on which the process is running.

Name	Action
DELIVERED	If the mail message was delivered successfully, this is set to yes and the calling process will be informed by Procmail. If we manually set this to yes *and* the message is not delivered, it will be lost without trace but the calling process will still believe that it was successfully delivered.
LASTFOLDER	This gives the name of the last file or directory to which a message was written.
MATCH	This holds the information extracted by the last regular expression operation.
$=	This holds the result of the latest scoring recipe. See the *procmailsc* manual page for more information.
$1, $2, ...; $@; $#	Just like the standard shell, this specifies the command-line arguments that Procmail was started with. • $1 is the first command-line argument, and so on. • $@ contains all arguments. • $# contains the number of arguments. Also see the SHIFT pseudo-variable.
$$	This holds the current process ID. This can be useful for creating temporary files unique to the process.
$?	This holds the exit code of the previous shell command.
$_	This holds the name of the current Procmail file that is being processed.
$-	This is an alias for LASTFOLDER.
	$= and $@ can't be used directly; we have to assign the value to another variable before it can be used for anything useful.

Message content variables

The main use for these variables is to access data held in the appropriate section but where the recipe has a flag that restricts the processing to the other part of the message. By using HB, we can access information across the whole of the message.

Name	Action
H	This holds the header information for the message being currently processed.
B	This holds the body of the message being currently processed.

Locking variables

Each of the variables in the following table control the names of any lock files and how long the recipe should wait for a lock to become free.

Name	Action
LOCKFILE	Assigning a value to this variable creates a global lock file that remains until LOCKFILE is assigned another value. This value may be either the name of another lock file to create or a null value to remove any lock.
LOCKEXT	Assigning a value to this allows us to override the extension used as part of the lock filename. This can be useful in identifying the process that has created the lock file.
LOCKSLEEP	If Procmail wants to create a lock on a file that is already locked by another process, it will go into a retry loop. The LOCKSLEEP variable specifies the number of seconds to sleep and wait before retrying to obtain the lock.
LOCKTIMEOUT	This specifies an age in seconds that the lock file must be of before it will be assumed that the lock file is invalid and will be overridden. If the value is 0 then the lock file will never be overridden. The default value is 1024 seconds.

Error-handling variables

In the event of an error in our recipe, we can decide what action to take by using any of these variables.

Name	Action
TIMEOUT	This specifies how long to wait for a child before telling the child process to terminate. The default is 960 seconds.
SUSPEND	This specifies how long to wait between NORESRETRY retries. Default is 16 seconds.
NORESRETRY	The number of times Procmail will retry before giving up when a serious system resource shortage occurs, such as out of disk space or the system has reached the maximum number of processes. The default value is 4 and, if the number is negative, Procmail will retry forever. If the resources do not become available during the retry period, the message will be discarded and classified as undeliverable.

Miscellaneous variables

The following table contains information about various Procmail variables that may be of use within our recipes:

Name	Action
LINEBUF	This sets a limit for the length of recipe lines that Procmail is ready to cope with. If we need to process very large regular expressions or store lots of data into MATCH, increase this value.
SHIFT	This is similar to the shift feature in normal shell processing. Assigning a positive number to this variable moves down Procmail's command-line arguments.
INCLUDERC	This instructs Procmail to load another file containing Procmail recipes. This new file is loaded and processed before Procmail continues processing the current file.
DROPPRIVS	This ensures that no root privileges are available when Procmail is executing as setuid or setgid. Setting this value to yes will make Procmail drop all its special privileges.

Printing Procmail variables

The following example will print most of the environment settings in response and will provide some information that could be helpful while trying to debug problems with Procmail. It is not expected that this is included in any production files, otherwise our log file could grow to be extremely large very quickly.

Create a file called rc.dump in the same directory as the other Procmail recipe files and place the following lines in the file:

 Please note that the quotes (") that appear at the start and end of the next example are required to ensure that the recipe operates correctly.

```
#
#  Simple Procmail recipe to dump variables to a log file
#
LOG="Dump of ProcMail Variables
MAILDIR is currently :${MAILDIR}:
MSGPREFIX is currently :${MSGPREFIX}:
DEFAULT is currently :${DEFAULT}:
ORGMAIL is currently :${ORGMAIL}:
SHELL is currently :${SHELL}:
```

```
SHELLFLAGS is currently :${SHELLFLAGS}:
SENDMAIL is currently :${SENDMAIL}:
SENDMAILFLAGS is currently :${SENDMAILFLAGS}:
UMASK is currently :${UMASK}:
SHELLMETAS is currently :${SHELLMETAS}:
TRAP is currently :${TRAP}:
EXITCODE is currently :${EXITCODE}:
LOGFILE is currently :${LOGFILE}:
LOG is currently :${LOG}:
VERBOSE is currently :${VERBOSE}:
LOGABSTRACT is currently :${LOGABSTRACT}:
COMSAT is currently :${COMSAT}:
PROCMAIL_OVERFLOW is currently :${PROCMAIL_OVERFLOW}:
TODO is currently :${TODO}:
HOST is currently :${HOST}:
DELIVERED is currently :${DELIVERED}:
LASTFOLDER is currently :${LASTFOLDER}:
\$= is currently :$=:
\$1 is currently :$1:
\$2 is currently :$2:
\$$ is currently :$$:
\$? is currently :$?:
\$_ is currently :$_:
\$- is currently :$-:
LOCKFILE is currently :${LOCKFILE}:
LOCKEXT is currently :${LOCKEXT}:
LOCKSLEEP is currently :${LOCKSLEEP}:
LOCKTIMEOUT is currently :${LOCKTIMEOUT}:
TIMEOUT is currently :${TIMEOUT}:
NORESRETRY is currently :${NORESRETRY}:
SUSPEND is currently :${SUSPEND}:"
```

Run the following command:

```
# procmail ./rc.dump
```

<CTRL-D>

This will create the following output:

```
# procmail ./rc.dump
<CTRL-D>
"Dump of ProcMail Variables
MAILDIR is currently :.:
MSGPREFIX is currently :msg.:
DEFAULT is currently :/var/spool/mail/root:
ORGMAIL is currently :/var/spool/mail/root:
SHELL is currently :/bin/bash:
SHELLFLAGS is currently :-c:
SENDMAIL is currently :/usr/sbin/sendmail:
SENDMAILFLAGS is currently :-oi:
UMASK is currently ::
SHELLMETAS is currently :&|<>~;?*[:
TRAP is currently ::
EXITCODE is currently ::
LOGFILE is currently ::
LOG is currently ::
VERBOSE is currently :1:
LOGABSTRACT is currently ::
COMSAT is currently :no:
PROCMAIL_OVERFLOW is currently ::
TODO is currently ::
HOST is currently :delta.adepteo.net:
DELIVERED is currently ::
LASTFOLDER is currently ::
$= is currently :0:
$1 is currently ::
$2 is currently ::
$$ is currently :9014:
$? is currently :0:
$_ is currently :./rc.dump:
$- is currently ::
LOCKFILE is currently ::
LOCKEXT is currently :.lock:
LOCKSLEEP is currently ::
LOCKTIMEOUT is currently ::
TIMEOUT is currently ::
NORESRETRY is currently ::
SUSPEND is currently ::
```

Recipes

Procmail recipes follow a simple format. However, there are a number of ways that Procmail can be instructed to interpret or implement the instructions in the rules based on a number of flags and the way that the rules and recipes are written.

Colon line

As we have already discovered, all rules so far have started with a `:0` followed by one or more flags and instructions. Historically a number followed the colon (`:`) to specify the number of conditions that were present in the rule. Current versions of Procmail determine the number of conditions automatically, and hence the value `0` is always used.

Locking

We have already discussed that we need to use a locking mechanism in order to stop more than one process trying to write to the same file at the same time. Of course this requirement varies with the type of process that the filter is attempting to invoke. For example, a filter that merely changes or assigns a value has no affect on any physical file and so no locking is required. Similarly, a filter that merely forwards the data on to another process or another recipient inherently does not need a lock to be applied. In most cases, automatic locking will be applied when Procmail realizes that it is writing to a file and will provide locking of the file itself. In some cases, it may be necessary to explicitly lock a resource.

To give some insight into when locking is applied automatically, not required at all, or requires manual locking to be enforced, here are some examples.

Automatic locking

Any rule that begins with `:0:` will apply automatic file locking. In this case, Procmail will automatically determine the name of the file that the mail is being delivered to and create a lock file. If the lock file already exists, it will wait for a period of time and retry to create the lock. When it finally creates the lock file, it will continue with processing. If it is unable to create the lock file, it will report an error and continue with the next rule.

The following rule uses automatic locking:

```
:0 <flags>:
```

Enforced locking

There may be a time, especially when processing mail by an external script, where enforced locking is required. In most cases, Procmail will determine the name of the file that the ultimate data is being written to by examining the process command line and looking where output is directed to. However, if the script takes care of choosing the output location itself, or if it relies on a file that may be altered by another Procmail process, a lock file must be specifically requested as follows:

```
:0 <flags> :scriptname.lock
```

You are unlikely to need to enforce locking in most of the scripts you write.

No locking

When forwarding to a pipeline that performs its own file or record-locking processes, such as storing a problem report in a database, no record locking is required. Similarly if the message is being forwarded to another user, the final delivery will take care of the record locking. The simple rule definition is:

```
:0 <flags>
```

Flags

In the examples we have looked at so far, we have allowed the default settings of Procmail to take effect. However, there are a number of flags that may be set to control how Procmail works.

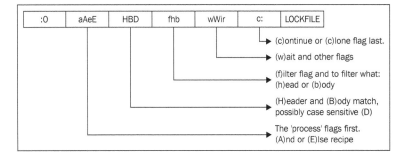

Default flags

If no flags are stated on the colon line of the recipe, Procmail will assume that the following flags (H, hb) have been used as default values.

Flag	Action
H	Only mail headers are scanned.
hb	Action line is passed both, headers and body of the mail data.

Scope of matching: HB

Normally, matching will take place across the whole of the mail package including both, the headers and the body of the mail. If the mail body could potentially be large and we know that we require the matches to be made against just the headers, it would be sensible to use the H flag to restrict the scope of the matching action to be across the headers only.

Conversely, it may sometimes be that we are looking for items of information, perhaps a repeated footer or signature that appears only in the body of the document, in which case we can use the B flag to restrict matching to the body only.

Flag	Action
H	Performs matching only across the mail headers.
B	Performs matching only across the mail body.
HB	Performs matching across the whole of the mail item including headers and body.

Scope of action: hb

By default, the action line processes the whole e-mail item including the headers and body. If it is required to process only one part of the mail data, it is possible to specify which part is passed to the action line.

Flag	Action
h	Pass only the headers to the action line for processing.
b	Pass only the body of the message to the action line for processing.
hb	Pass both, the headers and the message body, for processing. This is the default scope.

It is important to notice the difference between "scope of matching" and "scope of action". The value of the flag in the first case determines which part of the mail — header, body, or the entire mail — has to be scanned for matching. The value of the flag in the second case determines which part of the mail needs to be processed.

Flow control: aAeEc

This is probably the most complex set of flags to understand of all the Procmail flags. Examples later in the chapter will explain various ways of using these flags. Briefly the following may be assumed about each of the flags:

Flag	Action
A	The recipe will be processed only if the conditions of the previous recipe were met.
a	The recipe will be processed if the previous recipe's conditions were met and the operation was completed without error.
E	This is the opposite of A. The recipe will be processed if the previous recipe conditions were not met.
e	The recipe will be processed if the previous recipe conditions were met but the processing did not complete successfully.
c	This instructs the recipe to create a copy or clone of the original message and process this copy with any actions in a subprocess. The parent process continues processing the original copy of the message.

The c flag should be read as Clone or Copy. It is a common misconception that this flag should be interpreted as Continue. The Clone or Copy operation creates a separate copy of the data and a separate flow of execution is created to process that data, sometimes as a totally separate child process. When this clone recipe is complete, the parent continues execution with the original data intact.

Case sensitivity: D

Diehard Linux users are very much aware of case sensitivity and always view Capitals as being entirely different to capitals. However, the default operation of Procmail is to be case insensitive when matching strings. This means, for Procmail Capitals and capitals are identical, unless it is told that case sensitivity should be applied by means of the D flag.

Execution mode: fwWir

We can instruct Procmail how to process or execute the recipe and what actions to take if errors are encountered during the processing. Errors might not occur for smaller mail messages when the processing takes place only on the first few lines of data. However, for larger messages, the Linux shell may believe there is an error when the pipeline has read only a part of the available data.

The **Filtering Mode** of execution is important to understand. This terminology could be confusing as all that Procmail is designed to do is to filter mail. Think of the execution mode "filter" in the following way: The mail message we are processing would be piped through whatever is on the action line before it is actually piped on to Procmail (or at least the rest of our recipe). Another way of viewing the filter mode is as a conversion mode where the data is modified in some way and returned back to the controlling Procmail recipe for further execution.

Flag	Action
f	Pass the message contents through the recipe to an external pipeline process for processing and then take the output of the process line ready to replace the original message contents.
i	If a Linux pipeline process reads only part of its input and then terminates, the shell will send a SIGPIPE error signal to the Procmail program—the i flag instructs Procmail to ignore this signal. This should be used where it is expected that the pipeline process will return after processing only a part of the message.
r	The data passed to the pipeline process should be passed just as it is without any modifications.
w	By default, the Procmail process will spawn off a subprocess and continue its own processing. The w flag instructs Procmail to wait for the subprocess pipeline to complete before continuing with its own processing.
W	This works the same as w, but also hides any error or other output messages from the pipeline process.

Conditions

There are a number of condition types that could be applied to decide if a given recipe applies to a particular mail item. The idea of applying conditions correctly is to reduce the amount of unnecessary processing that is performed.

Condition lines always begin with an asterisk (*) character followed by one or more spaces. It is possible to apply multiple condition lines within a recipe, but they must all be grouped together on consecutive lines. The logical operation of the grouping is to perform an AND operation such that all the conditions must be applied before the action is executed.

```
:0
* condition1
* condition2
action_on_condition1_and_condition2
```

Applying a rule unconditionally

It may be required that a rule has to be applied to all messages regardless of any conditions. Such a rule could, for example, make a backup copy of the mail message to a mail folder or archive all mail for legal or corporate policy reasons.

The unconditional rule is implied by the lack of a conditional line. That is, the rule will always match.

```
# Save all remaining messages to DEFAULT
:0:
${DEFAULT}/
```

The unconditional rule is often used at the end of a nested chain of recipes to perform a final default action if the recipe has not delivered the mail. Remember that processing stops once a message has been delivered.

Tests with regular expressions

Those of us that are familiar with simple pattern-matching operations such as ? or * used commonly in matching of files in a file listing operation, may wonder if it is possible to create similar tests to match parts of a mail header or body. The good news is that there is an excellent feature known as **regular expressions** or **regex** for short. These provide a mechanism for very complex pattern-matching operations to be performed. In general, this feature matches very closely with the egrep command-line regular expressions. However, there are some important differences that experienced regex users should definitely be aware of, in order to understand how to write expressions tailored for Procmail operation. There is a complete section on writing regex later in this chapter.

Regular expressions may be run against the data portion of the mail message (header, body, or both) as defined by the flags or may be used to test a previously assigned variable.

Condition	Action
* regex	Tests the part of the message passed according to the flags against the regular expression. Normally this will process just the headers unless a B flag is given to indicate that the scope of matching was to process the body of the message.
* variable ?? regex	This is to compare the assigned variable against the regex for comparison.

Various pseudo-variables were listed earlier in the chapter and represent ways to access information that is contained within the Procmail application. These pseudo-variables can be compared in the same way as normal variables.

The following example will make a copy of all the mail items that contain a key phrase in the message body.

```
VERBOSE=1
:0cB:
* [0-9]+ Linux Rules [ok!]
${MAILDIR}/linuxrules/
VERBOSE=0
```

The following is a quick explanation of the operation of the previous example:

- We specify `:0cB:` to make sure that we search only through the body, and to make a copy so we still get the original message processed.

- If anywhere in the body there is a phrase that has one or more numbers followed by a `<SPACE>Linux Rules<SPACE>` followed by either o, k, or !, then a copy will be stored in the `linuxrules` folder.

Setting and unsetting the VERBOSE option before a rule is processed allows just that rule to be displayed in the log in more detail, which means less log file to search through while debugging.

Testing the size of a message part

In some cases, we may not want large messages to be processed by a recipe. In this situation, we can set a limit that the recipe will not match messages over a certain size. If we have users that use a slow data connection, perhaps using connectivity over a mobile phone connection, it can be useful to move all large items of mail into a separate folder for retrieval when the users are back at a better Internet connection.

Condition	Action
`* > number`	Will return `true` if the message size is larger than the given number of bytes.
`* < number`	Will return `true` if the message size is smaller than the given number of bytes.

Testing the exit code of an external program

If an external program is run to provide a part of the processing, the exit code may need to be checked to make sure that the process completed correctly or to perform a secondary operation to complete the overall processing.

```
? /unix/command/line | another/command
```

The ? instructs Procmail to pass the current message data to the Linux command line as standard input. The condition is successfully met if the command line exits with a zero exit code. While the command line is a pipeline of several processes, the exit code returned is that of the last program in the pipeline.

Any output printed to standard error by the pipeline is displayed in the log.

In this example, the body of the message is passed to the command pipeline and, if the phrase is found in exactly the third line (exit code 0), the message is filed in the folder.

The action of lines between the VERBOSE=1 and the VERBOSE=0 will be logged, but all lines outside this range will not be logged. This allows us to control the amount of logging taking place, and hence makes it easier to follow the log file activity.

```
VERBOSE=1
:0B:
* ? /bin/sed -n 3p | /bin/egrep "Linux Rules"
${MAILDIR}/linuxrules/
VERBOSE=0
```

Negation

Sometimes it is useful to be able to check if a particular condition does not exist in order to continue processing in a certain way. The **Exclamation** (!), or **Bang** as it is sometimes referred to, is used to reverse the value of the condition so that false becomes true and vice versa.

```
* ! condition
```

This tests for a negative result in the condition and returns true if the condition is not met.

Here we are looking for any item that was not sent directly to us and will be stored in a folder for later viewing.

```
:0:
* !^TO.*cjtaylor
${MAILDIR}/not_sent_to_me/
```

Variable substitution in conditions

Multiple $ flags may be used to force multiple substitution passes to be applied.

```
* $ condition
```

The $ instructs Procmail to process the condition with the normal sh rules to perform variable and back tick substitution before actually evaluating the condition. The substitution process will resolve variables ($VAR) into their values rather than processing them as literals. Any quoted strings will have their quotes removed and all other shell meta characters will also be evaluated. To have any of these characters passed through this substitution process, they should be escaped using the standard backslash (\) escape mechanism.

The following example is taken from the *procmailex* manual page, and even there it is described as being rather exotic, but it does serve as an example. Suppose you have a file in your home directory called .urgent, and the (one) person named in that file is the sender of an incoming mail. You would like that mail to be stored in $MAILDIR/urgent instead of in any of the normal mail folders it would have been sorted in. Then this is what you could do (beware, the file length of $HOME/.urgent should be well below $LINEBUF; increase LINEBUF if necessary):

```
URGMATCH=`cat $HOME/.urgent`

:0:
* $^From.*${URGMATCH}
$MAILDIR/urgent/
```

Action line

This is the line that does all of the processing activity. In most cases, this will mean writing to a physical file or folder. But it can also include forwarding mail to other users, passing data to a command or pipeline of commands or, in some cases, a number of successive actions to be performed as part of a compound recipe. If you want to perform more than one action, you can't just stack them one after the other — you need multiple recipes (possibly unconditional, and/or grouped in a pair of braces) and a colon line (and optionally conditions, of course) for each.

Also note that flags that affect the action line are not actually taking effect until the action is actually attempted. In particular, a c flag doesn't generate a clone of the message until its conditions have all been met.

Forwarding to other addresses

Global forwarding of all messages for a user account to another user account is a process that can be handled much more efficiently by Postfix itself. However, if some logic needs to be applied to decide what or where to send the message, then Procmail can assist.

Most mail transports will allow us to pass multiple e-mail addresses for onward transmission.

```
! user1@domain2.net user2@domain1.com user3 ...
```

The above action is functionally the same as passing the message to the following pipeline:

```
| $SENDMAIL "$SENDMAILFLAGS"
```

This is a special case for forwarding mail and instructs Procmail to extract the list of recipients from the original message's actual headers:

```
! -t
```

Here we will forward mail to our support team rather than handle it ourselves. The mail includes the phrase **support** in the subject line.

```
:0:
* ^Subject.*support
! support@adepteo.net
```

Feeding to a shell or command pipeline

Procmail allows a virtually unlimited amount of freedom in what can be done to an e-mail. One of the more powerful features of working with Procmail is its ability to forward an e-mail based on given criteria to an application program or script. A possible example would be to track support requests and have the entries stored directly into a database system where they can be tracked within a dedicated application.

The pipeline process is responsible for saving its output. The recipe's flags are able to tell Procmail to expect something else. By using the >> syntax, Procmail can determine a lock file to use. It is important to always use locking when writing to a file so as to avoid two operations writing to the same file at the same time and corrupting each other's data.

```
| cmd1 param1 | cmd2 -opt param2 >>file
```

It is possible to have the output of the command pipeline stored in a variable. This, by its own action, makes the recipe a non-delivering recipe.

```
VAR=| cmd1 | cmd2 ...
```

Please note that this syntax is allowed only on the action line. For the same result in a plain assignment, we could use back tick (`) operator.

```
VERBOSE=1
#Copy the data and pass the headers to the process
:0hc:
* ^Subject: Book Pipeline Example
#Copy so that the next recipe will still work
| cat - > /tmp/cjt_header.txt

#Final recipe so do not copy here, but pass the body
:0b:
| cat - > /tmp/cjt_body.txt

VERBOSE=0
```

Saving to a folder

This saves the output to a plain file. If only a filename is provided, the file will be created in the directory specified in the MAILDIR setting. Always make sure that you use some form of locking when writing to a plain file.

```
/path/to/filename
```

When saving to a directory, files will be created with sequentially numbered files within the directory.

Using a trailing (/) slash at the end of the path name instructs Procmail to store the item in a maildir formatted folder. The subfolders, cur, new, and tmp are created automatically.

```
directory/
```

Using /. at the end of the path name instructs Procmail to store the item in an MH formatted folder.

```
directory/.
```

If we want to store the data into several MH or maildir folders, we can list them all at the same time. The result will be that only one file will actually be written, the rest will be created as hard links.

Compound recipes

If we want to perform a number of conditional processes or actions on a matched item, then instead of a single action line we can specify a block of recipes to be used using the { and } characters. There must be at least one space after the { and before the } characters.

```
{

  # ... more recipes

}
```

The code between the braces can be any valid Procmail construct.

> Note that an action that is a variable assignment always has to go inside a set of braces: { VAR=value }. Using just VAR=value without the braces would result in the data being saved to a folder named VAR=value.

If we want a recipe that does not actually do any processing, perhaps as part of an if...else operation, we can use an empty set of { }, but the rules regarding the whitespace still apply and we need to ensure that there is at least one whitespace character between the two braces.

The following example takes the previous example and modifies it slightly so that only one test is performed and then a series of unconditional tests are run if the test passes:

```
VERBOSE=1
:0:
* ^Subject: Book Pipeline Example
  {
    #Copy so that the next recipe will still work
    :0hc:
    | cat - > /tmp/cjt_header.txt

    #Final recipe so do not copy here
    :0b:
    | cat - > /tmp/cjt_body.txt
  }
VERBOSE=0
```

Regular expressions

Procmail implements a form of regular expressions that operates slightly differently than other UNIX utilities. Here we cover the basic differences and guide the new user into the powerful world of regular expressions, their meanings, implementations, and uses.

We have already seen that Procmail matches are case insensitive unless the D flag is used. This is also true for regular expressions. Procmail also uses multiline matches by default.

Introduction to regular expressions

New users to the world of Linux and programming in general, may not be aware of the powerful features that regular expressions bring to processing data. In its simplest form, regular expressions can be understood as searching for a phrase or pattern anywhere in a body of data. The following simple example shows how we can match all mail items where the header and/or body contains the phrase mystical monsters and place the mail in a relevant folder.

```
:0 HB:
* mystical monsters
${MAILDIR}/monsters/
```

However, this filter would not match items that contained the phrase mystical monster or mystical-monsters, for example. So, the real power of regular expressions can be seen in the ability to describe text or data patterns in a simplified format and then search for matches to those patterns in a body of data. However, you should be careful not to be misled by the word *simplified*. The majority of regular expressions that you will come across in real life may well be anything but simple to read if written in the native format. Take the following example, which is intended to determine if a mail item is MIME encoded and store it in a suitable folder if it is:

```
:0:
* ^Content-Type: multipart/[^;]+;[ ]*boundary="?\/[^"]+
${MAILDIR}/mime/
```

The characters ., [, ^, ;,], +, ?, \, /, and " are special instructions rather than the literal ASCII character they normally portray. To understand these characters and their meanings, we will take a whirlwind tour through the most important examples.

The dot

This is the simplest and most common form of regular expression and simply means match any single character, (excluding a newline character, which is considered a special case). Consider the following expression:

```
:0
* Dragons ... mystical monsters
${MAILDIR}/result/
```

This would match any of the following phrases:

```
Dragons are mystical monsters
Dragons and mystical monsters
Dragons but mystical monsters
```

In fact, it will match any phrase with a three-character word between `Dragons` and `mystical`. If we wanted to match any length of word with three or more characters between `Dragons` and `mystical`, we could use the `?` or quantifier operation.

In case we want to match a literal '.' or more than one '.', we can escape any character that has special significance to a regular expression string by preceding it by a backslash '\' so that '\.' will literally match a '.' (period) and '\\' will literally match a '\' (backslash) character.

Quantifier operation

The question mark indicates that the preceding character should be matched zero times or one time only. So, the following lines of code will meet our requirements:

```
:0
* Dragons ....? Mystical monsters
${MAILDIR}/result/
```

This expression could be read as, "Match any word consisting of three or more characters followed by nothing or any one character".

The character preceding the `?` may also be a simple ASCII character in which case the expression would match as follows:

```
:0
* Dragons ..d? Mystical monsters
${MAILDIR}/result/
```

This could be read as, "Any two characters followed by either nothing or a letter `d`." Therefore this would match both `an` and `and` but not `are`.

The asterisk

The asterisk modifier works in a way similar to the quantifier operator, but means match zero or more of the preceding character except, of course, a newline. The .* is a very common sequence that you will find in a large number of recipes.

The following example will match all the messages that include the word choose followed by some other words followed by the word online:

```
:0
* ^Subject: Choose.*online
${MAILDIR}/result/
```

```
Subject: Choose discount pharmacy and expedite the service online.
Subject: Choose hassle free online shopping
Subject: Choose reliable online shopping site for reliable service and
quality meds
Subject: Choose reliable service provider and save more online.
Subject: Choose the supplier for more hot offers online
Subject: Choose to shop online and choose to save
```

The next example will look for "anything" (.*) followed by two or more exclamation marks (!!) and (!*):

```
:0
* ^Subject: .*!!!*
${MAILDIR}/result/
```

```
Subject: Breathtaking New Year sale on now!!! Get ready for it!!
Subject: Hey Ya!! New Year Sale on right now!!
Subject: It Doesn't Matter!!
```

The plus sign

The plus sign is very similar to the * except that it requires that there must be at least one instance of the character preceding the + in the regular expression.

If we consider our previous example, the next example will look for "anything" .* followed by two !! and at least one more (!+) exclamation marks.

```
:0
* ^Subject: .*!!!+
${MAILDIR}/result/
```

This would now give us a more restricted output where at least three ! in a row would be required.

```
Subject: Breathtaking New Year sale on now!!! Get ready for it!!
```

Restrictive matches using parentheses

So far, the matching patterns that we have been able to create are powerful but work in a rather unfocused way. For example, we can easily write a rule to find any three-letter word ending in t but cannot limit the matches to only a given set of words ending in t. To overcome this, we can replace the . or single character with a group of characters or sets of groups of characters in a list and then apply the quantifier operations to say exactly how many times these can be applied.

By careful use of the parentheses ( ), we can create groups of strings that we will use in the pattern matching rules. For instance, let us assume we are trying to split e-mails that are sent by a system script on a frequent basis. The script formats the subject line to have one of the following phrases in the subject line.

```
There is only one problem

There are 10 problems
```

The following regular expression will match the specific string we are looking for by matching any string that has one or more occurrences of the phrase is only one between there and problem.

```
There (is only one)+ problem
```

If we wanted to filter a list of words or phrases, we would need to use the **Alternation** feature.

```
There (is only one|are)+ problem
```

The | character separates lists of words that could be used to match against the pattern.

The following simple spam filter uses the alternation feature to search for text substitutions regularly used in a bid to avoid the simple word-based filters.

Creating a simple spam filter

With the growing number of spam messages that we receive every day, I am sure that some of you reading so far will have figured out that we could start to filter some of the regular messages that we receive on a daily basis. There are a number of specific spam filters that are designed to work closely with Procmail and offer a far larger set of tests and coverage for spam filtering. One such application, SpamAssassin, is covered in Chapter 8.

Take for example online casinos—a popular subject for spammers who encourage us to explore them. It is something that we are not usually interested in, and so we feel happy to filter all messages that contain the words "Online" and "Casinos" into a separate folder.

```
Subject: Online Casino
```

Part of the challenge for spammers is to write subject lines that we can read while spam filters find difficult to process. A simple way of doing this is to substitute commonly mistyped characters such as Zero (0) for letter O or letter o, 1 for L or l, and 4 for A or a.

So we could progress and write the rule as:

```
Subject: (o|0)n(1|l)ine casin(o|0)
```

The final iteration of this recipe is shown next where we are specifically looking for subject lines that contain both the words "online" and "casino" but to include the occasions where the word may be in different order each word is tested separately.

```
:0
* ^Subject: (o|0)n(1|l)ine
* ^Subject: casin(o|0)
${MAILDIR}/_maybespam/
```

While this would work quite well, it is not really efficient to have rules that work in this way and, as this sort of substitution is a common requirement for regular expressions, there is a special way of expressing these terms in the **Character classes**.

Character classes

Any sequence of characters contained in square brackets [ ] indicates that the listed characters are each to be checked in the expression. For common occurrences of sequences of characters such as the letters of the alphabet or a range of numbers, it is possible to use [a-z] or [0-9]:

- [a-e] means match all the letters a, b, c, d, e inclusive.
- [1,3,5-9] means match any of the numbers 1, 3, 5, 6, 7, 8, or 9.

The following example will find messages that embed numbers 0 and 1 within text strings so that they look like O and L or I.

```
:0
* ^Subject: [a-z]*[01]+[a-z]*
${MAILDIR}/_maybespam

Subject: Hot Shot St0ckInfo VCSC loadstone
Subject: M1CR0S0FT, SYMANNTEC, MACR0MEDIA, PC GAMES FROM $20 EACH
Subject: R0LEX Replica - make your first impressions count!
Subject: Small-Cap DT0I St0cks reimburse
Subject: TimelySt0ck DT0I Buy of the Week evasive
```

Start of line

If we want to match all of a wide range of characters and not match a small number of ranges, it is easier to specify the negative match using the ^ character.

```
[^0-9]
```

This means to match any string that begins with anything that is not a number between 0 and 9.

It is useful to add a start of line anchor to patterns we are searching for when we know that the pattern should start the line. For example, all headers must start on the beginning of the line, so searching for the following phrase:

```
Subject: any subject message
```

would also match headers that begin with a phrase such as:

```
Old-Subject:
```

To stop this, we can add the **Start of Line Anchor character** (^) and change the regular expression to:

```
^Subject: any subject message
```

End of Line

When we are planning to match strings that we know we should terminate, we can add the **End of Line Anchor character**, $, to the pattern to ensure that we match right to the end of the string as follows:

```
^Subject:.* now$
```

This will match any subject line that ends in the word now.

Further reading

Regular expressions are an enormous subject, but well worth learning as they are used by a large number of Linux tools and applications. There are many online resources related to regular expressions. Here are a few links to get started:

- `http://www.regular-expressions.info/`
- `http://en.wikipedia.org/wiki/Regular_expression`

As we briefly covered in the previous chapter, Procmail has a number of useful "pre-prepared" regular expressions or macros that provide a range of matches that are commonly used in Procmail recipes.

^TO and ^TO_

`^TO` was the original Procmail macro for handling "To" addresses. This has been superseded by the newer `^TO_` macro that was introduced in Procmail version 3.11pre4.

This catchall includes most headers that can include your address in them, such as `To:`, `Apparently-To:`, `Cc:`, `Resent-To:`, and so on.

In most cases, you should use the `^TO_` option as it has much better coverage.

 Although it would seem logical to have a similar macro to cover the source address details, note that there is *no* corresponding `^FROM` or `^FROM_` macro.

Here is the regular expression string from the Procmail source code:

```
"(^((Original-)?(Resent-)?(To|Cc|Bcc)|\
(X-Envelope|Apparently(-Resent)?)-To):(.*[^-a-zA-Z0-9_.])?)"
```

^FROM_MAILER

This macro recognizes a wide range of mail generation programs and is a useful catchall. However, new programs are being created all the time, so additional filters will nearly always be required.

Procmail expands this short macro into the following regular expression as taken from the Procmail source code.

```
"(^(Mailing-List:|Precedence:.*(junk|bulk|list)|\
To: Multiple recipients of |\
(((Resent-)?(From|Sender)|X-Envelope-From):|>?From )([^>]*[^(.%@a-z0-
9])?(\
Post(ma?(st(e?r)?|n)|office)|(send)?Mail(er)?|daemon|m(mdf|ajordomo)|
n?uucp|\
LIST(SERV|proc)|NETSERV|o(wner|ps)|r(e(quest|sponse)|oot)|b(ounce|bs\
\.smtp)|\
echo|mirror|s(erv(ices?|er)|mtp(error)?|ystem)|\
A(dmin(istrator)?|MMGR|utoanswer)\
)(([^).!:a-z0-9][-_a-z0-9]*)?[%@>      ][^<)]*(\\(.*\\).*)?)?$([^>]|$))
)"
```

^FROM_DAEMON

This takes a similar approach to the ^FROM_MAILER but is intended to identify messages from the more common Linux daemons and system processes.

Regular expression string from Procmail source code is given as:

```
"(^(((Resent-)?(From|Sender)|X-Envelope-From):|\
>?From )([^>]*[^(.%@a-z0-9])?(\
Post(ma(st(er)?|n)|office)|(send)?Mail(er)?|daemon|mmdf|n?uucp|ops|\
r(esponse|oot)|(bbs\\
.)?smtp(error)?|s(erv(ices?|er)|ystem)|A(dmin(istrator)?|\
MMGR)\
)(([^).!:a-z0-9][-_a-z0-9]*)?[%@>      ][^<)]*(\\(.*\\).*)?)?$([^>]|$))
"
```

The following example will store the daemon messages received in a folder that includes the year and month as part of the path. These variables ${YY} and ${MM} are assigned previously in the Procmail file and the necessary directories are also created.

```
:0:
* ^FROM_DAEMON
${YY}/${MM}/daemon
```

Advanced recipes

Here we are going to assemble the various items of Procmail capability into a few useful recipes that we can use as the basis for tools within our own organization. The first example is based on the traditional Vacation recipe that informs senders of the e-mail that may not be read by the recipient for some time. The second shows how to create the support to automatically file messages based on the date and the possible time of being processed. Finally, we will complete the rule started in the previous chapter to inform the user of large mail items that have been filtered into a separate folder.

Creating a vacation auto reply

This example is based upon the vacation example given in man procmailex and referred to briefly earlier in this chapter.

As we have already discussed, blindly and automatically responding to an e-mail is a very bad idea and has significant ramifications. First we must decide whether to send an auto reply. To do this, we need to make sure that conditions make sense and are satisfied. If so, headers (signified by the h flag) of the current message are fed to formail, a utility program that is part of the Procmail suite of utilities. formail then checks the vacation.cache file to find out if the sender has already received an auto reply. This is to make sure we are not sending multiple reports to a user. While this part of the processing is going on, our recipe will create a lock as vacation.lock.

The main reason for this is to avoid clashes when updating the cache, which could result in corruption of the cache information.

The recipe actually comprises two individual recipes. The first one provides the checks and recording of replies sent to ensure that we don't send duplicate or repetitive replies.

This recipe w, waits for a return from formail. Without the c, Procmail would stop processing after completing this recipe because it is a delivery recipe. It delivers headers to formail.

There is more to the TO_ and ^FROM_DAEMON conditions than what meets the eye.

TO_ $<logname> is satisfied if the user's login name appears in any recipient header **To:**, **Cc:**, **Bcc:**. This avoids sending auto replies to messages that were addressed to an alias or mail list, but not explicitly to our user.

!^FROM_DAEMON makes sure we do not auto reply to messages from any of the wide variety of daemons.

!^X-Loop: $RECIPIENT avoids replying to our own auto reply; notice that this X-Loop header is inserted into the auto replies we send out.

```
:0 Whc: vacation.lock
# Perform a quick check to see if the mail was addressed to us
* $^To_:.*\<$\LOGNAME\>
# Don't reply to daemons and mailinglists
* !^FROM_DAEMON
# Mail loops are evil
* !^X-Loop: $RECIPIENT
| formail -rD 8192 vacation.cache
```

The second part of the recipe takes place if the first one did not find a match in the cache. There are two reasons that the address may not have been found—either it has never been seen and so no reply has been sent, or it was seen so long ago that the entry has been forced out of the cache. In either case, a copy of the vacation message will be sent. The sender will never receive an automatic reply for every single message that they send—something that can really upset a prolific mail writer.

```
:0 ehc
# if the name was not in the cache
| (
    formail -rA"Precedence: junk" \
    -A"X-Loop: $RECIPIENT" ; \
    cat $HOME/.vacation_message \
    ) | $SENDMAIL -oi -t
```

Due to e, the previous recipe is executed if the preceding one returns an error status. In this case, it is not really an error, it is just the signal from formail that the address didn't exist in the cache file and we can go ahead with the auto reply. Notice that if in the preceding recipe the conditions are not met causing the formail cache check to be skipped, Procmail is clever enough to skip this recipe.

The headers of the current message are fed to the formail in this recipe, in order to construct the headers for the auto reply.

The c in this recipe causes the entire current message to be processed after this recipe. Typically, this means that it will be processed with no further recipes and that is how we get a copy in our mailbox. There is no need for a lock while executing this recipe, so none is used.

All that is required to send back to the sender of the original message is a copy of the message, and that is held in the file .vacation_message in the user's home directory.

Storing the message information outside the Procmail recipe makes it easy to allow your system users to easily update the message that they send out without risk of them breaking the actual recipe itself.

Organizing mail by date

You may not want to delete mail that you feel may be useful one day. This can easily lead to gigabytes of data being stored in a variety of locations. It is possible to filter some or all of our incoming mails into folders based on a combination of the year, month, and topic so that they can be tracked down easily.

A generic rule that is applied to every mail process ensures that the necessary directory structure exists.

```
#Assign the name of the folder by extracting the year and month
# parts from the external date command.
          MONTHFOLDER=`date +%y/%m`

#Unconditional rule to create the folder. Using the test
#command. we create the monthly folder if it does not exist.
          :0 ic
          * ? test ! -d ${MONTHFOLDER}
          | mkdir -p ${MONTHFOLDER}

#Alternative way of creating the folder using an assignment operation
          DUMMY=`test -d $MONTHFOLDER || mkdir $MONTHFOLDER`

#Now store any email matching 'meeting' in an appropriate folder
          :0:
          * meeting
          ${MONTHFOLDER}/meeting/
```

If you would prefer slightly more control over the output format or location, you may use these rules instead:

```
#This obtains the date formatted as YYYY MM DD, e.g. 2009 09 08
          date = `date "+%Y %m %d"`
#Now assign the Year YYYY style
          :0
          * date ?? ^^()\/
          { YYYY = $MATCH }
```

```
#Now assign the Year YY style
      :0
      * date ?? ^^..\/
      { YY = $MATCH }
#Now assign the Month MM style
      :0
      * date ?? ^^.....\/
      { MM = $MATCH }
#Now assign the Day DD style
      :0
      * date ?? ()\/..^^
      { DD = $MATCH }

#Create the various directory formats you are going to use
      DUMMY=`test -d ${YYYY}/${MM}/${DD} || mkdir -p ${YYYY}/${MM}/
${DD}`
      DUMMY=`test -d ${YY}/${MM} || mkdir -p ${YY}/${MM}`

#Now store the data in an appropriate folder using the variables
#YYYY, MM and DD setup above.
          :0:
          * ^FROM_DAEMON
          ${YYYY}/${MM}/${DD}/daemon/
```

Informing users about large mail

In the previous chapter, we introduced a very simple rule that stored all incoming mail over 100 KB in size in a `largemail` folder. This was useful in keeping the size of individual incoming mail folders from growing too large, but meant that a special check had to be made regularly to see if any mail had been filtered.

In this rule, we will now extract the headers and subject line, plus the first few lines of the original large e-mail message, and create a new message with a modified subject line. This modified message will be stored in the user's inbox at the same time as filtering the large original item into its separate `largemail` folder.

The main part of the test will be applied only if the size of the message is over 100,000 bytes in size, so we will need a structure similar to the following recipe to do the initial testing and decide if this is a large item or not:

```
:0:
* >100000
{
    MAIN PROCESS WILL GO HERE
}
```

Assuming that we do have a large item, we need to make a copy of the message using the c flag and store this copy in the `largemail` folder:

```
#Place a copy in the largemail folder
:0 c:
largemail/
```

Extracting the first part of the body of the message comes next and this can be done using a variety of options. In this case, we are going to strip off the first 1024 bytes of the message by waiting for the results of passing only the body of the message only to the system head command and telling it to return only the first 1024 bytes. The flags used here tell Procmail to wait for the results of the command-line process and to ignore any pipeline errors as the head command will only read part of the data being offered to it.

```
#Strip the body to 1kb
:0 bfwi
| /usr/bin/head -c1024
```

Now we need to rewrite the subject line, which is done using the `formail` program. This time, we pass just the headers to the command line and wait for the response.

In this case though, we need to obtain the current subject line so that we can pass it to the `formail` program as part of the modified subject line. We do this by doing a simple match on the subject contents and then passing the $MATCH variable, which now holds the subject line contents as an argument to the `formail` program. For neatness, we add the {* -BIG- *} wording before the original subject line to make it easy to sort and identify these messages.

```
#ReWrite the subject line
:0 fhw
* ^Subject:\/.*
| formail -I "Subject: {* -BIG- *} $MATCH"
```

Normal delivery of the message will then take place and the new shorter message will be stored in the inbox.

If we put all of this together, we end up with the following complete recipe.

```
:0:
* >100000
{
    #Place a copy in the largemail folder
    :0 c:
    largemail/
```

```
#Strip the body to 1kb
:0 bfwi
| /usr/bin/head -c1024

#ReWrite the subject line
:0 fhw
* ^Subject:\/.*
| formail -I "Subject: {* -BIG- *} $MATCH"
}
```

Procmail Module Library

As part of a community effort to avoid reinventing the wheel, the Procmail Module Library provides a collection of useful recipes contributed by Procmail users. The following introduction from the Procmail Module Library `http://freshmeat.net/projects/procmail-lib` describes the package as:

> *Procmail Module Library is a collection of many plug-in modules for the Procmail mail processing utility. The modules allow common tasks like parsing dates, times, MIME, and email addresses, forwarding mail, dealing with POP3, spam shielding, running email cron jobs, handling daemon messages, and more.*

Each of the modules, or Procmail included files, are comprehensively documented and show example usage. They can be used as supplied, with various configurable options or used as a basis of your own recipes. Many of the techniques we have illustrated in this chapter are used in the library along with some more sophisticated filtering methods based on the type of content within a message.

Putting it all together

We have covered a wide range of topics in this chapter, which we can now pull together. The following examples use each of the techniques shown in this chapter and are commonly used for e-mail processing. I hope that you find it useful in creating your own mail filtering strategy.

Creating a structure to base your own rules upon

Grouping related aspects of the Procmail rules and configuration will make your installation easier to maintain and less likely to create problems when making changes.

Within the main Procmail directory, create individual files following a consistent naming convention such as rc.main, rc.spam, rc.lists, and so on. Then include each of these into your main .procmailrc file as follows.

```
#This obtains the date formatted as YYYY MM DD
      date = `date "+%Y %m %d"`

#Now assign the Year YYYY style
      :0
      * date ?? ^^()\/
      { YYYY = $MATCH }
#Now assign the Year YY style
      :0
      * date ?? ^^..\/
      { YY = $MATCH }
#Now assign the Month MM style
      :0
      * date ?? ^^.....\/
      { MM = $MATCH }
#Now assign the Day DD style
      :0
      * date ?? ()\/..^^
      { DD = $MATCH }
#Create the various directory formats you are going to use
      DUMMY=`test -d ${YYYY}/${MM}/${DD} || mkdir -p ${YYYY}/${MM}/
${DD}`
      DUMMY=`test -d ${YY}/${MM} || mkdir -p ${YY}/${MM}`

#Make a backup copy of all incoming mail
      :0 c
      backup/
#Restrict the history to just 32 mail items
      :0 ic
      | cd backup && rm -f dummy `ls -t msg.* | sed -e 1,32d`
#Make sure that all mails have a valid From value
      :0 fhw
      | formail -I "From " -a "From "
#
## Don't include this unless we need to
## INCLUDERC=${HOME}/Procmail/rc.testing
##
## Now include the various process listings
INCLUDERC=${HOME}/Procmail/rc.system
INCLUDERC=${HOME}/Procmail/rc.lists
INCLUDERC=${HOME}/Procmail/rc.killspam
INCLUDERC=${HOME}/Procmail/rc.vacation
INCLUDERC=${HOME}/Procmail/rc.largefiles
INCLUDERC=${HOME}/Procmail/rc.virusfilter
INCLUDERC=${HOME}/Procmail/rc.spamfilter
```

Now for each of the listed `include` files, create the file as named and include the rules related to the container in that file. It then becomes a matter of commenting an `INCLUDERC` reference for temporarily isolating a section of processing for incoming mail. Be careful not to blindly cut and paste these examples without checking if each recipe performs as expected, especially in a production environment.

Rc.system

File informational system and daemon messages in a dated folder structure can be given as:

```
# Filter system mail messages into a dated folder structure.
# The variables YY and MM are defined in the calling recipe
# and each of the directories will have been created if necessary.
:0:
* ^From:.*root@delta.adepteo.net
${YY}/${MM}/daemon/

:0:
* ^From:.*root@ramsbottom.adepteo.net
${YY}/${MM}/daemon/


:0:
* ^TO_pager@adepteo.net
${YY}/${MM}/daemon/

:0:
* ^From:.*MAILER-DAEMON@delta.adepteo.net
${YY}/${MM}/daemon/

:0:
* ^From:.*me@localhost.com
${YY}/${MM}/daemon/
```

Rc.lists

Save all our subscribed mailing lists in dated folders for reading later.

```
# Mailing lists
# Store by date folder
# The variables DD and MM are defined in the calling recipe.
# and each of the directories will have been created if necessary.
:0:
* ^From:.*mapserver-users-admin@lists.gis.umn.edu
${YY}/${MM}/mapserver/
```

```
:0:
* ^TO_mapserver-users@lists.gis.umn.edu
${YY}/${MM}/mapserver/

:0:
* ^From:.*yourtopjob@topjobs.co.uk
${YY}/${MM}/jobs/

:0:
* ^Subject: silicon Jobs-by-Email Alert
${YY}/${MM}/jobs/
:0:
* ^Reply-To: Axandra Search Engine Facts <facts@Axandra.com>
${YY}/${MM}/lists/

:0:
* ^Subject: A Joke A Day
${YY}/${MM}/lists/

:0:
* ^List-Owner: <mailto:owner-tribune@lists.sitepoint.com>
${YY}/${MM}/lists/

:0:
* ^Reply-To: newsletter@192.com
${YY}/${MM}/lists/

:0:
* ^Subject: Developer Shed Weekly Update
${YY}/${MM}/lists/
```

Rc.killspam

Delete any mail from senders that match an address in our kill file.

```
#Kill file for known spammers
# If the sender is in the killfile then discard the mail into the bit
bucket
# Here we use the external command 'grep' to search our killfile for a
# matching sending sending by testing the return status from grep.
:0:
* ? grep -i `formail -rtzxTo:` $HOME/.killfile
/dev/null
```

Rc.vacation

Our holiday auto reply recipe:

```
#Vacation Replies
:0 Whc: vacation.lock
# Perform a quick check to see if the mail was addressed to us
* $^To_:.*\<$\LOGNAME\>
# Don't reply to daemons and mailinglists
* !^FROM_DAEMON
# Mail loops are evil
* !^X-Loop: $RECIPIENT
| formail -rD 8192 vacation.cache


:0 ehc
# if the name was not in the cache reply with the contents
# of our vacation message in the body of the email.
|  (
   formail -rA"Precedence: junk" \
   -A"X-Loop: $RECIPIENT" ; \
   cat $HOME/.vacation_message \
   ) | $SENDMAIL -oi -t
```

Rc.largefiles

To avoid clogging up our inbox with large messages, we file the large message in a folder and send ourselves a notification that we have received an oversized message.

```
#Assume that files larger than 100k are not spam
    :0 :
    * >100000
    {
        #Place a copy in the largemail folder
        :0 c:
        largemail/

        #Strip the body to 1kb
        :0 bfwi
        | /usr/bin/head -c1024

        #ReWrite the subject line
        :0 fhw
        * ^Subject:\/.*
        | formail -I "Subject: {* -BIG- *} $MATCH"
    }
```

Rc.viruses

Anything with an e-mail header indicating the message as a virus, file in a folder.

```
#Virus Filter
  #X-Virus-Status: Infected
  :0:
  * ^X-Virus-Status: Infected
  _virus/
```

Rc.spamfilter

Anything with an e-mail header indicating the message is spam, file in a folder.

```
#Spam Filter
:0fw
* < 256000
| spamc

# Mails with a score of 15 or higher are almost certainly
# spam (with 0.05% false positives according to
# rules/STATISTICS.txt). Let's put them in a
# different mbox. (This one is optional.)
#
# The regular expression below matches the SpamAssassin
# header with 15 asterisks or more.
#
:0:
* ^X-Spam-Level: \*\*\*\*\*\*\*\*\*\*\*\*\*\*\*
_almost-certainly-spam/

# All mail tagged as spam (eg. with a score higher than the
# set threshold)
 is moved to "probably-spam".
:0:
* ^X-Spam-Status: Yes
_probably-spam/
```

Summary

In this chapter, we have explored Procmail to discover a large number of services and a large amount of functionality that it can provide to help with getting our mail under control. Using the advanced features of Procmail we have discovered:

- The differences between delivering and non-delivering recipes
- How to order each recipe to avoid slow delivery times
- The use of Procmail variables and condition flags to control delivery
- Using regular expressions for sophisticated pattern matching
- The large number of available Procmail macros and their usage
- And finally, a number of example recipes to manage our mail effectively

While we have covered a lot, there is still a lot to be learned and there are a large number of resources available on the Web dedicated to this one particular application.

Hopefully you will now have a strong grasp of the core functionality of Procmail, how to implement it, and also how to go about exploring your real-life needs, and creating recipe sets that you can combine to create your own unique mail filtering strategy.

8
Busting Spam with SpamAssassin

Spam, or unsolicited commercial e-mail (UCE) as it is sometimes called, is the scourge of the Internet. Spam has increased relentlessly over the last ten years and now accounts for over half of all Internet bandwidth. One in six consumers have acted on spam e-mails, so there is a strong business case for keeping spam out of your users' inboxes. There are a variety of different spam solutions, ranging from outsourcing your spam entirely to no action at all. However, if you have your own e-mail server, you can add spam filtering very easily.

SpamAssassin is a very popular open source anti-spam tool. It won a Linux New Media Award-2006 as the "Best Linux-based Anti-spam Solution", and is considered by many to be the best free, open source, anti-spam tool, and better than many commercial products. In fact, several commercial products and services are based on SpamAssassin or previous versions of it.

In this chapter, you will learn:

- Why spam is difficult to deal with and why spam filters requires regular updates
- How to download, install, and configure SpamAssassin
- How to filter incoming e-mails with SpamAssassin.
- How to configure SpamAssassin to work on per-user or per-server basis
- How to configure popular e-mail clients to recognize the tags that SpamAssassin places in e-mails
- How to customize SpamAssassin to update new rules set automatically to keep your system's spam detection well tuned.
- How to integrate spam filtering with virus recognition using amavisd

Why filter e-mail

If you don't receive any spam, there may be no need to filter spam. However, once one spam message has been received, it is invariably followed by many more. Spammers can sometimes detect if a spam e-mail is viewed, using techniques such as Web bugs, which are tiny images in HTML e-mails that are fetched from web servers, and then know that an e-mail address is valid and vulnerable. If spam is filtered, the initial e-mail may never get seen, and consequently the spammer may not then target the e-mail address with further spam.

Despite legal efforts against spam, it is actually on the increase. In Europe and the US, the recent legislation against spam (Directive 2002/58/EC and bill number S.877 respectively) have had little effect and spam is still on the increase in both regions.

The main reason for this is that spam is a very good business model. It is very cheap to send spam, as little as one thousandth of a cent per e-mail, and it takes a very low hit rate before a profit is made. The spammer needs to turn just one spam in a hundred thousand or so into a sale to make a profit. As a result, there are many spammers and spam is used to promote a wide range of goods. Spamming costs are also negligible due to use of malware that uses innocent computers to send spam on their behalf.

In contrast, the costs of spam to the recipient are remarkably high. Estimates have varied, from 10 cents per spam received, through 1,000 dollars per employee per year, up to a total cost of 140 billion dollars globally in 2007 alone. This cost is mainly labor—distracting people from their work by clogging their inboxes and forcing them to deal with many extra e-mails. Spam interferes with day-to-day work and can include material that is offensive to most people. Companies have a duty to protect their employees from such content. Spam filtering is a very cheap way of minimizing the costs and protecting the workforce.

Spam is a moving target

Spam isn't static. It changes on a day-to-day basis, as spammers add new methods to their arsenal and anti-spammers develop countermeasures. Due to this, the anti-spam tools that work best are those that are updated frequently. It's a similar predicament to antivirus software—virus definitions need to be updated regularly or new viruses won't be detected.

SpamAssassin is regularly updated. In addition to new releases of the software, there is a vigorous community creating, critiquing, and testing new anti-spam rules. These rules can be downloaded automatically for up-to-date protection against spam.

Let's discuss some of the measures used by SpamAssassin to fight spam:

- **Open relays**: These are e-mail servers that allow spammers to send e-mails even though they are not connected to the owner of the server in any way. To counter this, the anti-spam community has developed **blocklists**, also known as **blacklists**, which can be used by anti-spam software to detect spam. These were mentioned in Chapter 5 as a list that your e-mail server should not appear on, as it may limit legitimate e-mail traffic. Any e-mail that has passed through a server on a blocklist is treated more suspiciously than one that has not. SpamAssassin uses a number of blocklists to test e-mails.

- **Keyword filters**: These are useful tools against spam. Spammers tend to repeat the same words and phrases again and again. Rules to detect these phrases are used extensively by SpamAssassin. These make up the bulk of the tests, and the user community rules mentioned previously are normally of this form. They allow specific words, phrases, or sequences of letters, numbers, and punctuation to be detected.

- **Blacklists and whitelists**: These are used to list known senders of spam and sources of good e-mail respectively. E-mails from an address on a blacklist are probably spam and are treated accordingly, while e-mails from addresses on a whitelist will be less likely to be treated as spam. SpamAssassin allows the user to enter blacklists and whitelists manually, and also builds up an automatic whitelist and blacklist based on the e-mails that it processes.

- **Statistical filters**: These are automated systems that give the probability that an e-mail is spam. This filtration is based on what the filter has seen previously as both spam and non-spam. They generally work by finding words that are present in one type of e-mail but not the other, and using this knowledge to determine which type a new e-mail is. SpamAssassin has a statistical filter called the **Bayesian filter** that can be very effective in improving detection rates.

- **Content databases**: These are mass e-mail detection systems. A lot of e-mail servers receive and submit e-mails to central servers. If the same e-mail is sent to thousands of recipients, it is probably a spam. The content databases prevent confidential e-mails from being sent to the server, by using a technique called **hashing** that also lowers the amount of data sent to the server. SpamAssassin can integrate with several content databases, notably Vipul's Razor (`http://razor.sourceforge.net/`), Pyzor (`http://sourceforge.net/apps/trac/pyzor/`), and the **Distributed Checksum Clearinghouse**, that is, **DCC** (`http://www.rhyolite.com/dcc/`).

- **URL blocklists**: These are similar to open relay blocklists, but list the websites used by spammers. In nearly all spams, a web address is given. A database of these is built so that spam e-mails can be quickly detected. This is a very efficient and effective tool against spam. By default, SpamAssassin uses **Spam URI Realtime BlockLists (SURBLs)**, without any further configuration required.

Spam filtering options

Spam can be filtered on the server or the client. The two approaches are explained next. In the first scenario, spam is filtered on the client.

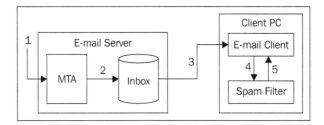

1. Mail is processed by the MTA.
2. The e-mail is then placed in the appropriate user's inbox.
3. The e-mail client reads all new e-mail from the inbox.
4. The e-mail client then passes the e-mail to the filter.
5. When the filter returns the results, the client can display the valid e-mail and either discard spam or file it in a separate folder.

In this approach, the spam filtering is always done by the client and is always done when new e-mail is processed. Often when the user may be present, so he or she may either experience a delay before e-mail is visible or there may be a period where spam e-mail is present in the inbox before the client software can filter the spam from view. The amount of spam filtering that can be performed on the client may be limited. In particular, the network tests such as open relay blocklists or SURBLs might be too time consuming or complex to perform on the user's PC. As spam is a moving target, updating many client PCs can become a difficult administrative task.

In the second scenario, the spam filtering is performed on the e-mail server.

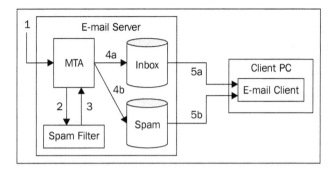

1.   Incoming e-mail is received by the MTA.

2.   It is then passed on to the spam filter.

3.   The results are then sent back to the MTA.

4.   Depending on the results, the MTA places the e-mail in the appropriate user's inbox (**4a**), or in a separate folder for spam (**4b**).

5.   The e-mail client accesses e-mails in the user's inbox and it can also access the spam folder if required.

This approach has several advantages:

•   The spam filtering is done when the e-mail is received, which may be any time of the day. The user is less likely to be inconvenienced by delays.

•   The server can specialize in spam filtering. It may use external services such as open relay blocklists, online content databases, and SURBLs.

•   Configuration is centralized, which will ease setup (for example, firewalls may need to be configured to use online spam tests) and also maintenance (updating of rules or software).

On the other hand, the disadvantages include:

•   A single point of failure now exists. However, with care, a broken spam filtering service can be configured around. If the service is not available, e-mail will still be delivered but spam will not be filtered.

•   All spam must be processed by one service. If this service is not scalable, large volumes of e-mail may affect mail delivery times, resulting in poor or intermittent filtering, or possibly even the loss of e-mail service.

Introduction to SpamAssassin

Spam filtering actually involves two phases — detecting the spam and then doing something with it. SpamAssassin is a spam detector and it modifies the e-mail it processes by putting in headers to mark whether it is spam. It is up to the MTA or the mail delivery agent in the e-mail system to react to the headers that SpamAssassin creates in an e-mail, to filter it out. However, it's possible that another part of the e-mail system could perform this task.

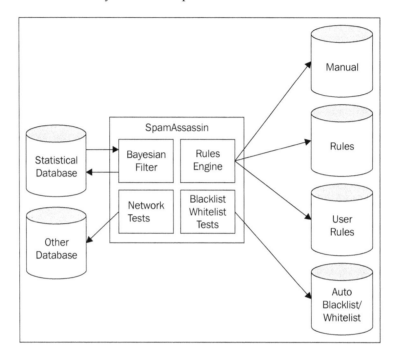

The previous figure gives a schematic representation of SpamAssassin. At the heart of SpamAssassin is its **Rules Engine** that determines which rules are called. Rules trigger whether the various tests are used, including the Bayesian Filter, the network tests, and the auto-whitelists.

SpamAssassin uses various databases to do its work, and these are shown too. The rules and scores are text files. Default rules and scores are included in the SpamAssassin distribution and, as we will see, both system administrators and users can add rules or change the scores of existing rules by adding them to files in specific locations. The Bayesian filter (which is a major part of SpamAssassin, and will be covered later) uses a database of statistical data based on previous spam and non-spam e-mails. The **Auto-Blacklist/Whitelist** also creates its own database.

Downloading and installing SpamAssassin

SpamAssassin is slightly different from most of the software that is used in this book. It is written in a language called **Perl**, which has its own distribution method called **CPAN** (**Comprehensive Perl Archive Network**). CPAN is a large website of Perl software (normally, Perl modules), and the term CPAN is also the name of the software used to download those modules and install them. Though SpamAssassin is provided as a package by many Linux distributions, we strongly recommend that you install it from source rather than use a package. This way, you will get the latest version of SpamAssassin rather than the one that was current when your Linux distributer created its release.

Most Perl users will build Perl modules using CPAN and experience no difficulties. CPAN can automatically locate and install any dependencies (other components that are required to make the desired component work properly). From a Perl point of view, using CPAN to install Perl modules is like using the rpm or apt-get commands in Linux. The basics are very simple and, once a system is configured, it generally works every time.

However, learning and configuring a new way of installing software may put off some people. A SpamAssassin release is distributed in source form, but administrators of **Red Hat Package Manager** (**RPM**) based systems can easily convert the latest SpamAssassin release into rpm format and then the regular rpm command can be used to install the package. The Debian repository is updated fairly quickly when SpamAssassin is updated and the regular apt-get commands can be used to install SpamAssassin. We strongly advise you to install via apt-get, CPAN, or using the rpmbuild command as described next, in preference to using an RPM provided by a distributor.

As SpamAssassin is a Perl Module, it appears on CPAN first. In fact, it is only released when it arrives at CPAN. Users of CPAN can download the latest version of SpamAssassin literally minutes after it has been released.

Support is also easier to obtain if SpamAssassin is built from source. Some distributors make unusual decisions when creating their RPM of SpamAssassin or may modify certain default values. These make obtaining support more difficult.

RPMs also take time to be delivered. Distributors need time to build and test new versions of software before they release them, and most software packages are not updated as quickly as SpamAssassin. So, Linux distributions may not provide the latest software, and what is provided can be several versions out of date.

Using CPAN

The prerequisites for installing SpamAssassin 3.2.5 using CPAN are as follows:

- **Perl version 5.6.1 or later**: Most modern Linux distributions will include this as a part of the base package.

- **Several Perl modules**: The current version of SpamAssassin needs the Digest::SHA1, HTML::Parser, and the Net::DNS modules. CPAN will install these if you configure it to follow dependencies, but there are many additional Perl modules that are optional and should be installed to get the best spam detection. CPAN will issue warnings with the module names, which will enable you to identify and install them.

- **C compiler**: This may not be installed by default and may have to be added using the `rpm` command. The compiler used will normally be called `gcc`.

- **Internet connection**: CPAN will attempt to download the modules using `HTTP` or `FTP`, so the network should be configured to allow this.

Configuring CPAN

If you've used CPAN before, you can skip to the next section, *Installing SpamAssassin Using CPAN*.

If a proxy server is required for Internet traffic, CPAN (and other Perl modules and scripts) will use the `http_proxy` environment variable. If the proxy requires a username and password, these need to be specified using environment variables. As CPAN is normally run as `root`, these commands should be entered as `root`:

```
# HTTP_proxy=http://proxy.name:80
# export HTTP_proxy
# HTTP_proxy_user=username
# export HTTP_proxy_user
# HTTP_proxy_pass=password
# export HTTP_proxy_pass
```

Next, enter this command:

```
# perl -MCPAN -e shell
```

If the output is similar to the following, the CPAN module is already installed and configured, and you can skip to the next section, *Installing SpamAssassin Using CPAN*.

```
cpan shell -- CPAN exploration and modules installation (v1.7601)
ReadLine support enabled
```

If the output prompts for manual configuration, as shown next, the CPAN module is installed but not configured.

```
Are you ready for manual configuration? [yes]
```

During configuration, the CPAN Perl module prompts for answers to around 30 questions. For most of the questions, selecting the default value is the best response. This initial configuration must be completed before the CPAN Perl module can be used. The questions are mainly about the location of various utilities, and the defaults can be chosen by pressing *Enter*. The only question for which we should change the default is the one about building prerequisite modules. If we configure CPAN to follow dependencies, it will install the required modules without prompting.

```
Policy on building prerequisites (follow, ask or ignore)? [ask] follow
```

Once CPAN is configured, exit the shell by typing `exit` and pressing *Enter*. We are now ready to use CPAN to install SpamAssassin.

Installing SpamAssassin using CPAN

To install SpamAssassin, enter the CPAN shell by typing the following command:

 # cpan

If the CPAN module is correctly configured, the following output (or something similar) will appear:

```
cpan shell -- CPAN exploration and modules installation (v1.7601)
ReadLine support enabled
```

Now, at the `cpan` prompt, enter the following command:

cpan> install Mail::SpamAssassin

The CPAN module will query an online database to find the latest version of SpamAssassin and its dependencies, and then install them. Dependencies will be installed before SpamAssassin. The following is the sample output:

cpan> install Mail::SpamAssassin

```
CPAN: Storable loaded ok (v2.18)
Going to read '/root/.cpan/Metadata'
  Database was generated on Mon, 03 Aug 2009 04:27:49 GMT
Running install for module 'Mail::SpamAssassin'
CPAN: Data::Dumper loaded ok (v2.121_14)
'YAML' not installed, falling back to Data::Dumper and Storable to
read prefs '/root/.cpan/prefs'
Running make for J/JM/JMASON/Mail-SpamAssassin-3.2.5.tar.gz
```

```
CPAN: Digest::SHA loaded ok (v5.45)
CPAN: Compress::Zlib loaded ok (v2.015)
Checksum for /root/.cpan/sources/authors/id/J/JM/JMASON/Mail-
SpamAssassin-3.2.5.tar.gz ok
Scanning cache /root/.cpan/build for sizes
..............................................................
.......DONE
CPAN: Archive::Tar loaded ok (v1.38)
Will not use Archive::Tar, need 1.00
Mail-SpamAssassin-3.2.5
Mail-SpamAssassin-3.2.5/t
Mail-SpamAssassin-3.2.5/sql
Mail-SpamAssassin-3.2.5/lib
....
    CPAN.pm: Going to build F/FE/FELICITY/Mail-SpamAssassin-3.00.tar.gz
```

SpamAssassin may require the user to respond to a few questions. The responses provided might affect the module configuration or only be part of the testing performed before installation.

```
    CPAN.pm: Going to build J/JM/JMASON/Mail-SpamAssassin-3
What e-mail address or URL should be used in the suspected-spam report
text for users who want more information on your filter installation?
(In particular, ISPs should change this to a local Postmaster contact)
default text: [the administrator of that system] postmaster@myfomain.
com

NOTE: settings for "make test" are now controlled using "t/config.
dist".
See that file if you wish to customise what tests are run, and how.

checking module dependencies and their versions...
```

SpamAssassin, as with many Perl modules, is very flexible. It can make use of features if they are available, and will work even if they are not. When using CPAN, you may see messages such as the following:

```
optional module missing: Mail::SPF
optional module missing: Mail::SPF::Query
optional module missing: IP::Country
optional module missing: Razor2
optional module missing: Net::Ident
optional module missing: IO::Socket::INET6
optional module missing: IO::Socket::SSL
optional module missing: Mail::DomainKeys
optional module missing: Mail::DKIM
optional module missing: DBI
optional module missing: Encode::Detect
```

If you install the modules mentioned, SpamAssassin will make use of them and this will improve e-mail filtering. You can abort the installation of SpamAssassin and install the modules using cpan `install Module::Name` commands.

If you let the build process complete, it will test the capabilities of the C compiler, configure and build the module, create documentation, and test SpamAssassin. At the end of the build, the output should be similar to the following:

```
chmod 755 /usr/share/spamassassin
   /usr/bin/make install    -- OK

cpan>
```

This indicates that SpamAssassin has been installed correctly. If SpamAssassin installation was successful, you can skip to the *Testing the Installation* section.

If the installation failed, the output may look like this:

```
Failed 17/68 test scripts, 75.00% okay. 50/1482 subtests
failed, 96.63% okay.
make: *** [test_dynamic] Error 29
/usr/bin/make test -- NOT OK
Running make install
make test had returned bad status, won't install without force
cpan>
```

If the output does not end with the `/usr/bin/make install -- OK` message, an error has occurred. Firstly, you should examine all the output for possible warnings and error messages, especially for prerequisite packages. If this does not assist, then avenues for support are described in the section *Testing the installation*.

Using the rpmbuild utility

If a version of Linux based on the Red Hat Package Manager format is used, SpamAssassin can be installed using the `rpmbuild` command. Download the SpamAssassin source from `http://www.cpan.org/modules/01modules.index.html` into a working directory, then issue the following command to build SpamAssassin:

```
# rpmbuild -tb Mail-SpamAssassin-3.2.5.tar.gz
   Executing(%prep): /bin/sh -e /var/tmp/rpm-tmp.ORksvX
   + umask 022
   + cd /root/rpmbuild/BUILD
   + cd /root/rpmbuild/BUILD
   + rm -rf Mail-SpamAssassin-3.2.5
   + /usr/bin/gzip -dc /root/Mail-SpamAssassin-3.2.5.tar.gz
   + /bin/tar -xf -
```

```
+ STATUS=0
+ '[' 0 -ne 0 ']'
+ cd Mail-SpamAssassin-3.2.5
+ /bin/chmod -Rf a+rX,u+w,g-w,o-w .
+ exit 0
Executing(%build): /bin/sh -e /var/tmp/rpm-tmp.zgpcdd
...
... (output continues)
...
Wrote: /usr/src/redhat/RPMS/i386/spamassassin-3.0.4-1.i386.rpm
Wrote: /usr/src/redhat/RPMS/i386/spamassassin-tools-3.0.4-1.i386.rpm
Wrote: /usr/src/redhat/RPMS/i386/perl-Mail-SpamAssassin-3.0.4-1.i386.
rpm
Executing(%clean): /bin/sh -e /var/tmp/rpm-tmp.65065
+ umask 022
+ cd /usr/src/redhat/BUILD
+ cd Mail-SpamAssassin-3.0.4
+ '[' /var/tmp/spamassassin-root '!=' / ']'
+ rm -rf /var/tmp/spamassassin-root
+ exit 0
```

It is possible that the installation will fail due to missing dependencies. These are Perl modules that SpamAssassin uses, and which are installed separately. Error messages often hint at the name of the dependency, as in the following installation:

```
# rpmbuild -tb Mail-SpamAssassin-3.2.5.tar.gz
    error: Failed build dependencies:
            perl(Digest::SHA1) is needed by spamassassin-3.2.5-1.i386
            perl(HTML::Parser) is needed by spamassassin-3.2.5-1.i386
            perl(Net::DNS) is needed by spamassassin-3.2.5-1.i386
```

In this case, the Perl modules `Digest::SHA1`, `HTML::Parser`, and `Net::DNS` are needed. The solution is to install it using CPAN. In some cases, SpamAssassin may require particular versions of packages, which may require the installed versions to be upgraded.

When installing SpamAssassin using CPAN, all the dependencies are installed automatically. However, while using the `rpmbuild` command, the dependencies need to be installed manually. Using CPAN is generally less troublesome than `rpmbuild`.

Using pre-built RPMs

SpamAssassin is packaged with many Linux distributions, and packages of new releases of SpamAssassin are often made available from other sources. As mentioned earlier, RPMs are not the recommended method of installing SpamAssassin but are more reliable than building from source on unusual platforms.

To install an RPM, simply download or locate it on the distribution CD, and install it using the `rpm` command. The following command can be used to install the RPM for SpamAssassin:

```
# rpm -ivh /path/to/rpmfile-9.99.rpm
```

Graphical installers can also be used to install SpamAssassin RPMs. The RPMs listed on the SpamAssassin website are usually the latest version of SpamAssassin and are complete. If these cannot be installed, the RPM provided by the Linux distribution should be installed instead.

Testing the installation

It is worth performing a few tests to ensure that SpamAssassin is installed correctly and the environment is complete. If you want to test a particular user account, you should log in to that account to perform the test.

SpamAssassin includes a sample spam e-mail and a sample non-spam e-mail. It can be tested by processing the sample e-mails. These e-mails are in the root of the SpamAssassin distribution directory. If you used CPAN to install SpamAssassin using the `root` user, then the path to this directory may be similar to `~root/.cpan/build/Mail-SpamAssassin-3.2.5/`, where `3.2.5` is the version of SpamAssassin installed. If the files cannot be located, download the SpamAssassin source from `http://www.cpan.org/modules/01modules.index.html` and unpack the source into a temporary directory. The sample e-mails are in the root of the unpacked source.

To test SpamAssassin, change to the directory containing `sample-spam.txt` and use the following commands. Example results are shown after each command.

```
$ spamassassin -t < sample-nonspam.txt | grep X-Spam
    [22674] warn: config: created user preferences file: /home/user/.
    spamassassin/user_prefs
    X-Spam-Checker-Version: SpamAssassin 3.2.5 (2008-06-10) on
    X-Spam-Level:
    X-Spam-Status: No, score=0.0 required=5.0 tests=none autolearn=haX-
```

```
$ spamassassin -t < sample-spam.txt | grep X-Spam
    X-Spam-Flag: YES
    X-Spam-Checker-Version: SpamAssassin 3.2.5 (2008-06-10) on
    X-Spam-Level: ***********************************************
    X-Spam-Status: Yes, score=1000.0 required=5.0 tests=GTUBE,NO_RECEIVED,
    X-Spam-Report:
    X-Spam-Prev-Subject: Test spam mail (GTUBE)
```

The output from the command using `sample-nonspam.txt` should have `X-Spam-Status: No`, and that using `sample-spam.txt` should have `X-Spam-Flag: YES` and `X-Spam-Status: Yes`.

SpamAssassin can verify its configuration files with the `--lint` flag and report any errors. By default, a clean installation of SpamAssassin should not have any errors, but once a site is customized, some rules may fail. In the following example, a `score` entry does not match a rule:

```
$ spamassassin --lint
    warning: score set for non-existent rule RULE_NAME
    lint: 1 issues detected. please run with debug enabled for more
    information
```

If the output includes warnings, something has gone wrong. It's worth fixing SpamAssassin before going on and using it. The best places to visit are the SpamAssassin Wiki (`http://wiki.apache.org/spamassassin/`), the archives of the SpamAssassin mailing lists (`http://wiki.apache.org/spamassassin/MailingLists`), and your favorite search engine. As with most open source projects, the developers are volunteers and appreciate users who search for the solution to their problem before posting a plea for help, as most problems have been encountered many times before.

Modified e-mails

In addition to the e-mail headers mentioned, SpamAssassin will modify an e-mail if it is thought to be spam. It takes the original e-mail and converts it to an e-mail attachment with a simple e-mail around it. SpamAssassin always wraps an e-mail if it detects a potential virus or other dangerous content. In its default configuration, it will add an envelope e-mail around the spam, but this can be turned off if desired. Consult the SpamAssassin documentation regarding the `report_safe` directive. The envelope e-mail looks like this:

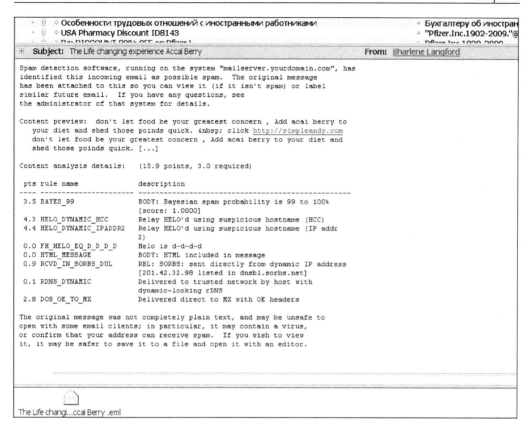

```
  ·  □  ◎ Особенности трудовых отношений с иностранными работниками      ◦ Бухгалтеру об иностран
  ·  □  ◦ USA Pharmacy Discount IDB143                                   ◦ "Pfizer.Inc.1902-2009."@
                                                                         ◦ Pfizer Inc 1939 2009
 ⊞   Subject:  The Life changing experience Accai Berry       From:  Sharlene Langford

 Spam detection software, running on the system "mailserver.yourdomain.com", has
 identified this incoming email as possible spam.  The original message
 has been attached to this so you can view it (if it isn't spam) or label
 similar future email.  If you have any questions, see
 the administrator of that system for details.

 Content preview:  don't let food be your greatest concern , Add acai berry to
    your diet and shed those poinds quick.   click http://simpleandy.com
    don't let food be your greatest concern , Add acai berry to your diet and
    shed those poinds quick. [...]

 Content analysis details:   (15.9 points, 3.0 required)

  pts rule name                description
  ---- -------------------     --------------------------------------------------
  3.5 BAYES_99                 BODY: Bayesian spam probability is 99 to 100%
                               [score: 1.0000]
  4.3 HELO_DYNAMIC_HCC         Relay HELO'd using suspicious hostname (HCC)
  4.4 HELO_DYNAMIC_IPADDR2     Relay HELO'd using suspicious hostname (IP addr
                               2)
  0.0 FH_HELO_EQ_D_D_D_D       Helo is d-d-d-d
  0.0 HTML_MESSAGE             BODY: HTML included in message
  0.9 RCVD_IN_SORBS_DUL        RBL: SORBS: sent directly from dynamic IP address
                               [201.42.32.98 listed in dnsbl.sorbs.net]
  0.1 RDNS_DYNAMIC             Delivered to trusted network by host with
                               dynamic-looking rDNS
  2.8 DOS_OE_TO_MX             Delivered direct to MX with OE headers

 The original message was not completely plain text, and may be unsafe to
 open with some email clients; in particular, it may contain a virus,
 or confirm that your address can receive spam.  If you wish to view
 it, it may be safer to save it to a file and open it with an editor.
```

The Life changi...ccai Berry .eml

Using SpamAssassin

Now that SpamAssassin is installed, we need to configure the system to use it. SpamAssassin can be used in many ways. It can be integrated into the MTA for maximum performance; it can run as a daemon or a simple script to avoid complexity; it can use separate settings for each user or use a single set of settings for all users; and it can be used for all accounts or just for the chosen ones. In this book, we will discuss using SpamAssassin in three ways.

The first method is with Procmail. This is the simplest method to configure and is suitable for low-volume sites, for example, less than 10,000 e-mails a day.

The second method is to use SpamAssassin as a daemon. This is more efficient, and can still be used with Procmail, if desired.

The third method is to integrate SpamAssassin with a content filter such as amavisd. This offers performance advantages, but occasionally the content filter does not work with the latest release of SpamAssassin. Problems, if any, are usually resolved quickly.

 To help you get the most out of SpamAssassin, Packt Publishing has published *SpamAssassin: A practical guide to integration and configuration*, (ISBN 1-904811-12-4) by Alistair McDonald.

Using SpamAssassin with Procmail

Procmail was covered in Chapters 6 and 7. If you have at least a basic understanding of Procmail, then what follows here should be easy to understand. If you jumped to this chapter and you don't know about Procmail, then it would probably be worthwhile reading Chapter 6, which discusses the basics of Procmail before continuing here.

Before we configure the system to use SpamAssassin, let's consider what SpamAssassin does. SpamAssassin is *not* an e-mail filter. A filter is something that changes the destination of an e-mail. SpamAssassin adds e-mail headers to an e-mail message to indicate if it is spam or not.

Consider an e-mail with headers like this:

```
Return-Path: <user@domain.com>
X-Original-To: jdoe@localhost
Delivered-To: jdoe@host.domain.com
Received: from localhost (localhost [127.0.0.1])
    by domain.com (Postfix) with ESMTP id 52A2CF2948
    for <jdoe@localhost>; Thu, 11 Nov 2004 03:39:42 +0000 (GMT)
Received: from pop.ntlworld.com [62.253.162.50]
    by localhost with POP3 (fetchmail-6.2.5)
    for jdoe@localhost (single-drop); Thu, 11 Nov 2004 03:39:42 +0000
(GMT)
Message-ID: <D8F7B41C.4DDAFE7@anotherdomain.com>
Date: Wed, 10 Nov 2004 17:54:14 -0800
From: "stephen mellors" <gregory@anotherdomain.com>
User-Agent: MIME-tools 5.503 (Entity 5.501)
X-Accept-Language: en-us
MIME-Version: 1.0
To: "Jane Doe" <jdoe@domain.com>
Subject: nearest pharmacy online
Content-Type: text/plain;
    charset="us-ascii"
Content-Transfer-Encoding: 7bit
```

SpamAssassin will add header lines.

```
X-Spam-Flag: YES
X-Spam-Checker-Version: SpamAssassin 3.1.0-r54722 (2004-10-13) on
    host.domain.com
X-Spam-Level: *****
X-Spam-Status: Yes, score=5.8 required=5.0 tests=BAYES_05,HTML_00_10,
    HTML_MESSAGE,MPART_ALT_DIFF autolearn=no
    version=3.1.0-r54722
```

SpamAssassin doesn't change the destination of the e-mail, all it does is add headers that enable something else to change the destination of the e-mail.

The best indication that an e-mail is spam is the X-Spam-Flag. If this is YES, SpamAssassin considers the mail to be spam and it can be filtered by Procmail.

SpamAssassin also assigns a score to each e-mail—the higher the score, the more likely that the e-mail is spam. The threshold that determines if an e-mail is spam can be configured on a system-wide or per-user basis. The default of 5.0 is a sensible default if you are using an unmodified installation of SpamAssassin without any custom rulesets.

Global procmailrc file

Let's suppose that we want to check all incoming e-mail for spam using SpamAssassin. Commands in the /etc/procmailrc file are run for all users, so executing SpamAssassin here is ideal.

The following simple recipe will run SpamAssassin for all users when placed in /etc/procmailrc:

```
:0fw
| /usr/bin/spamassassin
```

To place all spam in an individual spam folder, ensure that the global/etc/procmailrc file has a line specifying a default destination. For example:

```
DEFAULT=$HOME/.maildir/
```

If not, then add a line specifying DEFAULT. To filter spam into a folder, add a recipe similar to the following:

```
* ^X-Spam-Flag: Yes
.SPAM/new
```

This assumes that each user has a folder called SPAM already configured.

To place all the spam in a single, central folder, use an absolute path to the destination in the recipe:

```
* ^X-Spam-Flag: Yes
/var/spool/poss_spam
```

This will place all spam in a single folder, which can be reviewed by the system administrator. As regular e-mail may occasionally be wrongly detected as spam, the folder should not be world-readable, which leads to a more generalized statement.

 SpamAssassin will be run under the system account used by Postfix. This means that the Bayesian database and the auto-whitelists and blacklists will be shared by all users. From a security point of view, it's important that the various databases that SpamAssassin creates are not world-writable.

SpamAssassin stores user-specific files in the `~/.spamassassin/` directory. Here is a list of files that *may* be present for a user:

Files	Contents

`auto-whitelist`
`auto-whitelist.db`
`auto-whitelist.dir`
`auto-whitelist.pag`
	SpamAssassin creates a database of users who send ham (non-spam messages) and uses it to predict whether an e-mail from a particular sender is spam or ham. These files are used to track users.

`bayes_journal`
`bayes_seen`
`bayes_toks`
	SpamAssassin uses a statistical technique called Bayesian analysis. These files are used for this feature.

`user_prefs`	This file allows global settings to be overridden for a particular user. This file can contain configuration settings, rules, and scores.

Some of them may contain confidential data—for example, regular contacts will appear in the auto-whitelist files. Careful use of permissions will ensure that the files are not readable by regular user accounts.

Using SpamAssassin on a per-user basis

Perhaps some users don't receive spam, or there may be issues with users sharing whitelists and Bayesian databases. SpamAssassin can be run on an individual basis by moving the recipes to the `~/.procmailrc` of specific users. This should increase the filtering performance for each user, but increases disk space usage for each user and requires setting up each individual user account by modifying its `~/.procmailrc`.

A typical user's `.procmailrc` might look like this:

```
MAILDIR=$HOME/.maildir
:0fw
| /usr/bin/spamassassin
:0
* ^X-Spam-Flag: Yes
.SPAM/cur
```

As suggested, e-mail may sometimes be wrongly detected as spam. It's worthwhile reviewing spam to ensure that legitimate e-mails have not been wrongly classified. If the user receives a lot of spam, then wading through it all is time consuming, tedious, and error prone. Procmail can filter spam by checking the spam score written in the e-mail headers by SpamAssassin.

The low-scoring spam (for example, scoring up to 9) can be placed in one folder called `Probable_Spam`, while higher scoring e-mails (which are more likely to be spam) can be placed a folder called `Certain_Spam`.

To do this, we use the `X-Spam-Level` header, which SpamAssassin creates. This is simply the number of asterisks, related to the `X-Spam-Level` value. By moving e-mail with more than a certain number of asterisks to the `Certain_Spam` folder, the remaining spam is "Probable Spam". E-mail that is marked with `X-Spam-Flag: NO`, is obviously not spam.

The following `.procmailrc` file will filter high scoring spam separately from low scoring spam and non spam:

```
MAILDIR=$HOME/.maildir
:0fw
| /usr/bin/spamassassin
:0
* ^X-Spam-Level: \*\*\*\*\*\*\*\*\*\*\*\*\*\*\*\*
.Certain_Spam/cur
:0
* ^X-Spam-FLAG: YES
.Probable_Spam/cur
```

Using SpamAssassin as a daemon with Postfix

A daemon is a background process; one that waits for work, processes it, and then waits for more work. Using this approach actually improves performance (as long as there is sufficient memory) because responsiveness is improved — the program is always ready and waiting and does not have to be loaded each time spam tagging is required.

To use SpamAssassin as a daemon, a user account should be added — it's dangerous to run any service as `root`. As `root`, enter the following commands to make a user and a group called spam:

```
# groupadd spam
# useradd -m -d /home/spam -g spam -s /bin/false spam
# chmod 0700 /home/spam
```

To configure Postfix to run SpamAssassin, use SpamAssassin as a daemon. The Postfix `master.cf` file must be changed. Edit the file and locate the line that begins with `'smtp inet'`. Amend the line to add `-o content_filter=spamd` to the end.

```
smtp      inet  n    -    n    -    -      smtpd -o content_
filter=spamd
```

Add the following lines to the end of the file:

```
spamd unix -    n       n       -       -         pipe
    flags=R user=spam argv=/usr/bin/spamc
    -e /usr/sbin/sendmail -oi -f ${sender} ${recipient}
```

If the text is spread across several lines, any continuing line must begin with spaces as shown. The changes to the file define a filter called `spamd` that runs the `spamc` client for each message and also specifies that the filter should be run whenever an e-mail is received via SMTP.

On this line, `spamd` is the name of the filter and matches the name used in the `content_filter` line. The `user=` portion specifies the user context that should be used to run the command. The `argv=` portion describes the program that should be run. The other flags are used by Procmail and their presence is important.

Using SpamAssassin with amavisd-new

amavisd-new is an interface between MTAs and content checkers. Despite its name, amavisd-new is a well-established open source package that is well maintained. Content checkers scan e-mail for viruses and/or spam. amavisd-new is slightly different. Just like like spamd, it is written in Perl and runs as a daemon, but instead of accessing SpamAssassin via the spamc or spamassassin clients, it loads SpamAssassin into memory and accesses the SpamAssassin functions directly. It is therefore closely coupled to SpamAssassin and may need to be upgraded at the same time as SpamAssassin.

Unlike other Perl-based applications and utilities, amavisd-new is not available from CPAN. However, it is available in source form and RPM form for many distributions of Linux, and is also available for debian-based repositories. Details of versions available are listed on http://www.ijs.si/software/amavisd/#download. We recommend that if the version of SpamAssassin that your distributor offers is up-to-date, then you should use their package of both SpamAssassin and amavisd.

Installing amavisd-new from package

To install amavisd-new from package, use the rpm command for RPM-based distributions. amavisd-new has many dependencies, all of which are Perl modules. Each version may have different dependencies, which are listed in the install file that is a part of the package. The Perl prerequisites for version 2.6.2 are as follows:

```
Archive::Zip
BerkeleyDB
Convert::BinHex
Convert::TNEF
Convert::UUlib
Crypt::OpenSSL::Bignum
Crypt::OpenSSL::RSA
Digest::HMAC
Digest::Sha1
IO::Multiplex
IO::Stringy
MIME::Tools
Mail::DKIM
Net::CIDR
Net::DNS
Net::IP
Net::Server
Unix::Syslog
```

To view the prerequisites for a particular version of amavisd-new, download the source and unpack it as shown here, and read the install file.

```
$ cd /some/dir
$ wget http://www.ijs.si/software/amavisd/amavisd-new-2.6.2.tar.gz
$ tar xfz amavisd-new-2.6.2.tar.gz
$ cd  amavisd-new-2.6.2
$ vi INSTALL
```

Several of the dependencies may be installed already, as they are also used by SpamAssassin.

Installation prerequisites

Some RPM-based Linux distributions may automatically install the prerequisites as dependencies. For other distributions, all the prerequisites must be downloaded from CPAN and installed. This is easiest to accomplish with the cpan command. An alternative method is to download the source code for each prerequisite individually and install it with the following commands:

```
$ cd /some/directory
$ gunzip -c source-nn.tar.gz | tar xf -
$ cd source-nn
$ perl Makefile.pl
$ make test
$ su
# make install
```

Installing from source

amavisd-new has no makefile, configuration script, or installation routine. To install it, the sole executable script is copied to /usr/local/bin, and its attributes modified to ensure it cannot be modified by non-root users:

```
# cp amavisd /usr/local/sbin/
# chown root /usr/local/sbin/amavisd
# chmod 755 /usr/local/sbin/amavisd
```

The sample amavisd.conf file should be copied to /etc and its attributes should also be modified.

```
# cp amavisd.conf /etc/
# chown root /etc/amavisd.conf
# chmod 644 /etc/amavisd.conf
```

amavisd-new must be configured to run as a daemon, and so the sample `init` script should be copied to the appropriate directory.

```
# cp amavisd_init.sh /etc/init.d/amavisd-new
```

The `init` script should also be added to the system startup. Most Linux distributions use the `chkconfig` command to do this.

```
# chkconfig --add amavisd-new
```

Creating a user account for amavisd-new

To create a user account, first create a dedicated group using the `groupadd` command and then use the `useradd` command to add the user.

```
# groupadd amavis
# useradd -m -d /home/amavis -g amavis -s /bin/false amavis
```

Configuring amavisd-new

Several changes need to be made to the `/etc/amavisd.conf` file. This file will be parsed as Perl source, and syntax is important. Each line should end in a semicolon, and the casing is important. The following variable declaration lines should be changed to contain the following values:

```
$MYHOME = '/home/amavis';
$mydomain = 'domain.com';
$daemon_user = 'amavis';
$daemon_group = 'amavis';
$max_servers  =  5;              # number of pre-forked children
(default 2)
```

Ensure that the correct domain is specified for `$mydomain`. The number 5 specified for `$max_servers` is the number of daemons that will be run concurrently. If you have a modest amount of e-mail, for example less than ten messages a second, the default will be sufficient.

Within `/etc/amavisd.conf`, there is a section on SpamAssassin-related configuration settings:

```
$sa_tag_level_deflt  = 2.0;
$sa_tag2_level_deflt = 6.2;
$sa_kill_level_deflt = 6.9;
```

These three settings are used with the SpamAssassin score level associated with the e-mail being processed. The $sa_tag_level_deflt setting is the threshold at which ham is separated from spam and the X-Spam-Status and X-Spam-Level headers are added to an e-mail.

E-mails that score below this threshold do not have headers added, while e-mails above the threshold will have headers added. The $sa_kill_level_deflt setting is the threshold at which spam e-mail is rejected.

The default configuration is to reject spam. To forward spam to another e-mail address, locate the line specifying $final_spam_destiny or add one if it is not present, and make it read as follows:

```
$final_spam_destiny        = D_PASS;  # (defaults to D_REJECT)
```

The recipient of the spam has to be defined. Locate the line that specifies $spam_quarantine_to, and alter it or add one to contain an e-mail address. The $mydomain variable, which was configured earlier in this step, can be used to refer to the domain — remember to prefix the @ symbol with a backslash.

```
$spam_quarantine_to = "spam-quarantine\@$mydomain";
```

Now, amavisd-new should be started. Most Linux distributions use the following command:

```
# /etc/init.d/amavisd-new start
```

Configuring Postfix to run amavisd-new

Edit /etc/postfix/master.cf and locate this line:

```
smtp          inet  n       -       n       -       -       smtpd
```

Add these lines after it:

```
smtp-amavis unix  y  -              5                          smtp
    -o smtp_data_done_timeout=1200
    -o disable_dns_lookups=yes

127.0.0.1:10025 inet n              y--                        smtpd
    -o content_filter=
    -o local_recipient_maps=
    -o relay_recipient_maps=
    -o smtpd_restriction_classes=
    -o smtpd_recipient_restrictions=permit_mynetworks,reject
    -o mynetworks=127.0.0.0/8
    -o strict_rfc821_envelopes=yes
```

In the `smtp-amavis` line, the number 5 specifies the number of instances that can be used at once. This should correspond to the `$max_servers` entry specified in the `amavisd.conf` file.

Edit `/etc/postfix/main.cf` and add the following line near the end of the file:

```
content_filter = smtp-amavis:[localhost]:10024
```

Restart Postfix with the `postfix reload` command:

```
# postfix reload
```

Configuring e-mail clients

Instead of placing spam in a separate folder by using Procmail, this can be performed by the e-mail client. Most e-mail clients allow rules or filters to be created. These typically come into action when new e-mail is read or a folder is opened.

Rules in an e-mail client run on the value of an e-mail header. It is best to use the `X-Spam-Flag` and search for the value `YES`. The procedure to move tagged messages to a separate folder is outlined as follows:

1. Create a folder or mailbox for holding spam e-mail. The folder name should be intuitive, for example `Spam`.
2. Create a rule to be run when e-mails arrive. The rule should look for the text `X-Spam-Flag` in the message headers.
3. The action on the rule should be to move the e-mail to the `Spam` folder created in the first step.
4. Once the filter is created, send test messages, both spam and non-spam, to check that the filter works properly.

Microsoft Outlook

Microsoft Outlook is popular in large organizations. It integrates well with IMAP servers. Follow the next steps to configure Outlook to filter spam, based on the `X-Spam-Flag` in e-mail headers:

 These instructions are based on Outlook as shipped with Microsoft Office XP; other versions have similar configuration details.

1. Create a folder to store the spam. Click on the **Inbox** in the folder list to select it, right-click and select **New Folder** from the menu. Choose Spam, or another meaningful name and then click **OK**.

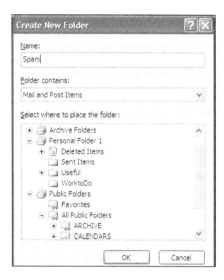

2. Click on the **Tools** menu and select **Rules and Alerts**. Click on **New Rule** to create a new rule.

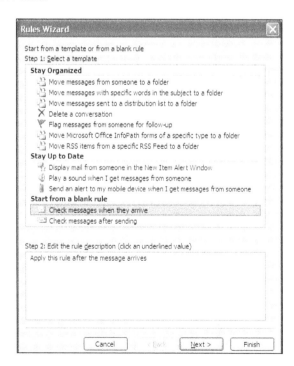

3. Select **Check messages when they arrive** from under **Start from a blank rule**. Click **Next**.

4. Check with specific words in the message header. This will allow Outlook to check the X-Spam-Flag e-mail header. Click on specific words to select the correct phrase.

5. In the next dialog, carefully enter **X-Spam-Flag: YES** and click **Add**. Then press **OK**, and click **Next**.

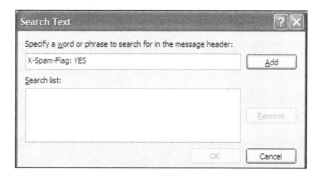

6. The next window offers a choice of actions. Choose **move it to the specified folder** and click on **specified**, which will display a list of folders.

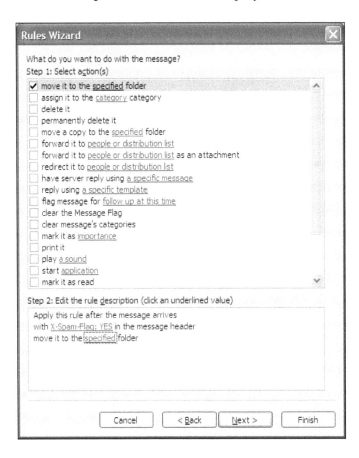

7. Choose the folder created earlier and press **OK**. Click **Finish**. There are no exceptions, so click **Next** again.

8. The Rules Wizard allows the rule to be run immediately on any existing messages in the Inbox. To do this, make sure that the checkbox next to **Turn on this rule is checked**.

9. Finally, click **Finish** and the rule is created and run on all messages in the Inbox.

Microsoft Outlook Express

Outlook Express is shipped with most versions of Windows up to and including Windows XP. It provides POP3 connectivity and many features such as HTML e-mail. Some e-mail clients, including Outlook Express, do not allow filtering on every e-mail header, but only on certain specific headers such as the `From:` and `Subject:` headers. By default, SpamAssassin writes only additional headers, but it can be configured to alter the `Subject`, `From`, or `To` headers of an e-mail. To do this, the `/etc/spamassassin/local.cf` file should be altered. This change can also be made on a per-user basis by editing `~user/.spamassassin/user_prefs`.

Add the following line to the file:

```
rewrite_header Subject *****SPAM*****
```

This will change the header of the e-mail to `*****SPAM*****`. The tag can be altered if desired.

Now that SpamAssassin configuration is complete, Outlook Express can be configured to act on the modified message subject. Follow these steps:

1. Create a folder for the Spam. To do this, select the **File** menu, click on **Folder**, and then on **New**. Type in **Spam**, or another descriptive name, as the folder name, and then click **OK**.

2. Select the **Tools** menu, then select **Message Rules**, and then **New**. On the next window, ensure that the conditions include **Where the Subject line contains specific words**, and the actions include **Move it to the specified folder**.

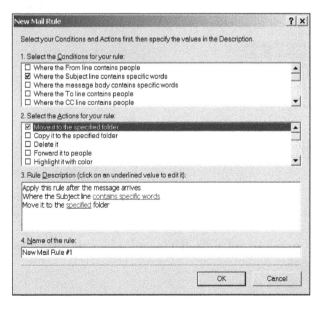

3. Click on **contains specific words**, and enter *******SPAM*******, or the alternative phrase chosen when configuring SpamAssassin. Click **OK**.

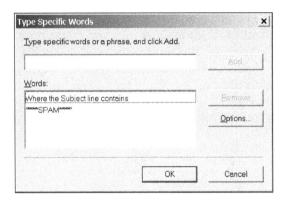

4. Click on **specified** in the next line of the **Rule Description**. Select the folder created and click **OK**.

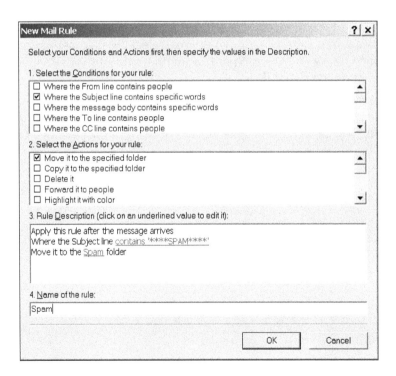

5. The rule is summarized. Give it a meaningful name, such as Spam, then click **OK** to save it.

Mozilla Thunderbird

Mozilla Thunderbird is a free, open source e-mail client with most of the features of Microsoft Outlook. It is available free at `www.mozilla.org/products/thunderbird/`. It has full filtering capabilities. To configure it, follow these steps:

1. Create a folder to store the spam. Click on the **File** menu and select **New | Folder**. Choose a location (the inbox should be fine) and a name, such as **Spam**. Click **OK**.

2. Click on the **Tools** menu and select **Message Filters**. Click on the **New** button to create a new filter.

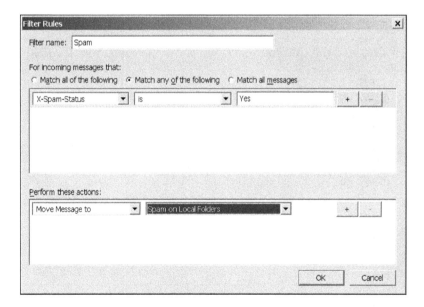

3. In the next dialog, choose a name for the filter such as **Spam**. Then select the **Match any of the following** button. In the left list, type **X-Spam-Status**, in the middle list select **is**, and in the right select **Yes**. In the box below, click on **Move Message to**, and select the folder created in the first step.

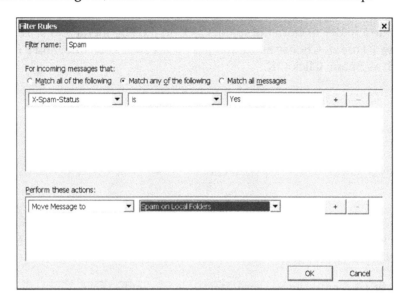

4. Click **OK**, and the rule summary will show the rule. Press **Run Now** to test the rule.

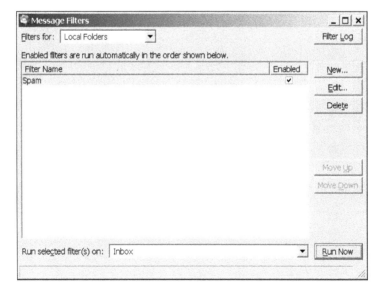

Customizing SpamAssassin

SpamAssassin is very configurable. Almost every setting can be configured on a system-wide or user-specific basis.

Reasons to customize

If SpamAssassin is so good, then why configure it? Well, there are several reasons why it's worth improving spam filtering with SpamAssassin.

- SpamAssassin by default (that is, when installed but not customized) typically manages to detect over 80% of spam. After adding a few customizations, the detection rate can be greater than 95%.

- Everyone's spam is different and one user's spam might look like another user's ham. By trying to be general, SpamAssassin may fail to filter spam for every user.

- Some of the features of SpamAssassin are disabled by default. By enabling them, the spam recognition rate is increased.

The following configuration options are discussed in this chapter:

- **Altering the scores for rules**: This allows rules to be disabled, poor rules to be given less weight, and better rules to be given a higher weight.

- **Obtaining and using new rules**: This can improve spam detection.

- **Adding e-mail addresses to white and blacklists**: This allows the e-mail from specified senders to always be treated as ham, no matter what the content is, or the opposite.

- **Enabling SpamAssassin's Bayesian filter**: This can increase filtering accuracy from 80% to 95% or more.

Rules and scores

The configuration files for standard, sitewide, and user-specific settings are saved in different directories as follows:

- Standard configuration settings are stored in /usr/share/spamassassin.

- Site-wide customizations and settings are stored in /etc/mail/spamassassin/. All files matching *.cf are examined by SpamAssassin.

- User-specific settings are stored in ~/.spamassassin/local.cf.

The bulk of the standard configuration files is devoted to simple rules and their scores.

A rule is typically a match for letters, numbers, or other printing characters. Rules are written using a technique called regular expressions, or regex for short. This is a shorthand method of specifying that certain combinations of characters will trigger the rule. A rule might try to detect a particular word, such as "Rolex", or it might look for particular words in certain orders, such as "buy Rolex online". The rules are stored in text files.

Default files are stored in `/usr/share/spamassassin`. These are files that are shipped with SpamAssassin and may change with each release. It's best not to modify these files or place new files in this directory, as an upgrade to SpamAssassin will overwrite these files. Most of the rules that SpamAssassin uses, and the scores applied to each rule, are defined within files in this directory.

The defaults can be overwritten by sitewide configuration files. These are placed in `/etc/mail/spamassassin`. SpamAssassin will read all files matching `*.cf` in this directory. Settings made here can overrule those in the default files. They can include defining new rules and new rule scores.

User-specific customizations can be placed in the `~/.spamassassin/local.cf` file. Settings made here can override sitewide settings defined in `/etc/mail/spamassassin`, and default settings in `/usr/share/spamassassin/`. New rules may be defined here, and scores for existing rules can be overridden.

SpamAssassin first reads all the files in `/usr/share/spamassassin` in alphanumerical order; `10_misc.cf` will be read before `23_bayes.cf`. SpamAssassin then reads all the `.cf` files in `/etc/mail/spamassassin/`, again in alphanumeric order. Finally, SpamAssassin reads `~user/.spamassassin/user_prefs`. If a rule or score is defined in two files, the setting in the last file read is used. This allows the administrator to override the defaults and a user to override the sitewide settings.

Each line in a rules file can be blank or contain a comment or a command. The hash or pound (#) symbol is used for comments. Rules generally have three parts, the rule definition, a textual description, and the score or series of scores. Convention dictates that all rule scores for rules provided by SpamAssassin should be located together in a separate file. That file is `/usr/share/spamassassin/50_scores.cf`.

Altering rule scores

The simplest configuration change is to change a rule score. There are two reasons why this might be done:

- A rule is very good at detecting spam, but the rule has a low score. E-mails that fire the rule are not being detected as spam.

- A rule is acting on non spam. As a result, e-mails that fire the rule are wrongly being detected as spam.

The rules that give a positive result when SpamAssassin is run are listed in the X-Spam-Status: header of the e-mail:

```
X-Spam-Status: Yes, score=5.8 required=5.0 tests=BAYES_05,HTML_00_10,
    HTML_MESSAGE,MPART_ALT_DIFF autolearn=no
    version=3.1.0-r54722
```

The rules applied to the e-mail are listed after tests=. If one continually appears in e-mail that should be marked as spam, but isn't, then the score for the rule should be increased. If a rule often fires in e-mail that is wrongly classified as spam, the score should be decreased.

To find the current score, use the grep utility in all the locations where a score can be defined.

```
    grep score.*RULE_NAME
$ grep score.*BAYES /usr/share/spamassassin/* /etc/mail/spamassassin/*
~/.spamassassin/local.cf
```

```
/etc/mail/spamassassin/local_scores.cf: score RULE_NAME 0 0 1.665 2.599
/etc/mail/spamassassin/local_scores.cf: 4.34
```

In the previous example, the rule has a default score that is overridden in /etc/mail/spamassassin/local_scores.cf.

The original score for the rule had four values. SpamAssassin changes the scores it uses, depending on whether network tests (for example, those that test open relays) are in use and whether the Bayesian Filter is in use. Four scores are listed, which are used in the following circumstances:

	Bayesian filter not in use	**Bayesian filter in use**
External tests not in use	1st score	3rd score
External tests in use	2nd score	4th score

If only one score is given, as overridden in `/etc/mail/spamassassin/ local_scores.cf`, it is used in all circumstances.

In the previous example, the system administrator has overridden the default score in `/etc/mail/spamassassin/local_scores.cf` with a single value in `/etc/mail/spamassassin/local_scores.cf`. To change this value for a particular user, their `~/.spamassassin/local.cf` might read:

```
score RULE_NAME  1.2
```

This changes the score used from `4.34`, set in `/etc/mail/spamassassin/ local_scores.cf`, to `1.2`. To disable the rule entirely, the score can be set to zero.

```
score RULE_NAME  0
```

Endless hours can be spent configuring rule scores. SpamAssassin includes tools to recalculate optimal rule scores, by examining existing e-mails, both spam and non spam. They are covered in detail in the book *SpamAssassin* published by Packt.

Using other rulesets

SpamAssassin has a large following, and the design of SpamAssassin has made it easy to add new rulesets, which are sets of rules and default scores for those rules. There are many different rulesets available. Most are based on a particular theme, for example finding the names of drugs often sold with spam or telephone numbers found in spam e-mails. Most custom rulesets are listed on the Custom Rulesets page of the SpamAssassin Wiki at `http://wiki.apache.org/spamassassin/CustomRulesets`.

As the battle against spam is so aggressive, rulesets have been developed that may possibly be uploaded daily. SpamAssassin provides this ability with the `sa-update` utility. You can choose to use `sa-update` on a regular basis, or to download a particular ruleset and keep it, or to manually update the rulesets that you choose. To obtain the best results in filtering spam, use of `sa-update` is recommended.

If you wish to install rulesets manually, the Wiki page gives a general description of each ruleset and a URL to download it. Once a ruleset has been chosen, we install it as follows:

1. In a browser, follow the link on the SpamAssassin Wiki page. In most cases, the link will be to a file with a name matching `*.cf`, and a browser will open it as a text file.

2. Save the file using the browser (normally, the **File** menu has a **Save as** option).

3. Copy the file to `/etc/mail/spamassassin`—the rules will be automatically run if the file is placed in this location.

4. Check that the file has scores in it, otherwise the rules will not be used.

5. Monitor spam performance to ensure that legitimate e-mail is not being detected as spam.

Adding rules to SpamAssassin will increase the memory used by SpamAssassin, and the time that it takes to process e-mails. It is best to be cautious and add new rulesets gradually, to ensure that the effect on the machine is understood.

You may manually monitor the ruleset and update it on your system using the same process.

If you choose to use `sa-update`, you should plan your use of it. sa-update can use several channels, which are basically sources of rulesets. By default, the channel updates.spamassassin.org is used; another popular channel is the OpenProtect channel, called `saupdates.openprotect.com`.

To enable `sa-update`, it must be run regularly, for example via cron. Add a cron entry to your system calling the following commands, to update the base rulesets:

```
sa-update
```

If you use an additional channel, the command might look like:

```
sa-update –channel saupdates.openprotect.com
```

> To protect against DNS poisoning and impersonation, SpamAssassin allows digital signing of rulesets. To use a signed ruleset, use the `-gpgkey` parameter to `sa-update`. The correct value to use with the `-gpgkey` parameter will be described in the SpamAssassin wiki page for the ruleset.

Whitelists and blacklists

SpamAssassin is very good at detecting spam, but there is always a risk of errors. By using a list of e-mail addresses that are known spam producers (a blacklist), e-mails from spammers who consistently use the same e-mail addresses or domains can be filtered out. With a list of e-mail addresses that are legitimate e-mail senders (a whitelist), e-mails from regular or important correspondents are guaranteed to be filtered as ham. This prevents the delay or non delivery of important e-mails that may otherwise be marked as spam.

Blacklists that list individual e-mail addresses have limited use—spammers normally use different or random e-mail addresses for each spam run. However, some spammers use the same domain for multiple runs. As SpamAssassin allows wildcards in its blacklisting, entire domains can be blacklisted. This is more useful for filtering out spam.

Manual whitelisting and blacklisting involves adding configuration directives to the global configuration file /etc/mail/spamassassin/local.cf and/or in ~/.spamassassin/user_prefs.

The whitelist and blacklist entries allow the ? and * characters to be used to match a single character or many characters respectively. So, if a whitelist entry read *@domain.com, then joe@domain.com and bill@domain.com would both match. For an entry that read *@yahoo?.com, joe@yahoo1.com and bill@yahoo2.com would match, but billy@yahoo22.com would not match. *@yahoo*.com would match all three examples.

The whitelist and blacklists rules do not immediately cause an e-mail to be tagged as spam or ham, even though the scores are heavily weighted. The default score for the USER_IN_WHITELIST rule is -100.0. It is technically possible that an e-mail may match a whitelist entry and still trigger enough other tests to result in it being marked as spam. Although in practice, this is unlikely to occur, unless the scores have been changed from the defaults.

To blacklist an e-mail address or whole domain, use the blacklist_from directive.

```
blacklist_from    user@spammer.com
blacklist_from    *@spamdomain.com
```

To whitelist an e-mail address or domain, use the whitelist_from directive.

```
whitelist_from    user@mycompany.com
whitelist_from    *@mytradingpartner.com
```

SpamAssassin has more complex rules for managing white and blacklists, as well as an automatic whitelist/blacklist. Both blacklists and whitelists can be specified as discrete items (blacklist joe@domain.com and bill@another.com) or as wildcards (blacklist every joe, and blacklist everyone from domain.com). The wildcards are particularly powerful, and care should be taken to ensure that legitimate e-mail is not rejected.

Bayesian filtering

This uses a statistical technique to determine if an e-mail is spam, based on previous e-mails of both types. Before it will work, it needs to be trained with e-mail that is known spam and also e-mail that is known non spam. It is important that the e-mail is correctly categorized, otherwise the effectiveness of the filter will be reduced. The learning process is done on the e-mail server, and the sample e-mails should be stored in an accessible location.

The `sa-learn` command is used to train the Bayesian filter with e-mail messages that are known ham or spam. The SpamAssassin installation routine will have placed `sa-learn` in the path, normally in `/usr/bin/sa-learn`.

It is used on the command line and is passed a directory, file, or series of files. For this to work, the e-mail has to be stored on the server or exported from the client in a suitable format. SpamAssassin recognizes `mbox` format, and many e-mail clients use a compatible format. To use `sa-learn`, a directory or series of directories can be passed in to the command:

```
$ sa-learn --ham ~/.maildir/.Trash/cur/ ~/.maildir/cur
    Learned from 75 message(s) (175 message(s) examined).
```

If the `mbox` format is used, the `mbox` flag should be used so that SpamAssassin searches the file for more than one e-mail.

```
$ sa-learn -mbox --spam ~/mbox/spam ~/mbox/bad-spam
    Learned from 75 message(s) (175 message(s) examined).
```

If SpamAssassin has already learned from an e-mail, `sa-learn` detects this and will not process it twice. In the example above, 100 of the 175 e-mails had been processed already and were ignored on this run. The remaining 75 e-mails had not been processed before.

If `sa-learn` is passed a number of messages, there may be no feedback for some time. The `--showdots` flag provides feedback in the form of dots (.) whenever an e-mail is processed.

```
$ sa-learn --spam --showdots ~/.SPAM/cur ~/.SPAM/new

. . . . . . . . . . . . . . . . . . . . . . .
    Learned from 20 message(s) (25 message(s) examined).
```

Once SpamAssassin has learned enough e-mails, it will begin to use the Bayesian filter automatically. It can be kept up-to-date by using the auto-learn feature.

Auto-learning should not be used without additional user input. There are two reasons for doing this.

- SpamAssassin occasionally gets spam detection wrong, and e-mail that is spam may be learned as an example of non spam. Auto-learning would confuse the Bayesian filter and decrease its effectiveness.

- The score threshold that an e-mail is auto-learned at is higher than that for detection as spam. In other words, an e-mail may be detected as spam, but not auto-learned. In this case, the rest of SpamAssassin is doing a fairly good job of detecting border-line spam (those with scores close to the threshold for spam), but the Bayesian filter is not being taught the e-mails.

To use automatic learning, set the `bayes_auto_learn` flag to 1. This can be configured sitewide in the `/etc/mail/spamassassin/local.cf` file, or can be overridden in a user's `~/.spamassassin/user_prefs` file. Two other configuration flags also affect auto-learning, and are the thresholds for learning ham and spam. These values are in the same units as SpamAssassin's score for each e-mail.

```
bayes_auto_learn          1
bayes_auto_learn_threshold_nonspam         0.1
bayes_auto_learn_threshold_spam            12.0
```

When auto-learning is enabled, any e-mail that is assigned a score of less than `bayes_auto_learn_threshold_nonspam`, is learned as ham. Any e-mail that is assigned a value greater than `bayes_auto_learn_threshold_spam`, is learned as spam.

It is recommended that the `bayes_auto_learn_threshold_nonspam` threshold is kept low (close to or below zero). This will avoid the situation where a spam e-mail that escapes detection is used as an example to train the Bayesian filter. Keeping the `bayes_auto_learn_threshold_spam` threshold high is to some extent a matter of choice; however, it should be above the scores of any e-mails that have been wrongly classified as spam in the past. This may occur up to a score of 10 for the default spam threshold of 5. Therefore, using an auto-learn threshold of less than 10 for spam may cause non spam to be accidentally learned as spam. If this happens, the Bayesian database will begin to lose effectiveness, and future Bayesian results will be compromised.

SpamAssassin keeps the Bayesian database in three files in the `.spamassassin` directory within a user's home directory. The format used is usually Berkeley DB format and the files are named as follows:

```
bayes_journal
bayes_seen
bayes_toks
```

The `bayes_journal` file is used as a temporary storage area. Sometimes it is not present. This file is generally relatively small, with a size of around 10 KB. The `bayes_seen` and `bayes_toks` files can each be several megabytes in size.

Other SpamAssassin features

This chapter has only scratched the surface of SpamAssassin's capabilities. If spam is a problem for an organization, SpamAssassin will reward further study. Some of the other features that it contains are as follows:

- **Network tests**: SpamAssassin can integrate with Open Relay Databases. (The 3.x distribution contains tests for over 30 databases, although not all of them are enabled by default.) Open Relay tests do not require a fast machine or lots of RAM, and so are relatively cheap tests to use. They have a fairly successful detection rate.

- **External content databases**: SpamAssassin can integrate with external content databases. These work in a participating network. All the participants send details of all the e-mails they receive to central servers. If the e-mails have been sent many times before, the e-mail is probably a spam that has been sent to many users. The services are designed so that no confidential data is sent.

- **Whitelist and blacklist**: SpamAssassin includes an automatic whitelist and blacklist, which work in a similar way to the manual lists described earlier. This is particularly effective at preventing regular correspondents from having their e-mail wrongly detected as spam.

- **Creating new rules**: New rules can be written and developed. Creating rules is not particularly difficult, with a little imagination and a suitable source of spam. System Administrators can rid their users of any persistent spam that fails to be detected with the default SpamAssassin rules.

- **Customizable headers**: The headers that SpamAssassin adds to e-mails can be customized, and new headers can be written. SpamAssassin will also attempt to detect viruses and Trojan software, and will wrap an e-mail address like that in a special envelope e-mail.

- **Multiple installations**: SpamAssassin can be installed on multiple machines, serving one or more e-mail servers. In very high volume e-mail systems, many spam servers may be run, each only processing spam. This leads to a high-throughput, high-availability service.

- **Customizable rule scores**: SpamAssassin includes tools to customize rule scores, based on samples of the spam and legitimate e-mail received at an organization. This helps to improve the filtering rate. With SpamAssassin 3.0, the tools were improved significantly, and the procedure to perform this is much less time consuming than it was in earlier versions.

Summary

In this chapter, you have seen how SpamAssassin can be obtained and installed. Three different methods of using SpamAssassin were presented, with suggestions on which option to choose for a particular installation.

Configuration of popular e-mail clients was also covered, namely Microsoft Outlook, Microsoft Outlook Express, and Mozilla Thunderbird.

9
Antivirus Protection

A common view is that Linux is not vulnerable to viruses, so why install an antivirus solution? While it is true that there are very few viruses for Linux, the primary objective is not to protect the mail server from infection, but to reduce or eliminate any risk to recipients. Your organization may have client PCs running Windows that are susceptible to viruses, or you could receive a virus laden e-mail that you may forward to a customer or business partner.

One of the many options for filtering with Procmail is to remove executable attachments from e-mails in order to protect your system from possible virus attacks. This will be, at best, a crude operation; at worst, it will remove files that do not contain viruses and possibly leave other infected documents such as scripts that are not executables.

It is also possible to scan e-mails on the client side. But in a company environment, it is not always possible to rely on every individual having their machines up-to-date and correctly installed with suitable virus checking software. The obvious solution is to run an efficient process on the server to ensure that all e-mail sent or received by the organization is correctly scanned for viruses.

There are a number of antivirus solutions available for Linux-based systems. We have chosen to focus on Clam AntiVirus, usually known as ClamAV. This is an open source software and regularly updates the database of viruses to be checked for before download.

In this chapter, we will learn about:

- The types of documents which may contain viruses that ClamAV can detect
- Installing and configuring the ClamAV components for detecting viruses
- Setting up procedures to maintain an up-to-date antivirus database
- Integrating ClamAV with Postfix to scan all incoming e-mail messages and attachments

- Extensively testing our installation with sample files containing test virus signatures and by using test e-mail bourne viruses

- Adding each ClamAV component into our system startup and shutdown procedures

Introduction to ClamAV

Clam AntiVirus is an open source antivirus toolkit for Linux, Windows, and Mac OS X. The main design feature of ClamAV was to integrate it with mail servers to perform attachment scanning and help filter out known viruses. The package provides a flexible and scalable multithreaded daemon (`clamd`), a command-line scanner (`clamscan`), and a tool for automatic updating via the Internet (`freshclam`). The programs are based on a shared library, `libclamav`, distributed with the Clam AntiVirus package, which you can also use with your own software.

The version of ClamAV we are going to use in this chapter is the latest stable version, 0.95.2, that has an up-to-date virus database and signatures to enable detection of over 580,000 viruses, worms, and Trojans including Microsoft Office macro viruses, mobile malware, and other threats. Although not covered in this book, it is also able to perform on-access scanning under Linux with suitable installation into the Linux kernel.

Document types supported

A wide range of document types can contain or spread viruses and ClamAV provides protection from the majority of them:

- **ELF** (**Executable and Linking Format**) files used by UNIX and UNIX-like operating systems such as Linux, Solaris, and OpenBSD.

- **Portable Executable** (**PE**) files (32/64-bit) compressed with UPX, FSG, Petite, WWPack32, and obfuscated with SUE, Yoda's Cryptor, and others. This is the standard format for Microsoft Windows Executables and one of the most common transports for viruses.

- Many forms of Microsoft documents can contain scripts or executables. The following document and archive types can be processed by ClamAV:
    - MS OLE2
    - MS Cabinet files
    - MS CHM (Compressed HTML)
    - MS SZDD
    - MS Office Word and Excel documents

- Support for other special files and formats include:
    - HTML
    - RTF
    - PDF
    - Files encrypted with CryptFF and ScrEnc
    - uuencode
    - TNEF (winmail.dat)
- Other common archive formats that may contain any form of document and that ClamAV can process include:
    - RAR (2.0)
    - ZIP
    - gzip
    - bzip2
    - tar
    - BinHex
    - SIS (SymbianOS packages)
    - AutoIt

Scanning of archives also includes the scanning of supported document formats held within the archives.

Downloading and installing ClamAV

As viruses are being discovered on an almost daily basis, it is well worth installing the latest stable version of ClamAV software. If your system already has ClamAV installed, it is possible that the installation may be based on an out of date installation package. It is highly recommended that you download and install the latest version from the ClamAV website to ensure the highest level of security against viruses on your systems.

Adding a new system user and group

You will have to add a new user and group to your system for the ClamAV system to use.

```
# groupadd clamav
# useradd -g clamav -s /bin/false -c "Clam AntiVirus" clamav
```

Installing from a package

There are a number of installation packages available for ClamAV and details can be found on the ClamAV website at `http://www.clamav.net/download/packages/packages-linux`.

 Due to licensing restrictions, most binary packages don't have a built-in RAR support. For this reason, we recommend that you install ClamAV from source until any licensing issues are resolved.

If you are using a Red Hat-based system, the installation may be performed using either of the following options, depending on which distribution you have installed:

```
# yum update clamav
```

or

```
# up2date -u clamav
```

If you are using a Debian-based system, the installation may be performed using the following command:

```
# apt-get install clamav clamav-daemon clamav-freshclam
```

 Make sure you are installing version 0.95.2 or higher as there are significant enhancements over previous versions. In general, you should always install the latest stable version available.

Installing from source code

Installing ClamAV from the original source code is not very difficult, and enables you to run any version you want and not just the version chosen by the package maintainer of your Linux distribution. The ClamAV source code can be downloaded from a number of mirrors accessible from the main ClamAV website (`http://www.clamav.net/download/sources`).

Requirements

The following elements are required to compile ClamAV:

- zlib and zlib-devel packages
- gcc compiler suite

The following packages are optional but highly recommended:

- bzip2 and bzip2-devel library
- UnRAR package

Building and installing

Once you have downloaded and unpacked the archive, cd to the directory, example, clamav-0.95.2. Before starting to build and install the software, it is well worthwhile reading through the INSTALL and README documents.

For most Linux systems, the simplest installation method can be reduced by following the steps listed here:

1. Run the configure utility to create the right build environment by running the configure command:

   ```
   $ ./configure --sysconfdir=/etc
   ```

2. After the configuration script is complete, you can run the make command to build the software executables.

   ```
   $ make
   ```

3. The final step, as root, is to copy the executables into the correct position for operation on the system.

   ```
   # make install
   ```

In the last step, the software is installed into the /usr/local directory and the config files into /etc as specified by the -sysconfdir option as shown.

At all stages you should check the processes output for any significant errors or warnings.

As with all packages built from the source code, you may wish to delete the unpacked archive after completion of the building, installing, and testing steps in this chapter.

Quick test

We can verify that the software is correctly installed, by trying the following test to scan the example test virus files in source directory recursively:

 The supplied test virus files do not contain real viruses and are harmless. They contain an industry agreed virus signature specifically designed for test purposes.

```
$ clamscan -r -l scan.txt clamav-x.yz/test
```

It should find some test files in the `clamav-x.yz/test` directory. The scan result will be saved in the `scan.txt` log file. Check the log file, paying particular attention to any warnings indicating that support for a particular file or archive format has not been compiled in. The tail of the log file should contain a summary similar to the following:

```
----------- SCAN SUMMARY -----------
Known viruses: 572081
Engine version: 0.95.2
Scanned directories: 2
Scanned files: 109
Infected files: 35
Data scanned: 1.39 MB
Data read: 1.18 MB (ratio 1.17:1)
Time: 2.057 sec (0 m 2 s)
```

Editing the config files

After installation of the software, two configuration files need to be edited. The first file, `/etc/clamd.conf`, is for the actual virus scanning software. Most of the important configuration options for this file are discussed in the following sections. The second configuration file, `/etc/freshclam.conf`, is covered later in this chapter. This is where we add the configuration options for the automatic virus database updates.

clamd

You have to edit the configuration file in order to use the daemon, otherwise `clamd` won't run.

```
$ clamd
   ERROR: Please edit the example config file /etc/clamd.conf.
```

This shows the location of the default configuration file. The format and options of this file are fully described in the `clamd.conf(5)` manual. The `config` file is well commented and configuration should be straightforward.

Examining the sample config file

The sample `config` file that is provided is very well documented with comments at every significant configuration value. Here are some key values that you may wish to modify:

```
##
## Example config file for the Clam AV daemon
## Please read the clamd.conf(5) manual before editing this file.
##

# Comment or remove the line below.
#Example
```

The `Example` line will cause the program to halt with a configuration error and is a deliberate inclusion to force you to edit the file before the software operates correctly. Placing a # at the beginning of the line will be enough to resolve this problem after you have finished editing the file.

```
# Uncomment this option to enable logging.
# LogFile must be writable for the user running daemon.
# A full path is required.
# Default: disabled
LogFile /var/log/clamav/clamd.log
```

It is well worth setting up a log file to enable you to check for errors and monitor correct operation over the first few weeks of operation. Thereafter, you can decide whether to stop the logging or leave it operational.

```
# Log time with each message.
# Default: disabled
LogTime yes
```

Enabling time stamping in the log files ensures that you can track down the time of the event being logged to aid in debugging problems and matching events to entries in other log files.

```
# Path to the database directory.
# Default: hardcoded (depends on installation options)
#DatabaseDirectory /var/lib/clamav
DatabaseDirectory /usr/local/share/clamav
```

Make sure that the database directory is correctly configured so that it is known exactly where the virus signature information is being stored. The installation process will have created the file `main.cvd`, and possibly `daily.cld`, as the database files containing the virus signatures.

```
# The daemon works in a local OR a network mode. Due to security
# reasons we recommend the local mode.

# Path to a local socket file the daemon will listen on.
# Default: disabled
LocalSocket /var/run/clamav/clamd.sock
```

Using local mode is an important configuration change and is required to ensure the security of the system on which ClamAV is installed.

```
# This option allows you to save a process identifier of the listening
# daemon (main thread).
# Default: disabled
PidFile /var/run/clamav/clamd.pid
```

This is useful to start and stop scripts. As shown in the previous example, the ClamAV directory must be writable.

```
# TCP address.
# By default we bind to INADDR_ANY, probably not wise.
# Enable the following to provide some degree of protection
# from the outside world.
# Default: disabled
TCPAddr 127.0.0.1
```

This is another security related configuration item to ensure that only local processes can gain access to the service.

```
# Execute a command when virus is found. In the command string %v
# will
# be replaced by a virus name.
# Default: disabled
#VirusEvent /usr/local/bin/send_sms 123456789 "VIRUS ALERT: %v"
```

This could be a useful feature to consider in some situations. However, with the wide range and frequency of virus delivery, this could prove to be a significant annoyance to have messages arriving throughout the night or day.

```
# Run as a selected user (clamd must be started by root).
# Default: disabled
User clamav
```

By creating a user especially for ClamAV, we can assign ownership of files and processes to this user ID and help improve security of the files by restricting access to only this user ID. Also, when running processes are listed on the system, it is easy to identify those owned by the ClamAV system.

freshclam

You have to edit the configuration file, otherwise `freshclam` won't run.

```
$ freshclam
   ERROR: Please edit the example config file /etc/freshclam.conf
```

A sample `freshclam` configuration file is also included in the source distribution. If you need more information about the configuration options and format, you should refer to the *freshclam.conf(5)* manual page.

Closest mirrors

A number of mirror servers are available on the Internet from which you can download the latest antivirus database. To avoid overloading any one server, the configuration file should be set up to make sure that the download is being taken from the nearest available server. The included `update` utility makes use of the DNS system to locate a suitable server based on the country code you are requesting.

The configuration file entry that you need to modify is `DatabaseMirror`. You may also specify the parameter `MaxAttempts` — number of times the database is downloaded from the server.

The default database mirror is `clamav.database.net`, but you are able to apply multiple entries in the configuration file. The configuration entry should be made using the format `db.xx.clamav.net`, where xx represents your normal two-letter ISO country code. For example, if your server is in the United States, you should add the following lines to `freshclam.conf`. The full list of two-letters country codes is available at `http://www.iana.org/cctld/cctld-whois.htm`.

```
DatabaseMirror db.us.clamav.net
DatabaseMirror db.local.clamav.net
```

If the connection to the first entry fails for any reason, an attempt will be made to download from the second mirror entry. You should not just use the default entry, as it may result in your server or IP address being blacklisted by the ClamAV database administrators for overloading and you may not able to obtain any updates at all.

Examining the sample config file

The sample `config` file that is provided is very well documented with comments at every significant configuration value. Here are some key values that you may wish to modify:

```
##
## Example config file for freshclam
## Please read the freshclam.conf(5) manual before editing this file.
## This file may be optionally merged with clamd.conf.
##


# Comment or remove the line below.
#Example
```

Make sure that this line is commented to allow the daemon to operate.

```
# Path to the log file (make sure it has proper permissions)
# Default: disabled
UpdateLogFile /var/log/clamav/freshclam.log
```

Enabling the log file is useful to track the ongoing updates that are being applied and to monitor the correct operation of the system during early testing stages.

```
# Enable verbose logging.
# Default: disabled
LogVerbose
```

The previous option enables more detailed error messages to be included in the update log file.

```
# Use DNS to verify virus database version. Freshclam uses DNS TXT
# records to verify database and software versions. We highly
# recommend enabling this option.
# Default: disabled
DNSDatabaseInfo current.cvd.clamav.net
# Uncomment the following line and replace XY with your country
# code. See http://www.iana.org/cctld/cctld-whois.htm for the full
# list.
# Default: There is no default, which results in an error when running
freshclam
DatabaseMirror db.us.clamav.net
```

This is an important configuration to reduce network traffic overheads and ensure that you are obtaining updates from a geographically close server.

```
# database.clamav.net is a round-robin record which points to our
# most
# reliable mirrors. It's used as a fall back in case db.XY.clamav.net
# is not working. DO NOT TOUCH the following line unless you know
# what you are doing.
DatabaseMirror database.clamav.net
```

As the instruction says—leave this line alone.

```
# Number of database checks per day.
# Default: 12 (every two hours)
Checks 24
```

For busy servers with lots of traffic, it is worthwhile to update the virus database at a more frequent interval. However, this is recommended only for systems running version 0.8 or higher of the ClamAV software.

```
# Run command after successful database update.
# Default: disabled
#OnUpdateExecute command

# Run command when database update process fails..
# Default: disabled
#OnErrorExecute command
```

To aid monitoring of the updates to configuration files, the options you have just seen are available to apply suitable actions if updates do or do not occur correctly.

File permissions

Following the previous recommendation, clamd will be run as the clamav user and by default, when started, freshclam drops privileges and switches to the clamav user. Therefore, ownership of the socket, PID, and log files specified in the configuration files seen in the previous example should be set up using the following commands to allow correct access:

```
# mkdir /var/log/clamav  /var/run/clamav
```

```
# chown clamav:clamav /var/log/clamav  /var/run/clamav
```

The user under which freshclam and clamd run can be changed in freshclam.conf and clamd.conf. However, you should verify that the ClamAV processes have access to the virus definition database if you change these parameters.

Post installation testing

Now that we have the main components of ClamAV installed, we can verify the correct operation of each component.

- `clamscan`—the command line scanner
- `clamd`—the ClamAV daemon
- `freshclam`—virus definitions updater

For these tests, we are going to need a virus or at least a non-destructive file that looks like a virus.

EICAR test virus

A number of antivirus researchers have already worked together to produce a file that their (and many other) products detect as if it were a virus. Agreeing on one file for such purposes simplifies matters for users.

This test file is known as the **EICAR (European Institute for Computer Anti-virus Research) standard antivirus test file**. The file itself is not a virus, it does not contain any program code at all, and is therefore safe to pass on to other people. However, most antivirus products will react to the file as though it really is a virus, which can make it a rather tricky file to manipulate or send via e-mail if you or the recipient has good virus protection systems in place.

The file is a text file consisting entirely of printable ASCII characters so that it can easily be created with a regular text editor. Any antivirus product that supports the EICAR test file should detect it in any file that starts with the following 68 characters:

```
X5O!P%@AP[4\PZX54(P^)7CC)7}$EICAR-STANDARD-ANTIVIRUS-TEST-FILE!$H+H*
```

When you are creating this file, you should take note of the following facts. The file uses only upper case letters, digits, and punctuation marks, and does not include spaces. There are a couple of common mistakes that can be made when recreating this file. These include ensuring that the third character is the capital letter O, not the digit zero (0), and that all 68 characters are one line, which must be the very first line in the file.

For more information on the EICAR antivirus test file, visit `http://www.eicar.org/anti_virus_test_file.htm`.

Testing clamscan

The first test we need to run is to make sure that the virus scanner is installed and that the virus definitions database is configured and included correctly. A virus database is supplied as part of the installation process.

The simplest way to do this is to create a copy of the EICAR test file on your server and then run the clamscan program. We are using the -i flag so that only infected files will be shown. You should get output like this:

```
$ clamscan -i testvirus.txt cleanfile.txt
LibClamAV Warning: ****************************************************
LibClamAV Warning: ***  The virus database is older than 7 days!  ***
LibClamAV Warning: ***   Please update it as soon as possible.    ***
LibClamAV Warning: ****************************************************
testvirus.txt: Eicar-Test-Signature FOUND
----------- SCAN SUMMARY -----------
Known viruses: 572031
Engine version: 0.95.2
Scanned directories: 0
Scanned files: 2
Infected files: 1
Data scanned: 0.00 MB
Data read: 0.00 MB (ratio 0.00:1)
Time: 2.310 sec (0 m 2 s)
```

Note the warning about an out-of-date virus database. This is normal and will be rectified during freshclam testing.

Testing clamd

By using the clamdscan program, we can again scan the test file, but do this by instructing the clamd process to do the scanning. This is an excellent test to make sure that the clamd daemon process is running.

The expected output should look something like the following:

```
$ clamdscan testvirus.txt
    /home/ian/testvirus.txt: Eicar-Test-Signature FOUND
    ----------- SCAN SUMMARY -----------
    Infected files: 1
    Time: 0.000 sec (0 m 0 s)
```

If the clamd daemon is not running it can be started using the # clamd command.

You should also check the clamd log file, as configured in clamd.conf, for any unexpected errors or warnings after running this test.

Testing freshclam

Using the `freshclam` program interactively we can update the virus database with the latest definitions. This test will update the database only once. We shall see later how to perform automatic updates. Using the following command (as superuser) we would expect output similar to the following:

```
# freshclam
ClamAV update process started at Wed Jul  8 14:21:01 2009
main.cvd is up to date (version: 51, sigs: 545035, f-level: 42, builder: sven)
Trying host db.us.clamav.net (207.57.106.31)...
Downloading daily-9543.cdiff [100%]
Downloading daily-9544.cdiff [100%]
nonblock_connect: connect timing out (30 secs)
Can't connect to port 80 of host 207.57.106.31 (IP: 207.57.106.31)
WARNING: getpatch: Can't download daily-9545.cdiff from db.us.clamav.net
WARNING: getfile: daily-9545.cdiff not found on remote server (IP: 64.246.134.219)
WARNING: getpatch: Can't download daily-9545.cdiff from db.us.clamav.net
Trying host db.us.clamav.net (64.246.134.219)...
WARNING: getfile: daily-9545.cdiff not found on remote server (IP: 64.246.134.219)
WARNING: getpatch: Can't download daily-9545.cdiff from db.us.clamav.net
WARNING: Incremental update failed, trying to download daily.cvd
Downloading daily.cvd [100%]
daily.cvd updated (version: 9546, sigs: 40746, f-level: 43, builder: ccordes)
Database updated (585781 signatures) from db.us.clamav.net (IP: 168.143.19.95)
```

From the output, we can see that the update process downloaded two differential updates successfully and failed with a network problem on the third. Downloading the differences between the latest and current database helps to reduce network traffic and server load. In this case `freshclam` detected the failure and downloaded the latest daily update to bring the virus database up-to-date with an increased number of virus signatures.

Now if you run the `clamscan` test again, you will notice that the out-of-date warning is no longer displayed.

You should also check that the `freshclam` log file contains output similar to the previous code after running this test.

Introduction to ClamSMTP

In order to scan all e-mail passing through the server, a software interface is required between Postfix and ClamAV. The interface we are going to use is **ClamSMTP**. The following introduction from the ClamSMTP site (`http://memberwebs.com/stef/software/clamsmtp/`) describes the SMTP virus filter as:

ClamSMTP is an SMTP filter that allows you to check for viruses using the ClamAV antivirus software. It accepts SMTP connections and forwards the SMTP commands and responses to another SMTP server. The 'DATA' email body is intercepted and scanned before forwarding. ClamSMTP aims to be lightweight, reliable, and simple rather than have a myriad of options. It's written in C without major dependencies.

Postfix is designed to allow external filters to be called to process mail messages and to return the processed data back to Postfix for onward delivery. ClamSMTP has been designed to work directly between Postfix and ClamAV to ensure efficient operation.

Some Linux distributions may have maintained packages for ClamSMTP, which can be installed via the relevant package manager. However, you should still complete the instructions that follow to configure and integrate ClamSMTP into Postfix.

The latest source code may be downloaded from `http://memberwebs.com/stef/software/clamsmtp/`, directly onto your Linux system using the `wget` command. Change to a suitable location to download and build the software. The command option for the current version (1.10) would be `wget <url>`.

```
$ wget http://memberwebs.com/stef/software/clamsmtp/clamsmtp-1.10.tar.gz
```

You should check the website for the latest version that you can download. After you have downloaded the file, unpack the contents of the file using the `tar` command.

```
$ tar xvfz clamsmtp-1.10.tar.gz
```

This will create a directory structure with all the relevant files contained below the current directory.

Building and installing

Before building and installing the software, it is well worthwhile reading through the `INSTALL` and `README` documents.

For most Linux systems, the simplest installation method is as follows:

1. Run the `configure` utility to create the right build environment by running the `configure` command.

   ```
   $ ./configure --sysconfdir=/etc
   ```

2. After the configuration script is complete, you can run the `make` command to build the software executables:

   ```
   $ make
   ```

3. The final step, as `root`, is to copy the executables into the correct position for operation on the system:

```
# make install
```

In the last step, the software is installed into the `/usr/local` directory and the config files into `/etc`.

At all stages, you should check the processes output for any significant errors or warnings.

Configuring into Postfix

Postfix provides support for mail filtering by passing mail items through external processes. This operation can be performed either before or after the mail has been queued. The way communication between Postfix and `clamsmtp` works is by pretending that `clamsmtp` is itself an SMTP server. This simple approach provides an easy way to create a distributed architecture whereby different processes could be working on different machines to spread the load in very busy networks. For our use, we will assume that we are using only one machine with all software running on that machine.

The `clamsmtp` filter interface was designed specifically to provide an interface between ClamAV and the Postfix mail system. The filter is implemented as an after-queue filter for antivirus scanning.

The first configuration option requires adding lines to the Postfix `main.cf` file:

```
content_filter = scan:127.0.0.1:10025
receive_override_options = no_address_mappings
```

The `content_filter` instruction forces Postfix to send all mail through the service named `scan` on port `10025`. The scan service will be the one that we set up using `clamsmtpd`. The instruction for `receive_override_options` configures Postfix to perform `no_address_mappings`. This prevents Postfix from expanding any e-mail aliases or groups, which otherwise would have resulted in duplicate e-mails being received.

The second configuration change needs to be made to the Postfix `master.cf` file.

```
# AV scan filter (used by content_filter)
scan      unix  -       -        n       -       16      smtp
          -o smtp_send_xforward_command=yes
          -o smtp_enforce_tls=no
# For injecting mail back into postfix from the filter
127.0.0.1:10026 inet  n -        n       -       16      smtpd
          -o content_filter=
```

```
            -o receive_override_options=no_unknown_recipient_checks,no_
    header_body_checks
            -o smtpd_helo_restrictions=
            -o smtpd_client_restrictions=
            -o smtpd_sender_restrictions=
            -o smtpd_recipient_restrictions=permit_mynetworks,reject
            -o mynetworks_style=host
            -o smtpd_authorized_xforward_hosts=127.0.0.0/8
```

 The formatting of the files is very important. You should ensure that there are no spaces around the = (equal) sign or , (commas) in the text you added.

The first two lines, do the actual creation of the `scan` service. The remaining lines set up a service for accepting mail back into Postfix for delivery. The rest of the options are there to prevent a mail loop occurring and to relax address checking. When these changes have been made, you need to get Postfix to reread the modified configuration files by using the following command:

```
# postfix reload
```

Configuring clamSMTP

You have to create the configuration file, /etc/clamsmtpd.conf, otherwise clamsmtpd won't run:

```
$ clamsmtpd
```

```
clamsmtpd: configuration file not found: /etc/clamsmtpd.conf
```

A sample clamsmtp.conf configuration file is included in the source distribution doc directory. This needs to be copied to the correct location and edited before the clamsmtp software will operate correctly.

```
# cp clamsmtpd.conf /etc/clamsmtpd.conf
```

The format and options of this file are fully described in the clamsmtpd.conf(5) manual.

Examining the sample config file

The sample config file that is provided is very well documented with comments for each significant configuration value. Here are some key values that you may wish to modify.

```
# The address to send scanned mail to.
# This option is required unless TransparentProxy is enabled
OutAddress: 127.0.0.1:10026
```

As we are using just one machine in this configuration, we should specify the `OutAddress` option as `127.0.0.1:10026` to match the option specified in `master.cf`.

```
# The maximum number of connection allowed at once.
# Be sure that clamd can also handle this many connections
#MaxConnections: 64

# Amount of time (in seconds) to wait on network IO
#TimeOut: 180

# Keep Alives (ie: NOOP's to server)
#KeepAlives: 0

# Send XCLIENT commands to receiving server
#XClient: off

# Address to listen on (defaults to all local addresses on port 10025)
#Listen: 0.0.0.0:10025
```

This address matches the option specified in `main.cf`.

```
# The address clamd is listening on
ClamAddress: /var/run/clamav/clamd.sock
```

This should match the `LocalSocket` option in the `clamd.conf` file.

```
# A header to add to all scanned email
#Header: X-Virus-Scanned: ClamAV using ClamSMTP

# Directory for temporary files
#TempDirectory: /tmp

# What to do when we see a virus (use 'bounce' or 'pass' or 'drop'
Action: drop
```

Throw away the message.

```
# Whether or not to keep virus files
#Quarantine: off

# Enable transparent proxy support
#TransparentProxy: off

# User to switch to
User: clamav
```

It is important to make sure that the processes are run as the same user as you use to run `clamd` or you may find that each process has problems accessing the other's temporary files.

```
# Virus actions: There's an option to run a script every time a virus
is found.
# !IMPORTANT! This can open a hole in your server's security big
enough to drive
# farm vehicles through. Be sure you know what you're doing.
!IMPORTANT!

#VirusAction: /path/to/some/script.sh
```

We are now ready to perform the start up of the `clamsmtpd` process. You should start this as `root` and verify that the process is present and running with the user id of `clamav`.

 # clamsmtpd

If you have problems starting the service, make sure that the `clamd` (the ClamAV daemon) is running, and that it is listening on the socket you specified. You can set this in `clamd.conf` using the `LocalSocket` or `TCPSocket` directives (be sure that you only uncomment one of those lines). You should also make sure that the `ScanMail` directive is set to `on`.

Testing e-mail filtering

Viruses, by definition, are things that we would prefer to avoid having any contact with at all. But in order to be certain that our filtering and detection processes are working correctly and that we are fully protected, we need to have access to a virus for testing purposes. Using real viruses for testing in the real world in a production ready environment is rather like setting fire to the trash can in your office to see whether the smoke detector is working. Such a test will give meaningful results, but with unappealing risks and unacceptable side effects. Therefore, we need our EICAR test file that can safely be mailed around and which is obviously non-viral, but which your antivirus software will react to as if it were a virus.

Testing mail-borne virus filtering

The first test is to check that you can still receive mail.

```
$ echo "Clean mail" | sendmail $USER
```

You should receive your mail with the addition of the following line in the header:

```
X-virus-scanned: ClamAV using ClamSMTP
```

If you did not receive the mail, check the system, postfix, and clamd log files. If necessary, you can also stop and restart the `clamsmtpd` daemon with the `-d 4` option for extra debugging output.

The second simple test of scanning for mail-borne viruses can be performed by simply sending yourself a copy of the EICAR virus as an e-mail attachment.

The sample EICAR virus file must be created as an attachment to an e-mail. The following command chain from the Linux command prompt will send a very simple uuencoded attachment copy of the virus-infected file.

```
$ uuencode testvirus.txt test_virus | sendmail $USER
```

If everything is working and configured correctly, you should not receive the mail, as `clamsmtp` was instructed to drop the message. The absence of the message does not prove everything is working, so check the system or postfix log files for an entry similar to the following:

```
Jul  8 19:38:57 ian postfix/smtp[6873]: 26E66F42CB: to=<ian@example.
com>, orig_to=<ian>, relay=127.0.0.1[127.0.0.1]:10025, delay=0.1,
delays=0.06/0/0.04/0, dsn=2.0.0, status=sent (250 Virus Detected;
Discarded Email)
```

This proves the simple case of detecting a straightforward attachment containing a virus.

Of course, in the real world, viruses are slightly more clever than your average e-mail attachment. Thorough testing is required to be sure that the filtering is set up correctly. Luckily, there is a website (http://www.gfi.com/emailsecuritytest/) available to send e-mails to you that contain the EICAR virus encoded within e-mails in a wide range of ways. Currently it supports 17 individual tests.

Thorough e-mail-borne testing

The site http://www.gfi.com/emailsecuritytest/ requires you to register the e-mail address you wish to test and sends a confirmation e-mail to that address. In this e-mail is a link to follow that confirms that you are the valid user in control of that e-mail address. You are then able to send any or all of the 17 virus and e-mail client exploit tests to this e-mail address. If any of the virus bearing e-mails end up unfiltered in your inbox, then the installation has failed.

However, there are some test messages on the site that are not strictly viruses and so are not detected by the ClamAV process. This is because the messages do not themselves contain viruses and so there is nothing to find and therefore, nothing to stop.

By definition, ClamAV traps only malicious code. The gfi (http://www.gfi.com/emailsecuritytest/) site sends this type of test messages. The nature of these messages is that they have some malformed MIME tags that can fool Outlook clients. It is not the job of an antivirus program to detect such messages.

Automating update of virus data

ClamAV is provided by volunteers, and the servers and bandwidth that are used to enable the software and virus database to be distributed are voluntarily funded. As such, it is important to ensure that there is a balance between the frequency of checking for updates to maintain an up-to-date database and overloading the various servers.

The ClamAV group recommends the following: If you are running ClamAV 0.8x or higher, you can check for database updates as often as four times per hour provided you have the following option in freshclam.conf: DNSDatabaseInfo current.cvd.clamav.net.

If you don't have that option, you must stick with one check per hour.

Setting up auto updating

The virus database files for ClamAV can be downloaded from the ClamAV servers in a variety of ways. This includes using automated or manual tools such as wget. However, this is not the preferred way of doing the updates.

The freshclam utility we installed earlier with ClamAV is the preferred method to perform updates. It will download the latest antivirus database automatically on a regular basis. It can either be set up to work automatically from a cron entry or from the command line, or it can run as a daemon process and handle its own scheduling. When freshclam is started by a user with root privileges, it drops the special privileges and switches user ID to the clamav user.

`freshclam` uses the capabilities of the DNS system to obtain details of the latest version of virus database that is ready to be downloaded and where it can be obtained from. This can significantly reduce the load on your own as well as remote systems, as in most cases the only action performed is a check with the DNS server. Only if a newer version is available, it will attempt to perform a download.

We are now ready to start the `freshclam` process. If you have decided to run it as a daemon process, then simply execute the following command:

```
# freshclam -d
```

Then check that the process is running and that the log file is being updated correctly.

The other method available is to use the `cron` daemon to schedule the `freshclam` process to run at a regular period. To do this, you will need to add the following entry to the `crontab` file for either the `root` or the `clamav` user:

```
N * * * *       /usr/local/bin/freshclam -quiet
```

 `N` can be any number of your choice between `1` and `59`. Please don't choose any multiple of 10, because there are already too many servers using those time slots.

Proxy settings are only configurable via the configuration file, and `freshclam` will require strict read-only permissions for the owner of the config file when `HTTPProxyPassword` is enabled. For example,

```
# chmod 0600 /etc/freshclam.conf
```

The following is an example of proxy settings:

```
    HTTPProxyServer myproxyserver.com
    HTTPProxyPort 1234
    HTTPProxyUsername myusername
    HTTPProxyPassword mypass
```

Automating startup and shutdown

If you installed any or all of the ClamAV and ClamSMTP components via a package manager rather than from source, the necessary startup scripts may have been provided. Check to see if the necessary scripts have been included in the boot startup sequence.

If you have installed ClamAV from the source code, the following scripts are examples for starting and stopping the necessary daemons at boot time. Depending on your distribution, the file locations may vary and you may need to execute additional commands to set run levels for each script. Please consult your distributions documentation.

ClamSMTP

One of the contributed scripts that are available in the ClamSMTP sources is a script to be used for automatically starting and stopping the operating daemon when the system is booted. Check that the path names in the script match those in the config file and the installed directory, and then execute the following command from the root of the ClamSMTP source tree:

```
# cp scripts/clamsmtpd.sh /etc/init.d/clamsmtpd
```

After copying the file, make sure that the script has execute permissions and is not modifiable by anyone other than the system root user.

```
# ls -al /etc/init.d/clamsmtpd
-rwxr-xr-x 1 root root 756 2009-07-09 15:51 /etc/init.d/clamsmtpd
```

Add the script to the system startup.

```
# update-rc.d clamsmtpd defaults
```

ClamAV

Next is an example script to start and stop the clamd and freshclamd daemons at boot time. As before, verify the path names, adapt the script to your needs, and copy the script to the system initialization directory before adding it to the system startup.

If freshclam is run as a cron job, rather than as a daemon, then remove the lines that start and stop the freshclam process from the script.

```
#!/bin/sh
#
# Startup script for the Clam AntiVirus Daemons
#

[ -x /usr/local/sbin/clamd ] || [ -x /usr/local/bin/freshclam ] ||
exit 0

# See how we were called.
case "$1" in
  start)
```

```
                echo -n "Starting Clam AntiVirus Daemon: "
                /usr/local/sbin/clamd
                echo -n "Starting FreshClam Daemon: "
                /usr/local/bin/freshclam -d -p /var/run/clamav/freshclam.pid
                ;;
     stop)
                echo -n "Stopping Clam AntiVirus Daemon: "
                [ -f /var/run/clamav/clamd.pid ] && kill `cat /var/run/clamav/
clamd.pid`
                rm -f /var/run/clamav/clamd.socket
                rm -f /var/run/clamav/clamd.pid
                echo -n "Stopping FreshClam Daemon: "
                [ -f /var/run/clamav/freshclam.pid ] && kill `cat /var/run/
clamav/freshclam.pid`
                rm -f /var/run/clamav/freshclam.pid
                ;;
     *)
                echo "Usage: clamav {start|stop}"
                ;;
esac
```

Monitoring log files

It is important to monitor the log file on a regular basis. Here you will be able to track the regular updating of the virus database and make sure that your system is as well protected as possible.

Regular update messages should appear similar to the following:

```
Received signal 14, wake up
ClamAV update process started at Wed Jul  8 15:42:27 2009
main.cvd is up to date (version: 51, sigs: 545035, f-level: 42, builder: sven)
daily.cvd is up to date (version: 9546, sigs: 40746, f-level: 43, builder: ccordes)
-------------------------------------
```

Occasionally new software will be released and will need to be updated. In this case, you will get warning messages in the log file, such as the following:

```
Received signal 14, wake up
ClamAV update process started at Mon Jul  6 09:05:44 2009
WARNING: Your ClamAV installation is OUTDATED!
WARNING: Local version: 0.94.2 Recommended version: 0.95.2
DON'T PANIC! Read http://www.clamav.net/support/faq
main.cld is up to date (version: 51, sigs: 545035, f-level: 42, builder: sven)
daily.cld is up to date (version: 9538, sigs: 38480, f-level: 43, builder: ccordes)
-------------------------------------
```

In cases when there are Internet connection problems or the remote files themselves are unavailable while being updated, the process may log transient error messages. No action needs to be taken provided that these errors do not persist.

Disinfecting files

A common request is for files to be disinfected automatically before being forwarded on to the final recipient. In the current version (0.95), ClamAV cannot disinfect files. The following information is available from the ClamAV documentation.

> *We will add support for disinfecting OLE2 files in one of the next stable releases. There are no plans for disinfecting other types of files. There are many reasons for it: cleaning viruses from files is virtually pointless these days. It is very seldom that there is anything useful left after cleaning, and even if there is, would you trust it?*

Summary

We have now installed and configured a very efficient antivirus system for checking all incoming e-mails for infected attachments, and have significantly secured our systems—both the server and the workstation—against attack.

Our Mail Transport Agent, Postfix, can now filter all messages using the ClamAV daemon via the ClamSMTP content filtering interface, to scan and detect a wide range of threats against a database of virus signatures. Using `freshclam`, we have ensured that our detection database has been kept up-to-date to guard against the latest threats and any new viruses released. Constant vigilance is still required to make sure that software and files are always kept totally up-to-date in this ongoing battle.

10
Backing Up Your System

In order to recover from catastrophic loss of service in case of a major hardware or software malfunction, it is absolutely essential to have a backup. The backup is supposed to let you restore the software (or rather the software's configuration) and other data that you need to reestablish your service. This includes the users' mails, the system's mail queue, and their authentication data among other things.

This chapter will guide you through the steps necessary to safeguard your system from failure and, if failure occurs, how to recover from it. After reading through this chapter you will know:

- What backup options are available
- What data we need to back up
- The storage considerations for our backup media
- How to perform incremental and full backups for the mailboxes
- The steps required for a complete file system restore
- How to restore an individual e-mail
- How to backup our server configuration
- Setting up automated backup schedules

Backup options

Choosing the most appropriate backup option is always a trade-off. You have to juggle the cost of downtime to a business, the price and availability of backup media and hardware, the value of user data (in our case, users' e-mails), and the staffing costs to manage the backup operations.

For our small office e-mail server, we are going to present a simple but reliable solution, using tried and trusted techniques and tools employed by numerous administrators over many years.

Any backups we take need to be stored on backup media. The most convenient solution is to have a spare Linux machine, with a number of hard drives, networked to our e-mail server, preferably located in another building. Storing backups off site is essential if we want to protect ourselves from a catastrophic event such as fire.

If a remote server is not available, an alternative could be some hot-swappable external hard drives connected to the server, or even, in a pinch, a DVD burner. Magnetic tape drives are also an option, but often the cost of the tape drive and media is greater than the server. If removable media is the only option then don't leave the backups stacked on top of the server or in a desk drawer, move them to a safe off site location. It may be convenient to retain a local copy of the latest backup media on site to respond more quickly to urgent recovery situations.

RAID

RAID is an acronym for a **Redundant Array** of **Inexpensive** (or **Independent**) **Disks**. By using multiple disks in a RAID setup, data is spread across the disks, but the array is viewed by the operating system as a single device. By replicating and dividing the data throughout the array, the tolerance to disk failure can be reduced significantly, increasing data reliability and possibly I/O performance. If a hard disk fails in the array, the old disk can be swapped out and replaced with a new disk. The RAID controller, either a hardware or software controller, then reconstructs the data. For more information on RAID and the various configuration options available, visit `http://en.wikipedia.org/wiki/RAID`.

However, RAID, by itself, is not a backup solution. A file or e-mail that has been deleted, whether accidentally or maliciously, cannot be recovered. RAID does not protect from user error or serious hardware failure such as a power surge that fries the server or even fire damage.

Increasing data availability using RAID is a good thing, but is not an alternative to a proper backup and recovery strategy.

Image backups

A disk image backup program will copy data from a hard disk, sector by sector with no regard to any files or structure on the disk. The backup is an exact image of the disk—the master boot record, partition tables, and all data.

In the event of a major hardware failure, the steps to restore a system are as follows:

1. Replace or repair failed hardware.
2. Boot a Linux live CD containing the disk image restore program.
3. Write the image of each disk from the backup.
4. Reboot.

Superficially, this looks like an attractive and quick approach to restore service quickly and easily. However, there are number of problems inherent in using disk images for backup.

*   Restoring a disk image to a new disk of a different size or geometry is often not possible.

*   The new hardware will almost certainly be of a different configuration (motherboard, network card, disk controllers, and so on.), and the restored Linux kernel may not have the necessary drivers to boot successfully.

*   Disk images are big. The image is the total size of the disk, not just the size of the data stored on it. The space requirements of multiple disk images soon adds up.

*   Recovery of an individual user file is quite cumbersome. The disk image would need to be restored to a spare disk, mounted on a running system and, once found, copied to the desired location.

Total system failures happen rarely and the perceived convenience and speed of an image restore is often outweighed by the flexibility of file system backups.

File system backups

Unlike image backups, file system backups understand the structure of the file system and consequently the data on the hard disk. Therefore, only the allocated portions of the disk are copied and the free space is not copied. The backup is for all files in the file system rather than sector by sector.

Because file system backups are done this way, it means that it is possible to copy only the files that have changed since the last backup, resulting in smaller subsequent backup files.

In the event of a major hardware failure, the steps to restore a system are as follows:

1. Replace or repair failed hardware.
2. Install the Linux distribution.
3. Install the mail server applications in this book.
4. Apply any patches.
5. Restore application configuration data backups.
6. Restore user data backups.
7. Reboot

Compared to image backups, this approach will take slightly longer and involves more steps, but does have a number of advantages.

- Replacement disks need not be of the same size or geometry.
- As long as your Linux distribution supports the new hardware, there are no compatibility issues.
- Backup file sizes are much smaller.
- Restoration of individual files is much simpler.

As mentioned before, major system failures are not that common. Although the steps to complete a full restore are a little more cumbersome than image backups, the advantages of smaller and faster backups along with the ease of selective restoration of user data are significant.

To reduce the likelihood of an unexpected disk failure, system tools are available to monitor the health of disk drives. For more information, visit `http://en.wikipedia.org/wiki/S.M.A.R.T.`.

Ad hoc backups

File system backups back up whole file systems only, not individual files or directories. Occasionally we may wish to take a copy of just a few files after a significant configuration change to one of our applications.

Using standard Linux tools such as `tar` or `cp`, important changed files can be copied to a directory on a file system that is part of the normal backup schedule.

What to back up

The big question always associated with backups is, "What should we back up?"

There are many things that contribute to our final decision. Of course, we want to back up our server's configuration because it is essential to our server's functionality. But we also want to back up the users' data because it is a valuable asset to our business. Is there a company policy that says people may use e-mail for private communication? If there is, should we back up those messages as well?

We should only back up what we need to restore the system to a functional state. This saves space on the backup media and shortens the time required to perform a backup and restore if necessary.

After all, the space on any backup media is limited and thus precious. It is more important to back up all the users' mails than to have a complete backup of the /tmp directory. Also, the less data we back up, the less time is required to perform the backup, thus returning our system's resources (CPU cycles, I/O bandwidth) more quickly to their main purpose—handling users' mails.

The following is list of items we need to backup to get a working system:

- System inventory
- Installed software that the services require
- Software configuration files
- Users' credentials
- Users' mailboxes
- Log files (for billing purposes and end user requests)
- Postfix mail queue

The following sections describe each of these items discussed.

System inventory

In the event of a partial or total hardware failure, it is useful to make a note of our current system layout. In most cases, replacement hardware will often be as good as, if not better, than our current setup. In order to restore our system, we will need to know how disks are partitioned and how the mount points organized. It would be difficult to restore our users' data onto a disk that is too small.

Using the output from following commands, we will have enough information to recreate our disk layout:

```
# fdisk -l > disk_layout.txt
```

This command prints out the partition table for each disk and saves the output to a file.

```
# df -h >> disk_layout.txt
```

This command appends the capacity and usage of each mount point to our file.

```
# mount >> disk_layout.txt
```

The `mount` command lists the current mount points, which we append to the file.

Additional information may be in the file /etc/fstab, which we will backup later.

Obtaining a list of installed software

In order to restore our installed software, we need to have a list of software currently installed.

In Debian, this is given by the following command. The installed_software.txt file contains the current state of which software on the system is installed/not installed.

```
# dpkg --get-selections > installed_software.txt
```

With an RPM-based distribution, that would be:

```
# rpm -qa > installed_software.txt
```

In a Debian-based system, this file can later be used to install the same set of software.

```
# dpkg --set-selections < installed_software.txt
# dselect
```

In the dselect utility, select i for install and then confirm the installation.

With an RPM-based distribution, that would be:

```
# yum -y install $(cat installed_software.txt)
```

 The commands just discussed list only the software installed via a package manager. If you have installed software from source, then make a note of the application and version you installed.

System configuration files

The server will not perform its expected duties without these. As a minimum, the configuration files that need to be backed up are:

- /etc/courier: This directory holds Courier-IMAP's configuration data.
- /etc/postfix: This directory holds Postfix's configuration data.

The directory tree /etc includes items such as network settings, routings, and much more, which we would otherwise need to memorize. It is recommended to backup the whole /etc tree.

 If you have installed software from source with configuration files in non-standard locations, be sure to include those configuration files in your backup candidate list.

Authentication data

Users cannot authenticate themselves using their username and password combination without this. The data that needs to be backed up depends on the way the authentication is done and would include three files— /etc/passwd, /etc/shadow, and /etc/group, along with a MySQL database (if the users' credentials are stored in that database).

The users' mailboxes

This is where the users' mails are stored. This includes the whole directory tree of /home and below. This is the bulk of our backup—vast amounts of data.

Log files

We should at least store the logs generated by Postfix and Courier. These will be needed to process user requests such as, "Where did my mail go?". If users are billed based on mail volume sent and/or received, we will definitely need a backup of Postfix's logs.

As Postfix's and Courier's logs are normally written by the system's syslogd daemon, we need to check the /etc/syslog.conf file to see where these logs go. Both programs log their messages with the syslog mail facility.

To ensure complete coverage, it is wise to back up the whole directory tree of /var/log.

The mail queue

It may or may not make sense to back up the Postfix queue of a working system, depending on the situation.

With Postfix, e-mail messages hit the disk at least twice.

- The first time that the e-mail messages hit your drive is when they are being accepted by Postfix; they are written to Postfix's `queue_directory` before delivery continues.

 More disk I/O may be generated by a virus scanner or a program that detects spam (for example, `clamav` and `spamassassin`).

- If it's mail for local domains, our server is the final destination for these mails and their lifespan in the `queue_directory` is extremely short. They hit the queue, just to be delivered to the user's mailbox immediately afterwards. That's the second time they hit the disk.
- If it's mail that goes to other domains (because the server acts as a relay), then Postfix will immediately contact the recipient's mail server and try to deliver the message there. Only in case of problems will the queue ever contain a significant number of e-mails not yet delivered. These problems are:
  - **The** `content_filter` **is slow or not operational**: For example, `clamsmtp` or any other product.
  - **Remote sites have problems**: Large free e-mail providers often have problems and thus may not be able to accept our e-mails immediately.

In both these cases, the deferred queue will fill up with mail that's still to be delivered and that should obviously be backed up in case of a failure. If the server is very busy, there may be quite a bit of deferred mail in the queue.

The Postfix mail queue includes the directory tree `/var/spool/postfix` and below.

What not to back up

We do not need to back up all of the installed binaries as these can simply be reinstalled using the aforementioned "list of installed software". Of course this assumes that the installation media is available when we need to reconstruct our system. As security conscious administrators, we keep our system up-to-date by installing the vendors' patches. Over the course of time, the versions of the installed and subsequently patched software will differ significantly from the versions that came on the installation media. If these updates can be installed via the Internet (for example using Red Hat's up2date or Debian apt-get), we don't have to keep them on site.

So, we don't just need the installation media, but also a complete set of updates, as the configuration of our installed software may work only with the latest, greatest patched version.

Backing up users' e-mail

We will be using dump to backup the whole partition containing our mailboxes. The dump command copies files on a file system to a specified disk, tape, or other media.

Some of the reasons for using it are:

- It is incredibly fast (in my tests, the network is the bottleneck)
- It is simple (one command suffices)
- It can run unattended (for example, as `cron` job)
- It does not need any additional software to be installed
- It does not need a GUI
- It is very mature having been around since AT&T UNIX Version 6, circa 1975

The `restore` command performs the opposite of `dump`. A backup of a file system taken using `dump` can be restored as the complete file system or you can selectively restore certain files or directories.

Mail storage

We recommend putting the mailboxes (`/home`) on a separate partition for many reasons.

- File system maintenance can be performed independently from other parts of the system (simply unmount `/home`, perform an `fsck`, mount it again).
- It is possible to put that partition on a separate disk or on a RAID, thus separating the users' I/O (on that partition) from the system's I/O (logs, mail queue, virus scanner).

Most important of all:

- Using `dump`/`restore`, we can dump whole partitions. (OK, that's not entirely true, but a `dump`/`restore` is done easily only with whole partitions.)

- An overfull partition containing the mailboxes will not negatively influence the system's ability to write log files or other important system information. If all the data (logs, mailboxes, the system files) were on a single partition, filling this partition would cause logging to stop.

Both Courier and Postfix use the Maildir format for users' mailboxes. They store each piece of mail as a separate file allowing easy restore operations even for single mails.

Backup operations are very easy with the Maildir format.

- "Back up an e-mail" corresponds to "back up a file to the backup media".

- "Restore an e-mail" corresponds to "restore a file from the backup media".

- "Back up a mailbox" corresponds to "back up a Maildir and all its subdirectories to the backup media".

- "Restore a mailbox" corresponds to "restore a Maildir and all its subdirectories from the backup media".

Using dump

There are basically two approaches to backing up data. The simple method stores all data, whenever we perform a backup. This is called a full backup. Its advantage is the simplicity, and its main disadvantage is the sheer amount of data that needs to be stored on the backup media. This problem is addressed by the concept of the incremental backup. An incremental backup saves the changes only since the last incremental (or full) backup.

If the space on the backup media allows for a full backup everyday, we can do that for the sake of simplicity. That way we only need to look at the last intact backup to restore all the data.

Incremental backups are simple. The backup software needs to back up only those files and directories that have recently been created or changed since the last backup.

If the space doesn't allow for that simple solution, we could use this scheme instead:

- Perform a full backup every week

- Do six incremental backups, one each day

If we need to restore from scratch, restore the last full backup, then restore up to six incremental backups. That way we lose at most one day of mail—which is as close as we can get with a daily backup interval. Later we shall see more sophisticated incremental backup strategies to reduce the number of incremental restorations required after restoring a full dump.

For detailed information on dump(8) and restore(8) see the system manual pages.

We shall now look at the actual task of backing up the mailboxes using the dump command.

Full dump

We're now about to perform a full backup of the partition containing our users' Maildirs. In this example, this partition will be /dev/sdb1 (the first partition of our SATA disk). So, we will want to back up /dev/sdb1.

To find out which partition we need to back up on our system, we need to examine the output of the mount command:

```
# mount
/dev/sda1 on / type ext3 (rw,relatime,errors=remount-ro)
tmpfs on /lib/init/rw type tmpfs (rw,nosuid,mode=0755)
/proc on /proc type proc (rw,noexec,nosuid,nodev)
sysfs on /sys type sysfs (rw,noexec,nosuid,nodev)
varrun on /var/run type tmpfs (rw,nosuid,mode=0755)
varlock on /var/lock type tmpfs (rw,noexec,nosuid,nodev,mode=1777)
udev on /dev type tmpfs (rw,mode=0755)
tmpfs on /dev/shm type tmpfs (rw,nosuid,nodev)
devpts on /dev/pts type devpts (rw,noexec,nosuid,gid=5,mode=620)
fusectl on /sys/fs/fuse/connections type fusectl (rw)
lrm on /lib/modules/2.6.27-14-generic/volatile type tmpfs
(rw,mode=755)
/dev/sdb1 on /home type ext3 (rw,relatime)
```

As we can see, /home is the partition of /dev/sdb1.

Our plan is to use the dump tool to create the backup for this partition. This backup data needs to go to our backup medium, which could be another disk, a tape or, in our case, a disk in the remote backup server.

There are various methods to get data across the network, one of them being ssh. It is a network protocol that facilitates secure communications between two devices.

To get our backup data across the network onto another disk in the backup server, we use the power of Linux to marry the dump program and ssh protocol.

The output of the dump program will be fed into gzip to compress the dump, then fed to ssh, which in turn spawns another program dd on the backup server to finally write that data onto its disk.

The following lines of code give a full dump of the partition containing the mailboxes to a file on a remote system. We are assuming that the mailboxes are on the partition /dev/sdb1 mounted as /home.

As root, run the following commands:

```
# dump -0 -u -b 1024 -f - /dev/sdb1 | \
      gzip -c | \
      ssh user@backup-host.domain.com \
      dd of=/backupdirectory/$(date +%Y%m%d%H%M%S).home.dump.0.gz
```

The command looks complicated, so let's break it down in each of the steps:

- dump -0 -u -b 1024 -f - performs a level 0 (full) dump of the partition /dev/sdb1 (which contains /home in our example) using a block size of 1024 (for maximum performance) and updates (-u) the file /var/lib/dumpdates after the dump had been successful. The -u option is important because it records the date and time of this dump, so subsequent incremental dumps can determine which files have been changed or created since the last dump. The output of the dump goes to a file (-f) specified as (-), which indicates stdout, the standard output.

- As the dump data goes to standard output (stdout), we can pipe that output into gzip to compress the size of the dump. The -c option tells gzip to write the compressed output to stdout.

- The compressed level 0 dump output is then piped to the ssh command, which makes a remote connection to the system backup-host.domain. com logging in as user. Once logged in, the remote system executes the dd command. We recommend the use of the key-based authentication scheme that ssh offers. This way, the backup can run unattended, as nobody has to enter the password needed to log in as user on backup-host.domain.com.

- On the remote server, the final step is to write the output using the dd command. The output filename is specified by the of option to dd. The output filename has been constructed in such a way as to easily identify the file system, the date and time the dump was taken, the level of the dump, and the suffix .gz to indicate that this dump file has been compressed. The filename portion $(date +%Y%m%d%H%M%S) is a shell expansion performed on the local system (not the remote system) to output the current date and time in YYYYMMDDHHMMSS format. The final output filename will be something similar to 20090727115323.dump.0.gz.

For more information on each of the commands, see the system manual pages for dump, gzip, ssh, dd, and date.

The output will look similar to the following:

```
# dump -0 -u -f - /dev/sdb1 | gzip -c | \
        ssh backup@nas1 dd of=backups/$(date +%Y%m%d%H%M%S).home.dump.0.gz
  DUMP: Date of this level 0 dump: Mon Jul 27 15:39:09 2009
  DUMP: Dumping /dev/sdb1 (/home) to standard output
  DUMP: Label: none
  DUMP: Writing 10 Kilobyte records
  DUMP: mapping (Pass I) [regular files]
  DUMP: mapping (Pass II) [directories]
  DUMP: estimated 1400920 blocks.
  DUMP: Volume 1 started with block 1 at: Mon Jul 27 15:40:11 2009
  DUMP: dumping (Pass III) [directories]
  DUMP: dumping (Pass IV) [regular files]
  DUMP: Volume 1 completed at: Mon Jul 27 15:41:23 2009
  DUMP: Volume 1 1400910 blocks (1368.08MB)
  DUMP: Volume 1 took 0:01:12
  DUMP: Volume 1 transfer rate: 19457 kB/s
  DUMP: 1400910 blocks (1368.08MB)
  DUMP: finished in 72 seconds, throughput 19457 kBytes/sec
  DUMP: Date of this level 0 dump: Mon Jul 27 15:39:09 2009
  DUMP: Date this dump completed:  Mon Jul 27 15:41:23 2009
  DUMP: Average transfer rate: 19457 kB/s
  DUMP: DUMP IS DONE
1629153+1 records in
1629153+1 records out
834126574 bytes (834 MB) copied, 129.964 s, 6.4 MB/s
# ssh backup@nas1 ls -l backups/*.gz
-rw-r--r-- 1 backup backup 834126574 2009-07-27 15:41 backups/20090727153909.home.dump.0.gz
#
```

This next example will simply write the backup data to a directory—no stdout wizardry this time!

The following lines of code give a full dump of the partition containing the mailboxes to a file on a separate disk to hold the backups:

```
# dump -0 -u -f /backupdirectory/fulldump /dev/sdb1
```

This is, of course, much faster and simpler than sending all the data across the network via ssh with the data encryption and decryption carried out during the transit (which takes a lot of time and CPU power), but if our server is burnt to cinders, a backup on a built-in hard drive won't help at all.

Keep in mind that /backupdirectory/fulldump can also be an NFS mount or an SMB mount. This would give you both, the advantage of a simple command line and an off site backup. So, make sure you do have an offsite backup. It's easy enough either way.

Incremental dumps

Incremental dumps are performed in exactly the same way as a full dump except that we change the level option from 0 to either 1, 2, or 3, and so on depending on how many changes we wish to back up. Remember, a level number above 0 tells dump to copy all files new or modified since the last dump of a lower level. This is best illustrated with some examples. For clarity, we shall be simply dumping to a file, but in practice we would normally use the same sequence of commands as discussed using `gzip`, `ssh`, `dd`, and so on.

Let's assume our level 0 dump was taken on Sunday night. The first incremental dump (level 1, indicated by the `-1` option) is then taken on Monday night like this:

```
# dump -1 -u -f mon.dump.1  /dev/sdb1
```

This saves everything that is new or has changed since the last full dump to `mon.dump.1`. This dump file will be much smaller than the previous full dump containing only the changes made on Monday. Assume, on the following day we repeat this level 1 dump

```
# dump -1 -u -f tue.dump.1  /dev/sdb1
```

The second incremental dump, `tue.dump.1`, will contain all the changes made on Monday and Tuesday because a level 1 dump will back up everything that has changed since the level 0 dump. In order to recover the system back to the latest backup, we would have to restore only Tuesday's backup. Therefore one might consider that the dump taken on Monday is now obsolete; however, should a user wish to recover a file created on a Monday and accidentally deleted on a Tuesday, our first backup is still required.

Repeatedly performing level 1 dumps allows for very quick recovery as only two dump files need to be restored, the level 0 dump and the latest level 1 dump. The downside is that each subsequent dump file grows in size and takes longer and longer to complete. This scheme is sometimes called differential backup.

An alternative is to use additional dump levels to reduce the size of each backup file.

For example, the following sequence of commands perform a number of incremental backups after our initial level 0 dump:

```
# dump -1 -u -f mon.dump.1  /dev/sdb1
# dump -2 -u -f tue.dump.2  /dev/sdb1
# dump -3 -u -f wed.dump.3  /dev/sdb1
# dump -4 -u -f thu.dump.4  /dev/sdb1
```

In this example, each day's dump file contains only the new and changed files since the previous dump. Each dump operation from Tuesday onwards will complete more quickly and result in smaller file sizes than in our previous example. However, recovery will take longer. To recover to the latest backup, we would need to restore our full dump, then restore each of the incremental dumps from Monday through Thursday in order.

Trying these examples on a small temporary file system might be a useful exercise in order to understand the interaction between different levels of dumps. Each dump file can be examined using the following command:

```
# restore -t -f filename
```

For the curious, the file `/var/lib/dumpdates` can also be examined after each dump to verify the date and level of each dump.

As was stated at the beginning of this chapter, everything is a trade-off, so choosing the appropriate backup strategy involves balancing media costs, personnel costs, and recovery time.

So far, all of our backups have been performed with the disks mounted, which makes verifying the backup impossible. The reason for this is that data we were just backing up is constantly in flux. Remember that each file represents an e-mail. Whenever a user gets new mail or deletes old mail, the state of the file system changes. Users constantly get mail, read mail, and delete mail, even when they're about to perform a backup.

The `restore` command does have the `-C` option to compare a dump with the original disk contents, but this is sensible only if the file system we are dumping is unmounted. In most cases, unmounting each file system is not practical and would interrupt service significantly.

Using restore

All the data that has been backed up will need to be restored before it can be used.

This can be done in two ways, interactively or non interactively.

Interactive restore

To restore data from a dump interactively, we need to copy the dump from our backup media onto our system or perform the selection of files to restore on the computer we stored the dump in. If we are extracting only a few files, this can be performed in a temporary directory and the resulting files can be moved to the correct location once the restore has been completed. For larger numbers of files, for example a whole user account, we can cd to the ultimate destination before starting the restore.

For an interactive restore, run the following command:

```
# restore -i -f /backupdirectory/subdir/dumpfile
>
```

The > is the prompt of the interactive interface to restore. It is a spartan interface with limited commands available. It allows navigation through the dump as if we were on a live file system. Use ls and cd to show directory contents or change directories. Issue ? to get a list of supported commands.

Once we have found the data we want to restore, type either of the following commands:

- > add directoryname
- > add filename

This adds the particular directoryname and all data below it, or just the filename to the set of files that need to be restored. Repeat for additional files or directories.

Once we are done with adding all the data that needs to be recovered, we issue the extract command.

```
> extract
You have not read any volumes yet.
Unless you know which volume your file(s) are on you should start
with the last volume and work towards the first.
Specify next volume # (none if no more volumes): 1
set owner/mode for '.'? [yn] n
```

The output shown in the previous screenshot relates to volume numbers on magnetic tape. A dump file may have been split over a multi-volume tape set, but when dealing with dump files on hard disk, choose volume 1. We would normally select n to retain the current ownership and permissions of the working directory.

Once the necessary files have been extracted, issue the following command:

```
> quit
```

Do this with the last full dump and each incremental dump in order, up to the last incremental dump available. This makes sure that we restore all changes since the last full backup.

 If the data we are restoring hasn't changed between two dumps, we will not find it in the second incremental dump at all.

Non-interactive restore across the network

The manual approach makes sense if we want to restore just a few mailboxes. If we want a complete recovery of all mailboxes, we need to use the non-interactive scheme. This doesn't need additional storage space on the target system, as the dump data is being piped across the network.

Recreate the file system on our newly installed, freshly partitioned hard disk and mount it:

```
# mke2fs -j /dev/sdb1
# mount /dev/sdb1 /home
```

The -j option to mke2fs creates a ext3 journaling file system on /dev/sdb1 and it's mounted as /home.

Please note that we need to recreate the data using the same file system you used when creating the backup!

Let the restore begin.

```
# cd /home
# ssh user@backup-host.domain.com \
      dd if=/backupdirectory/20090601030034.home.dump.0.gz | \
      gunzip -c | restore -r -f -
```

Just like when we performed the backup across the network, we now do the same with the restore.

```
ssh user@backup-host.domain.com
```

The previous line executes the following command as the user on the backup-host.domain.com host, although this time with the dd command using the if option to read the compressed dump file and sending the output to stdout.

```
dd if=/backupdirectory/20090601030034.home.dump.0.gz
```

The output is piped across the network and fed into gunzip to uncompress the file and ultimately piped to restore -r -f -. The -r option instructs restore to rebuild the whole file system from the dump file's contents to the original locations using the original permissions and ownerships. If you wish, you may use the -v option with restore for verbose output.

 It is necessary to ensure we are located in the correct directory before issuing the restore command, otherwise serious damage may occur to an existing file system.

The output from the restore will look something like this:

```
# ssh backup@nas1 dd if=backups/20090727153909.home.dump.0.gz \
    | gunzip -c | restore -r -f -
restore: ./lost+found: File exists
1629153+1 records in
1629153+1 records out
834126574 bytes (834 MB) copied, 71.4752 s, 11.7 MB/s
#
```

The warning about the existence of lost+found is normal and can be safely ignored.

This operation should then be repeated for each incremental dump file that is required to return the system to the required state. If we restore the incremental dumps in the wrong order, we will get the error "Incremental tape too low" or "Incremental tape too high". Once we have received one of these errors, we cannot complete the full restore and must restart the restoration from the level 0 dump.

When using the -r option to the restore command, it will create the file restoresymtable. This is a checkpoint file that the restore command uses when we are restoring multiple dumps as an aid to help the next restore command determine which directories or files need updating, creating, or deleting.

Once the file system has been completely restored and verified, we should remove the restoresymtable file. If this file is included in the next dump, the old restoresymtable file could end up overwriting the one that is being created at that time and prevent additional dumps from being restored.

As the final step, perform a level 0 dump of the newly restored file system.

Backing up configurations and logs

There are two approaches to the backup of configuration data and important log files.

- **Store the data on our backup media**: Using this method, we will back up directly to our backup server.

- **Add the data to our backup schedule**: This approach will include the necessary files as a part of our user data backup.

Either case is equally valid and is really a matter of personal preference.

As a reminder, earlier we made a list of the important parts of the system that require backup. These were:

Important part of the system	Example command
System inventory	`disk_layout.txt`
List of installed software	`installed_software.txt`
System configuration files	`/etc`
Authentication data	`/etc/password /etc/groups /etc/shadow`
Log files	`/var/log`
Mail queue	`/var/spool/postfix`

As each system is different, you should ensure that the example commands given next cover all the necessary files.

Transferring configurations and logs to backup media

To keep it simple, we just use the `tar` tool to create an archive of the files and directories listed previously, and store it in the same directory as the full or incremental dumps on the backup server:

```
# tar cz disk_layout.txt installed_software.txt \
    /etc /var/log /var/spool/postfix | \
    ssh user@backup-host.domain.com \
    dd of=/backupdirectory/$(date +%Y%m%d%H%M%S).config.tar.gz
```

Alternatively, we can create the `tar` archive on the `/home` file system and have it backed up as part of our normal backup schedule.

```
# mkdir -p /home/config
```

```
# chmod 600 /home/config
```

```
# tar czf /home/config/$(date +%Y%m%d%H%M%S).config.tar.gz \
      disk_layout.txt installed_software.txt \
      /etc /var/log /var/spool/postfix
```

In both cases, we use the `tar` command with the options `c` to create an archive, `z` to compress, and `f` as the output archive name. Also note that we have restricted access to the `/home/config` directory as it contains archives with sensitive information that should be protected.

For more information on `tar`, please see the system manual pages.

Restoring the configuration

Depending on the method used earlier, restoring our configuration and log files is relatively simple. We can either copy the required archive from the backup server or use the archive directly from `/home/config`. In either case, untarring the archive is performed using the following commands:

```
# mkdir tmpdir
```

```
# cd tmpdir
```

```
# tar xzf xxxxx.config.tar.gz
```

Note that we have created and moved into a temporary directory before expanding the archive. If our current directory was / when we executed the `tar` command, we would have overwritten all the files in `/etc`, `/var/log`, and `/var/spool/postfix` with potentially undesirable results.

Now that we have untarred the archive, we can compare and copy the files we need to restore.

Automating backups

Now that we have seen how to back up our system, we need to put in place an automated procedure to remove the drudgery of manually invoking `dump` at regular intervals.

The manual pages for dump do provide some guidance on how often to back up and at which level to reduce restoration time.

> *In the event of a catastrophic disk event, the time required to restore all the necessary backup tapes or files to disk can be kept to a minimum by staggering the incremental dumps. An efficient method of staggering incremental dumps to minimize the number of tapes follows:*
>
> *Always start with a level 0 backup. This should be done at set intervals, say once a month or once every two months, and on a set of fresh tapes that is saved forever.*
>
> *After a level 0, dumps of active file systems are taken on a daily basis, using a modified Tower of Hanoi algorithm, with this sequence of dump levels:*
> *3 2 5 4 7 6 9 8 9 9 . . .*
> *For the daily dumps, it should be possible to use a fixed number of tapes for each day, used on a weekly basis. Each week, a level 1 dump is taken, and the daily Hanoi sequence repeats beginning with 3. For weekly dumps, another fixed set of tapes per dumped file system is used, also on a cyclical basis.*
>
> *After several months or so, the daily and weekly tapes should get rotated out of the dump cycle and fresh tapes brought in.*

This sequence of dumps looks rather bizarre and needs a little more explanation. Working through the process will illustrate how we minimize the size of dumps taken and reduce the number required to restore.

Once the level 3 dump is taken, restoration is only a matter of restoring the dumps 0 and 3. After the second day, the level 2 dump will back up everything changed since the last dump at a lower level, that is, level 0. This renders the level 3 dump ineffective. The level 5 dump then backs up the changes since the level 2 dump. As the sequence progresses using higher and lower levels to skip days, previous dumps become ineffective and are no longer required to complete a full restore. Each of the dumps should still be retained, in case we need to restore individual files deleted by accident at some later time.

By the end of the week, a level 1 dump is performed rendering all the previous weeks' dump levels obsolete, and the sequence restarts until the end of the month when a new level 0 dump is taken.

The following table illustrates which dump levels are taken for each day and the number of restorations required to recover the data to the latest version:

Day of month	Dump level	Restore levels required
1	0	0
2, 9, 16, 23, 30	3	0, 1*, 3
3, 10, 17, 24, 31	2	0, 1*, 2
4, 11, 18, 25	5	0, 1*, 2, 5
5, 12, 19, 26	4	0, 1*, 2, 4
6, 13, 20, 27	7	0, 1*, 2, 4, 7
7, 14, 21, 28	6	0, 1*, 2, 4, 6
8, 15, 22, 29	1	0, 1

 During the first week, the level 1 dumps (marked with *) are not required during the restoration process. From the eighth day, the level 1 dump is always required.

As we can see from the table, even at the end of a month only a few dumps are required to restore our data, rather than several dozen when creating incremental daily dumps.

With our monthly backup schedule, a simple script and the addition of some entries to cron will complete the automated backup process.

Backup script

The following example bash script will archive our system configuration and log files, and dump the requested file system to a remote backup server. This is only a sample script and should be modified to suit your needs. Any error checking and logging has been omitted for clarity.

```
#!/bin/sh

# The name of the dump, e.g. home or users
NAME=$1

# The partition to dump, e.g. /dev/sdb1
DEVICE=$2

# The dump level, e.g. 0 or 3 etc.
LEVEL=$3
```

```
# ssh login name and host
#
USERNAME=user
BACKUPHOST=backuphost

# Take a system inventory.
#
/sbin/fdisk -l > /tmp/disk_layout.txt
/bin/df -h >> /tmp/disk_layout.txt
/bin/mount >> /tmp/disk_layout.txt

# Installed software (Debian)
#
/usr/bin/dpkg --get-selections > /tmp/installed_software.txt

# Archive our system configuration and logs
#
/bin/tar cz /tmp/disk_layout.txt /tmp/installed_software.txt \
    /etc /var/log /var/spool/postfix | \
    /usr/bin/ssh $USERNAME@$BACKUPHOST \
    /bin/dd of=$(date +%Y%m%d%H%M%S).config.tar.gz

# Perform the dump to the remote backup server.
#
/usr/sbin/dump -u -$LEVEL -f - $DEVICE | \
    /bin/gzip -c | ssh $USERNAME@$BACKUPHOST \
    /bin/dd $(date +%Y%m%d%H%M%S).$NAME.dump.$LEVEL.gz"

# Remove temporary files.
#
rm -f /tmp/disk_layout.txt /tmp/installed_software.txt

exit 0
```

The script expects 3 parameters — the name of the dump, the partition to be dumped, and the dump level.

The typical usage is as follows:

```
# remote-dump.sh home /home 0
```

The previous script archives /etc each time it runs. You may wish to move these commands to a separate script to perform this task weekly or even monthly. This is particularly important if the script will be used to dump other file systems as well.

Old dump files from previous months are not removed by the script and could fill up our backup server preventing future backups. It is prudent to put procedures in place to either remove or archive old dump files depending on the organization's data retention policy.

Adding crontab entries

Running our backup script automatically each night is just a matter of using the entries from our backup schedule table and executing the script to dump the correct partition. The following example `crontab` entries execute our script each night at 02:10 to dump `/home`. On the first of each month, a level 0 dump is performed and then a weekly level 1 dump is performed every seven days after that. The other entries implement the modified "Towers of Hanoi" algorithm.

```
10 02 1 * * /bin/remote-dump.sh home /home 0
10 02 2,9,16,23,30 * * /bin/remote-dump.sh home /home 3
10 02 3,10,17,24,31 * * /bin/remote-dump.sh home /home 2
10 02 4,11,18,25 * * /bin/remote-dump.sh home /home 5
10 02 5,12,19,26 * * /bin/remote-dump.sh home /home 4
10 02 6,13,20,27 * * /bin/remote-dump.sh home /home 7
10 02 7,14,21,28 * * /bin/remote-dump.sh home /home 6
10 02 8,15,22,29 * * /bin/remote-dump.sh home /home 1
```

Once our automated backup procedure has been put in place, we need to keep an eye out for any errors and verify the integrity of the dump files on the remote server.

Verifying restoration procedures

Even with the best planning in the world, things go wrong and always at the most inconvenient moment.

Taking a proactive approach to disaster recovery with good planning and practice will highlight any problems at an early stage before it is too late. Verifying the integrity of system backups is only really possible by restoring them and checking that the restored system is fully operational.

You should ask yourself questions such as, "What actions are necessary if the remote server fails?" Do you repair the backup server first or switch to another server to reduce the size of the window without backups? If the mail server fails, are you familiar with the restoration procedures? Is replacement hardware available at short notice, for example, on a Sunday?

There are many horror stories of administrators diligently taking backups only to find that when required the backups are useless because of a tape drive error or a minor syntax error in the backup script that overwrites valid dump files with bad data.

Invent scenarios for yourself and practice a full bare metal restore on spare hardware, or the recovery of an individual users' e-mail.

Verifying that your restoration procedures work will give you the confidence that you can recover from data loss.

Summary

In this chapter, we described how to back up e-mail and the mail server configuration. We started off with an introduction to what you should consider worth backing up and ended with a sophisticated solution using automated full and incremental backups.

In particular, we described the process using the `dump` command, and how to take copies of our data. We used the `restore` command to recover a complete file system and selective files.

This chapter guides you through the process of backing up and restoring your server's precious data. It shows why to back up, what data to back up, the different backup and restore methods, and a procedure to take automatic daily backups.

After implementing all the procedures we have shown you in this chapter, you will sleep a lot better and, in any case, your users will love the range and functionality your system can offer.

Index

Writing for Packt

We welcome all inquiries from people who are interested in authoring. Book proposals should be sent to authors@packtpub.com. If your book idea is still at an early stage and you would like to discuss it first before writing a formal book proposal, contact us; one of our commissioning editors will get in touch with you.

We're not just looking for published authors; if you have strong technical skills but no writing experience, our experienced editors can help you develop a writing career, or simply get some additional reward for your expertise.

About Packt Publishing

Packt, pronounced 'packed', published its first book "Mastering phpMyAdmin for Effective MySQL Management" in April 2004 and subsequently continued to specialize in publishing highly focused books on specific technologies and solutions.

Our books and publications share the experiences of your fellow IT professionals in adapting and customizing today's systems, applications, and frameworks. Our solution-based books give you the knowledge and power to customize the software and technologies you're using to get the job done. Packt books are more specific and less general than the IT books you have seen in the past. Our unique business model allows us to bring you more focused information, giving you more of what you need to know, and less of what you don't.

Packt is a modern, yet unique publishing company, which focuses on producing quality, cutting-edge books for communities of developers, administrators, and newbies alike. For more information, please visit our website: www.PacktPub.com.

PACKT
PUBLISHING

SpamAssassin: A Practical Guide to Configuration, Customization and Integration

ISBN: 978-1-904811-12-1   Paperback: 240 pages

In depth guide to implementing antispam solutions using SpamAssassin

1. Implement the right antispam solution for your network and your business requirements

2. Learn how to detect and prevent spam

3. Optimize SpamAssassin for all major mail servers and clients

4. Discover how to use SpamAssassin as a service

Hacking Vim: A cookbook to get the most out of the latest Vim editor

ISBN: 978-1-847190-93-2   Paperback: 228 pages

From personalizing Vim to productivity optimizations: Recipes to make life easier for experienced Vim users

1. Create, install, and use Vim scripts

2. Personalize your work-area

3. Optimize your Vim editor to be faster and more responsive

Please check **www.PacktPub.com** for information on our titles

CUPS Administrative Guide

ISBN: 978-1-847192-58-5   Paperback: 248 pages

A practical tutorial to installing, managing, and securing this powerful printing system

1. Install and configure the CUPS server and set up clients

2. Manage printers through the command line and web interface and manage users

3. Monitor the CUPS server along with filtering and file typing

4. Secure your CUPS server

5. Integrating with other systems like LPDs and Mac

Qmail Quickstarter: Install, Set Up and Run your own Email Server

ISBN: 978-1-847191-15-1   Paperback: 152 pages

A fast-paced and easy-to-follow, step-by-step guide that gets you up and running quickly

1. Qmail Basicsy

2. Storing and retrieving of emails

3. Virtualisation

4. Hosting Multiple Domains, Encryption, and Mailing Lists

Please check **www.PacktPub.com** for information on our titles

www.ingramcontent.com/pod-product-compliance
Lightning Source LLC
Chambersburg PA
CBHW062049050326
40690CB00016B/3026